Life's
Unexpected
Moments

LIFE'S UNEXPECTED MOMENTS

Dorothy Collins

DOROTHY COLLINS

In Memory of my late daughter Bonnie.
She inspired me to publish the novels I wrote.

And

Thank you to Terry Unger in appreciation of her encouragement.

Chapter One

When Chrissy woke up, she found herself tied to a man. She looked at him in horror. Who was this man? She had never met him before. Why was she bound to him? He was sleeping or unconscious.

Then she noticed the blood on his temple. She realized her head hurt too. She tried to move her hand to feel her head, but someone tied her too tightly to the man.

Chrissy studied his features. He didn't look sinister. A broad forehead, a gentle facial structure, and lips of tenderness. Now, why did I think that? That is dumb. How do I know his lips are tender?

Then a foreboding came over her as she recalled. This man was the one who hit her. The terror set in again. If he hit her, how come they were tied together?

She tried to stop her body from touching his, which was difficult with the ropes binding them. Should she try to wake him? No, she knew he was evil. He didn't look sinful. But she distinctly remembered him chasing her and hitting her. It was all coming back. She had gone to the door of 721 Langley Street. This man had come up behind her. Some sixth sense had made her move sideways to escape his arms. Then she ran back down the stairs, with him in pursuit. He was yelling, "Stop."

She had an appointment to see the lady at 721 Langley Street regarding a job about interior decorating. Mrs. Frank Doherty, yes, that is the name.

Chrissy was having trouble getting her thoughts in order. The bump on the head must have been more severe than she thought. Could he have hit her with something? No, he reached out for her. She fell, hitting her head on the iron gate post. Then she must have passed out.

How could we be tied together? Where are we?

The man was starting to make moaning sounds. Was he aware that he was tied to her? His eyes fluttered, then opened and closed quickly. She was still wearing a look of fear. He was waking up, and she couldn't get away from him.

Chrissy tried to look around with limitations. They were tied together tightly with her facing him. So that she could only move her head partway to the side. Who is this man? Why had he been after her? Was it her or Mrs. Frank Doherty he wanted? Could it be that he had the wrong person? After all, he probably didn't even know that she would be there, or had he followed her?

Again, he moaned, and she kept trying to look around. They seemed to be in a garage. There were some cars, very expensive classic cars.

Clearly not 721 Langley Street, had they been moved? Who had moved them? Now, why was she so sure it wasn't that address? Because the Langley house she saw did not look elaborate enough to have these expensive cars.

Again, the man tried to open his eyes. Open, close, then open with a look of bewilderment.

"Who are you?" his voice was weak and gruff and slightly raspy as though his throat was dry.

"Who are you? That is more to the point. Why were you chasing me?"

"Chasing you? I wasn't chasing you. Where are we?" He was trying to look past her head.

"I don't know. I know you were chasing me," Chrissy said firmly.

"Look, we are tied together, so we had better get along until we are free. Make that if we get free."

"We had better be free. I can't stay here. I have another appointment at four," Chrissy said dumbly. She wouldn't be going anywhere. "You were chasing me, and that was why I fell trying to get away from you." Chrissy jutted out her chin, accentuating her statement.

He closed his eyes, shook his head as if to clear it. Then relaxed his head on the pavement as though he had passed out.

"Hey, you wake up. I want to know why you were chasing me?"

"I have no idea," he replied without opening his eyes.

Chrissy tried to wriggle away from him. His eyes flew open again.

"Don't do that we are too closely linked and . . ."

"Just like a man to think of sex at a time like this. Well, Buster, think again. This is not a turn on for me. Got that?"

"Look, it is no turn-on for me either, but if you keep rubbing against me like that, things will be out of my hands. Do I make myself clear?" he said through clenched teeth. His eyes closed again.

"Fine, you sleep, and I will scream to get attention." She opened her mouth to scream.

He leaned forward and placed his mouth over hers. The kiss was to silence her, but he wasn't stopping. His mouth was devouring her, and she realized she wasn't pulling away. How could this be happening? She hadn't bothered with men since Todd passed away. The kiss had escalated into such an erotic kiss that she found herself responding. Then it sunk in. Chrissy pulled her mouth away as far she could.

"Yuck. Why did you do that? I don't know you."

"I know, but it was the only way I could think of to stop you from screaming. Now, let's calmly think this out before we act. Okay?"

"Just as long as you promise me no more kissing. Promise?"

"Okay, I promise." His eyes closed again.

"Open your eyes. I insist. You can't sleep now."

"I am not sleeping. I am trying to clear my head of the sledgehammers that are making morgue music in my head. It helps to have my eyes closed."

Chrissy looked at his face showing pain lines. Her head was not feeling great. She closed her eyes too, and it did feel better this way.

Her eyes flipped open, hearing a noise. It sounds like boots, construction, or army boots, not a good sound. They stopped.

Then a voice said, "I was just going to check on the prisoners," murmurs in the background. "All right." The boots headed back the way they came. Chrissy sighed with relief.

"Who are you?" Chrissy implored.

"I am John Taylor. I work as a Private Investigator."

"Fine, so why were you investigating me?"

"I wasn't. I was trying to warn you away from that house. There was a homicide there, and I was trying to stop you from entering."

"Mrs. Frank Doherty?"

"No, her husband, I presume. Somebody stabbed him three times in the chest. Now, why were you there?"

"I was trying to reach his wife to arrange an appointment for the next day. I couldn't keep the one for tonight. She wouldn't answer the phone, and there was no answering machine. As I was in the area, I thought I would drop in and tell her in person or leave a note," Chrissy remembered more clearly now. "What were you doing there?"

"I was following a man for my client. He disappeared into the house and didn't come out. When I went in, he was gone. I noticed a body on the living room floor. I continued out the back to find the man I was following. He wasn't around, so I came back to the front of the house. When I saw you there, I tried to warn you away before the police came."

"Well, if you were the one chasing me, how come we are tied together here? Wherever here is?"

"Someone hit me over the head when I knelt beside you. I didn't hit you. You tripped and fell against the iron gate post."

"Who hit you?" she asked.

"I don't know. I didn't hear him or see him."

"Could it have been the man you were following?"

"No, I doubt it. This man must have been hiding in the shrubs near the front gate where you fell."

"What did the man do that you were following?"

"He had violated his parole and was planning on leaving the country. Uncle Sam hired me to keep an eye on him."

"Who is Uncle Sam?"

"A member of the Calgary Police Department."

"Why would they hire you?"

"Because I used to be a cop, and they are usually shorthanded with injuries and guys on vacation. So, they inquired if I would keep an eye on him."

"Why do you think it wasn't him?"

"Because the guy that hit me had boots on and the guy I was following didn't. Now, who are you?"

"Chrissy Lambert. I am an Interior Decorator. I was supposed to meet with Mrs. Doherty tonight, but I have to go to my son's concert. Why am I telling you all this?" she stopped.

"Because you like my face, I guess," John closed his eyes. The hammer wasn't quite as active, but it was still falling and resounding in his brain.

"John, that isn't the reason. I get carried away talking sometimes," Chrissy paused then went on. "Do you know why someone killed Frank Doherty?"

"No, and I don't know if that is his name. I took your word for it that if Doherty was the lady's name. Then I presumed that the body or the man found dead would be her husband."

"You know that sounded pretty muddled, but I figured out what you're trying to say, I think."

"Look, if you had the drums in your head that I have. Then you would not criticize me, okay?"

"If you say so. Does your head hurt much on the outside? You have blood on your temple." Chrissy was studying his head.

"Yes. I wonder what the thug used to hit me? How is your head?"

"Better than yours, but I do feel a bit woozy."

"You took quite a header into that post. I can't see any blood, only a bump on your forehead."

"Who do you think is holding us?" Chrissy asked.

"I would have to say it is whoever totaled the guy on the floor back there. Perhaps they think we saw more than we thought we did, or they think we did."

"That doesn't sound any better than what I thought you said before. You do have a problem, or is talking in circles normal for you?"

"No, only when my head is deeply wounded. Then it doesn't seem to want to work properly," John replied in a worried voice.

"You should have your head looked at by a doctor," Chrissy

volunteered.

"Would you like to suggest that to Mr. Boots when he arrives back here?" John replied. Right on cue, Mr. Boots arrived.

"I see you two are awake. You should stand up in my presence, don't you think?" With that, his huge hands came out and grasped them both and hauled them to their feet, as though he was picking up 50 pounds instead of two adults.

Lying down, they were close enough, but standing up, it was a case of being glued together. The weight rearranged meant Chrissy had flattened breasts against his chest. He didn't want to breathe too profoundly or expand his torso. That would be unthinkable.

Just then, John started to cough and cough. Oh dear, that led to other bodily expansions that were plain to both of them. Chrissy wasn't looking him in the face anymore.

John apologized. "Sorry." But saying sorry wasn't about to alleviate the matter. Not while glued together. Chrissy was well-endowed in the breast area. Oh, dear!! Now he was beyond an apology, way beyond.

Mr. Boots was leering at Chrissy. She turned her head forward again, and her nose brushed John's chin. They both pulled their heads backward. Absurdly, John said, "what do you think our chances are of getting these ropes loosened? We will get numb from lack of circulation."

"What are you complaining about? You never had it so good." Another leer by Mr. Boots. "Now, I will have to ask you to walk into the house. One of you will have to walk backward. Who will it be?"

"You can't make us do that. It is impossible. Now untie us, right now," Chrissy insisted.

"No can do. Now, who wants to go backward? Make up your mind quickly, or I will help you along at knifepoint."

"Oh, so did you do Frank Doherty in?" Chrissy asked.

John shook his head 'no,' trying to give Chrissy the high sign not to let on she knew anything. But she had said it. Now, he felt they were in trouble for sure.

Chrissy opened her mouth to say something else when John planted his lips on hers, trying to speak simultaneously, 'be quiet,' which wasn't easy. He hoped she got the message as she pulled her head away. She glared at him but kept her mouth shut.

Mr. Boots drew his knife out of its sheath.

John said, "I will go backward," maneuvering around in tiny steps until his back was towards the house.

"This is not going to work," Chrissy said plaintively.

Mr. Boots commented, "it had better work." He thrust his hand forward until the knifepoint was against John's cheek.

"Chrissy, on the count of three, move the right foot forward. One Two Three." Chrissy moved her foot forward as John drew his back. Then they repeated it with the other foot.

She moved her feet in unison with John until they reached the second car, which was longer. John bumped into the tail end, throwing him off balance. They both fell. John yelled at Chrissy, "why didn't you warn me?" He had hit his head again on the cement, with Chrissy landing on top of him. His body cushioned her from being hurt.

"Don't yell at me. I can't see through your body, you know," Chrissy yelled back.

Mr. Boots grabbed them both and hauled them to their feet.

"Next time you fall, someone gets slashed. Do you understand? Now move."

John was counting again, and they started moving in unison. Chrissy was leaning her head sideways to look around him.

"Door coming up, probably a raised step."

"One two three, halt," John said. They both stopped. He leaned his head away to the left so she could see past him.

"Yes, a raised step about 3 inches."

"Come on, get moving," Mr. Boots directed, digging the knifepoint in John's face. John was counting again. "Raise your foot when you think we are at the step."

"Raise," Chrissy said.

She lifted her foot, but John couldn't because they were too closely tied, catching his heel. He tripped on the step. His body went sideways, bringing Chrissy with him. They didn't fall because of the doorjamb, but Chrissy was lying against him again in their off-balance stance.

She knew their bodies were being too intimate. She tried to be detached. But the man's lower body kept reacting to the brush of her body parts that were best kept separate from male contact.

Chrissy's face was a profusion of reds and pinks, embarrassed by his obvious response to her body, which he seemed to have a great deal of trouble controlling.

She turned to Mr. Boots. "It is impossible to negotiate that stair when so closely tied. Now, release these ropes immediately, or I won't move any further." John was dying inside. *Fine, she will refuse to move, but it is me that has the knife embedded in his cheek. She isn't going to shed blood, but I will.*

Again, the knifepoint nicked into his cheek, causing blood to run down his face.

"Please, Chrissy, try." *'I promise to try and control my body's reaction to you.'* John was silently pleading. They pushed off the doorjamb and tried to move in sync again. But again, John couldn't bend his leg at the same time as Chrissy.

"It can't be done, John. Untie us, or we will never get through this doorway." At the same time, she butted Mr. Boots knocking the knife out of his hand. It fell to the floor. When he bent over, John threw himself at Chrissy, bumping her over. They both landed on top of Mr. Boots and flattened him. Mr. Boots' breath whooshed out of his body, plastering him to the floor. Chrissy was on her back on top of him with John lying on top of her. Mr. Boots was face down and lying helpless. But she had Mr. Boots where she wanted him.

"Will you untie these ropes now? We are not moving until you promise to release us," Chrissy was threatening.

Once they got off Mr. Boots, John thought he wouldn't have to keep his promise. *What was the matter with this girl that she believed in promises? Such an innocent. She probably believes in Santa Claus and the tooth fairy too.*

"All right. All right, I will untie you, I promise," Mr. Boots said in a muffled voice still plastered to the ground.

"John, roll to your right." John debated ignoring her. *He didn't believe in Mr. Boots' promise.* Chrissy was glaring at him for not responding.

"John, I said roll to your right." Chrissy hit him with her head to emphasize her request. He got clipped on the nose. It now hurt as bad as his head, so he rolled before she had his nose bleeding. She rolled with him. They continued rolling until he was on top of her. When she tried to roll away, he stayed firm, not budging.

"John, roll-off me," Chrissy's voice was threatening. John grinned.

"Chrissy, you ordered me to roll, and I rolled. I can't help it if this is the way we ended up." Chrissy was still trying to roll, but he wasn't cooperating.

"You lummox, get off me." Chrissy was throwing daggers with her eyes. "John, I am going to kill you when we get out of this," Chrissy yelled.

Now Mr. Boots was on his feet. He came over to them. They both were expecting to be dragged to their feet, but instead, Mr. Boots started untying the ropes holding their legs together. When the ropes fell away, he lifted them to their feet again. Now only their upper bodies were too close.

"Now move," ordered Mr. Boots loudly.

John gave Chrissy a grin. "Do you want to put your leg between my legs, or will I put my leg between yours? You have a choice, darling, and I suggest you hurry." John knew Mr. Boots had his knife again.

Chrissy rammed her leg between John's. "Ugh, naughty, naughty, that wasn't nice." They were on the move again, easier with their legs free.

Chrissy said through gritted teeth, "be thankful I didn't raise my leg at the same time, the way you have been acting. You know what I mean, too human, in my opinion. Too male too."

But they were making slow progress even though their legs were free because John couldn't see where he was going. Chrissy wasn't directing him either.

John finally bumped into a door with a thump. The door opened with a jerk. John fell backward. Chrissy's weight landed on top of him, expelling all the air from his lungs.

"Well, well, what do we have here?"

John looked past Chrissy's head to see a man he recognized. "Mr. Hammond, what are you doing here?"

"Well, I happen to live here. Hello John. I didn't know it was you.

Release them," Mr. Hammond looked sternly at Mr. Boots.

Mr. Boots untied the rest of the ropes. Chrissy rolled away immediately like John was a snake wanting to coil itself around her.

"Help them up, Geoffrey."

Geoffrey grabbed Chrissy and pulled her up, brushing his hand across her chest. She brought her arms up to ward him off.

John had maneuvered to his feet on his own. *Now what?*

They were in a room that appeared to be a study. John was observing Mr. Hammond. He didn't look threatening in any way.

"Sorry, John, I had no idea it was you. Can you understand my amazement to find you here like this?" Mr. Hammond waved Mr. Boots off. "Geoffrey, I won't be needing you now."

"All right, Mr. Hammond, what is this all about?" John enquired.

"John, you have to understand that Geoffrey doesn't have much upstairs. He isn't too good at thinking things out, reacting with brute force. He must have got you mixed up with someone else."

John knew he would have to play along to get Chrissy out of there safely.

"Yes, Geoffrey must have made a mistake."

"Introduce me to your friend, John."

"Chrissy, meet Mr. Hammond. I don't know your first name."

"Alan."

"Alan, meet Chrissy Lambert."

"How do you do, Chrissy Lambert." Alan held out his hand.

Chrissy looked at his hand then raised her eyes to his.

"You expect me to greet you with a handshake after the humiliation you and your bruiser put me through?"

"Sorry, Miss Lambert. I apologize for Geoffrey. He can be a bit overbearing at times."

"Overbearing is not strong enough. Don't you mean overpowering and physically scathing?"

"Miss Lambert, I would be careful if I were you. Just a word of advice. I don't take kindly to rudeness from my guests. Do we understand each other?"

Before Chrissy could answer, John jumped in, "Alan, Miss Lambert is a bit upset about being tied to me, and my body didn't act too kindly to her proximity. So, that is why she is upset, isn't that right, Chrissy?" John held her arm squeezing it, hoping that she would realize her folly at speaking out, and the consequences if she continued. "I am sorry, Chrissy, but you are well endowed, and I was only reacting accordingly. A male would have to be dead from the feet up if they didn't respond as I did."

Chrissy wrenched her arm free. "Let go of me. I hate to be manhandled."

John dropped her arm, like a hot potato and held his hands up in surrender.

Mr. Hammond laughed. "Yes, I can see your point; proximity to Miss Lambert could be a problem.

Chrissy glared at both men but didn't respond, for which John was thankful. She figured from John's deference to Mr. Hammond that the situation could be lethal if not treated with care, so she had wisely clammed up.

"John, you understand I can't let you leave here without an understanding. You will forget about your trip. Blindfolds will be necessary when you leave. You do understand, don't you?"

John knew their days were numbered if they showed any interest in this place or today's events. But his first responsibility was to Chrissy and getting her away from there safely. So, his reply was a logical answer. "Of course."

"Geoffrey, John and Miss Lambert will be leaving now," Alan said in a raised voice. Geoffrey's immediate appearance meant he was just outside the door. He took an arm of each of them and lifted them along as they left the room. Mr. Boots was tall with a sturdy body, and his weight was solid muscle.

John and Chrissy glided along in his tight grip of persuasion. John called out. "It was nice to see you again, Mr. Hammond," to which there was no reply, only a grunt from Geoffrey.

They were taken to the garage, stopping beside the limousine. Geoffrey opened the door and reached into a pocket on the back of the seat and extracted some black scarves. Blindfolds must be a standard way of traveling in this car.

Geoffrey blindfolded them both. John was thankful that Chrissy was silent now. He did not want Geoffrey upset in any way until they were away from here.

They were both shoved forcefully into the limo. John sprawled over Chrissy, and she immediately gave him an elbow. John grunted and quickly straightened in his seat beside her.

The limo started to move to the accompaniment of classical music. Surely it was for Mr. Hammond's benefit as John doubted Geoffrey was a Beethoven fan.

The limo traveled the winding road for about an hour. Then by the sounds of the traffic joined a highway. John didn't remove the blindfold, although his hands were free. As long as Chrissy was beside him, he would cooperate to the fullest. He was hoping she would do the same.

They were traveling at a fast pace for another hour, turning onto an off-ramp. Then quickly turned left, then right then left shortly after then right. The limo seemed to be in a maze of short streets. John lost track of where they were with the transitions left to right so frequently.

Then the car stopped. Geoffrey opened the door on Chrissy's side. He quickly dragged her out, whisking the blindfold off, and shoving the door shut before John could get out. John almost had his leg caught in the door. Geoffrey moved to the front seat without comment to Chrissy. She grabbed for the limo door as Geoffrey locked it. John removed his blindfold and was trying to open the door to no avail. It had a unique locking system controlled by the driver.

"John, my phone number is 555-7777, call me."

He could see her mouth moving but couldn't hear clearly, and he had missed the first part but caught the 7777 by the movement of her mouth. He figured it must be her telephone number. Chrissy could not see in the window. She just hoped John could see her and hear her.

Chapter Two

Chrissy had no idea where she was or which way to go. No one in sight to ask. It was night time in an abandoned area. It was an industrial district from the dark buildings and the lack of vehicles.

She thought she had a reasonably good handle on this city of hers but obviously not. Where to go? Which way? She had no purse. She was almost in a panic when a truck came towards her. She waved a hand, signaling it to stop. But it kept going without pause.

Chrissy had to find a taxi or find a telephone. But there seemed to be a lack of both on these vacant streets. She had walked about three blocks when she heard another truck coming from behind. She whipped around. It appeared to be the same truck. She stepped off the curb onto the roadway, moving across the street. She planned to place herself in the truck's path. Would it stop? That was the chance she would have to take. The truck stopped, but only just two feet from her. Too close for comfort.

"Hey lady, what are you doing? Do you want to get yourself killed?"

"No, I need help. I was kidnapped, then blindfolded. They dropped me off here, but I have no idea where I am. Can you take me to a taxi or a police station?"

"No police station near here, but I can help you find a taxi. Are you hurt?"

"No, only my pride. I thought I knew this city so well, but I realize now I don't," Chrissy said in a pitiful voice. then added, "I did have a head injury, which made me unconscious at one point."

"I will get you out of here, but I have a couple more stops. So, it will be a few minutes longer before I can help you. Now hop in."

She went around the truck and climbed in.

"I am Tad Mousier. Who kidnapped you?"

"I am Chrissy Lambert. I don't know who they were other than their names."

"Why did they kidnap you?"

"Because I was in the wrong place at the wrong time. Otherwise, I wouldn't be in this predicament." Chrissy started to shake when she realized how close she had come to being killed. First by the murderer than by Mr. Hammond and Geoffrey, then this truck.

Tad could see she wasn't doing well, maybe going into shock, so he abandoned his deliveries and headed into the city core. He took her to a hospital emergency. Tad put his arm around Chrissy as he led her inside and up to the nurse's station.

"This woman has a head injury and maybe going into shock. She was kidnapped and released."

The nurse pushed a button, and running steps sounded from the direction of the corridor rooms. Tad eased Chrissy's shaking body down into the wheelchair the nurse was holding. Two doctors in green appeared.

"What happened to her?" The doctor was feeling for her pulse.

"She was kidnapped and then released. At least that is what she told me." The one doctor whipped her away while the other doctor stayed to ask questions.

"Do you know if she has injuries?"

"I asked her, but she said no at first, then mentioned being unconscious from a head injury. Her name is Chrissy Lambert. She said she was in the wrong place at the wrong time. That is all I know. She stopped me by walking in front of my truck. I was making deliveries. She appeared disoriented as to where she was. She seemed to be going into shock, so I brought her here."

"Okay, thanks, we will take care of her." Bill turned away and went after the doctor with Chrissy. Upon entering the room, he said,

"Gord, someone kidnapped her, and she told the truck driver she was unconscious at one point. So, I think we're dealing with a head injury and shock. Nurse, I want heated blankets."

Gord was administering an IV into her hand. "Her pulse was erratic, but her vital signs are only a shade off." He looked down at the girl. "Chrissy, are you okay? Did someone hurt you?"

She was still shaking, wrapped in a nest of heated blankets that the nurse had put around her.

"No . . . No, they took me somewhere. Then the kidnapper brought me back. I was tied and blindfolded, but they didn't hurt me physically."

"But the driver said you mentioned you were unconscious with a head injury."

"But that wasn't the kidnappers."

"Why were you kidnapped?"

"I was told someone was stabbed, but I didn't see anything. I was just in the wrong place at the wrong time."

"Where was this?"

"721 Langley Street. They said there was a dead body inside. A man chased me, and I fell and hit my head on an iron gatepost knocking myself out apparently. When I came to, a man and I were tied together. It was the man that chased me. We were in a garage, but I have no idea where," her words were starting to slither.

The doctor checked the bump on her head. But there was no sign of blood, although there was a protruding nodule and some bruising.

Bill indicated to Gord that an x-ray was needed to be sure. Chrissy's eyes kept closing.

"Gord, we had better get the police involved. Darcy, will you make that call, please?" asked Bill as he headed for the door. "I will arrange for the x-ray on her head. You make that call to the police and inform them she was kidnapped and released." Gord exited the room too.

"Are you warm enough now?" questioned the nurse.

Chrissy just wanted to go to sleep and wake up from this horrible nightmare and forget it all.

The nurse removed the extra pillow and eased her down. Chrissy closed her eyes dosing off but awoke during the x-ray exam. After the x-ray, they wrapped her in more warm blankets, and she drifted off to sleep from the sedative.

A young policeman was sitting watching Chrissy sleep. He was enjoying her pretty face with delicate features. He had a strong urge to protect her from whatever she had encountered. When she awoke, her eyes were deep blue but unfocused. He gave her a minute to come completely awake.

Her expression changed to a fearful look. The man started to talk.

"It is all right. You are safe now. My name is Officer Hanley, and you are?"

She tried to push yourself up to a sitting position then dropped her head back down. She still felt woozy.

"I am Chrissy Lambert." Her voice was little more than a whisper.

"Do you want some water?"

"Yes, please."

After pouring some, he put his hand gently under her head and raised her slightly, tipping the cup to her lips. She took a few dainty sips then a gulp.

"Where do you live? Is there someone I can contact for you? A husband? Father? Mother?" he paused after each one.

"My neighbor is looking after my son. He is four."

"Your son's name is?"

"Jared. My neighbor is Nancy Marshall. What time is it?"

"It is 10:13," looking at his watch.

"Oh, I have missed Jared's concert for his day school." Chrissy's face showed her distress. "I have to talk to Nancy right now. She will be so worried, and so will Jared."

"I'll get the nurse to bring in a phone. I am sure she can do that." Officer Hanley went in search of a nurse.

She was worried about Jared but also wondering how much to tell the police. Would John have problems if she told about Mr. Hammond? They evidently knew each other, although neither man expressed how.

Of course, she would tell the police. She didn't owe John anything. He was the one who attacked her in the first place. John might be covering himself when he tried to warn her away. In the end, he had been caught along with her by Geoffrey.

Officer Hanley reappeared. "The nurse is bringing a phone. Now Mrs. Lambert, would you like to explain what happened to you?"

"Well, I struck my head on an iron gate post when a man was chasing me. When I came to, we were bound together in a garage somewhere."

"Who was the man?"

"John somebody," Chrissy said vaguely.

"Where were you when you hit your head?"

"721 Langley Street. John said there was a stabbed man inside. He said he was trying to warn me away. We were in a garage when I came to."

"Do you think the man who kidnapped you was the murderer?"

"I have no idea. They didn't reveal anything when they were talking to us."

"Was there more than one man?"

"Yes, one called Geoffrey, and the other man was Alan," Chrissy said as though that was the limit of her knowledge.

"You don't know any last names?"

"Not that I can recall. My head is sore, and my mind is hazy."

A nurse arrived with a phone. Chrissy dialed the number and waited.

"Hello, Nancy." "Yes, I am all right now. I am in the hospital." "What hospital am I in?" She looked at the police officer.

"Stanhope General on Kensington Street."

"You heard, that didn't you?" "Well, it is a long story. But I am okay, just a bump on the head. How is Jared?" "I am so sorry I missed his concert. I will explain everything when I get there." "I'm not sure when. The doctor has to release me. I came in because I was going into shock." "Yes, as soon as I can," Chrissy hung up the phone.

Officer Hanley picked up the receiver and dialed a number.

"Hello, Mac. I am at Stanhope General hospital with Mrs. Lambert. She says there is a homicide at 721 Langley Street. Do you know anything about it? Well, maybe you should check it out. I should be back in half an hour." Officer Hanley hung up. Chrissy's eyes were closed as if she was asleep.

"Mrs. Lambert?" Her eyes popped open. "Do you know where you were taken and held?"

"No, I was unconscious going and blindfolded when I left."

"Why did they release you?"

"They said they had made a mistake. We were the wrong people. They drove us back to the city. They dropped me out in the industrial area, but they kept John and drove away."

"Can you describe the men involved?"

"John was about 6 feet, muscular but not a bodybuilder type with black wavy hair and brown eyes. He was wearing black pants and a pullover."

"Alan was about the same height as John with sandy hair and grey eyes, hefty build but well-groomed."

"Geoffrey has a huge bodybuilder physic along with brown hair, green eyes, and missing teeth. I think two. The way Alan spoke, Geoffrey, is Alan's bodyguard." Chrissy hesitated. "I think that is all I can remember," she wore a puzzled look.

The doctor came in. "Your x-rays didn't show any problems. The nurse said your vital signs are normal now. So, you can get dressed and leave. I strongly recommend that if your head bothers you at all that you contact your doctor. Also, be careful where you go as you don't want a repeat of what just happened."

"Thank you, doctor."

After the doctor left, Chrissy asked, "Officer Hanley, would you mind leaving while I get dressed?"

"No, but I'll wait outside. I will drive you home. I am sure you need a ride."

"My car?" she said in horror.

"I take it that the car is still at 721 Langley Street?"

"Yes, when I last saw it. I lost my purse there because I haven't seen it since I regained consciousness."

"We will call that way first. Where do you live?"

"Ambrose Street. Can I get dressed now?"

"Certainly." He left the room, pulling the door closed.

When Mrs. Lambert appeared, she had on a rumbled, stylish pink suit with the look of a well-established confident business woman.

She held herself well and walked confidently. The only evidence of her ordeal was a slight droop to her shoulders and a sad look on her face.

"Mrs. Lambert, are you ready now?"

She walked beside the officer out the door. The stares of curiosity of the waiting patients followed her.

When they were driving to 721 Langley, Officer Hanley said, "you know, I think I should drive you home. I doubt you are in a proper condition to drive. You can pick up your car tomorrow."

"No, I have to find my purse. I won't be able to sleep otherwise. I need my keys. Honest, I am fine now." Chrissy wasn't entirely convincing, but he did know how women were about their purses. Valerie, his sister, couldn't go without one hiked over her shoulder.

They arrived at the house with a feeling of dread, red, blue, and white whirling strobe lights illuminating the night. There were police cars all over the place and an ambulance.

Her car was sitting amongst this sea of white cars. There was no way she could move her vehicle anytime soon. Just then, another car arrived. A man in a business suit got out. He was a short man with a stern face like he never found anything in life to smile about. Officer Hanley said, "that is the coroner. I guess there was a homicide here this afternoon like you said."

Chrissy looked towards the house lit up like a Christmas tree. Lights in every window, as well as the veranda and the garage.

Where was Mrs. Frank Doherty? She wondered.

She headed for the front gate. Her purse must be around here somewhere. The light from the veranda and garage didn't quite reach the street area. The flashing strobe lights were only casting a fleeting glimpse of the ground. So, Officer Hanley went back to his car to get a flashlight. Upon his return, Chrissy could see there was no purse.

A white light appeared from behind them, swinging back and forth like a lighthouse illumination but still no purse. Did someone find it earlier and pick it up, or did the police on their arrival?

A man spoke. "What are you doing here?" Chrissy's pink suit stood out in the white light. He grabbed hold of Chrissy and looked towards the other flashlight questioningly.

Officer Hanley shone the flashlight on his face then away. "This lady lost a purse here this afternoon. We are trying to locate it. That is her car." Waving a hand towards the group of police cars.

The man was prodding Chrissy towards the house. She was trying to drag herself away from him.

"Mrs. Lambert wasn't involved in the slaying. Someone kidnapped her then released her. I was the one that phoned in the homicide after talking to her," said Officer Hanley. He had a hand on Chrissy, pulling her away from the man.

"And you are?" The detective continued pulling Chrissy towards the house.

"Officer Hanley of the 89th precinct. I responded to the call from the hospital where she was taken by a truck driver who found her dazed from a head injury."

"I am Detective Delaney. I am holding Mrs. Lambert here until I say she can be released. Do you understand?" he was still trying to pull her towards the house.

"She had nothing to do with this. She has a son waiting for her anxiously." Officer Hanley and Chrissy were still resisting the detective's firm grasp.

"I don't care what you think. I am detaining her here until I am satisfied that she is not involved. Do I make myself clear?"

"Yes, sir." The officer let go of Chrissy. She caromed into the detective as he again pulled her relentlessly toward the house. She regained her balance.

"Let go of me," she yelled. "I have had enough manhandling today."

"Fine, but you are coming into the house until I say you can leave." He had released her arm. Then he turned to the officer. "Hanley, you won't be needed here."

"But Mrs. Lambert shouldn't be driving in her state." Hanley didn't like the detective pulling rank on him. He still felt sorry for Chrissy and her plight, having this oaf dragging her around using no finesse. After all, she had been through enough already today.

"I will see she gets home. I said you are dismissed. You are out of your district here."

"Sorry, Mrs. Lambert," Officer Hanley gave her a woeful look, backing away, still reluctant to leave her.

"Thank you, Officer Hanley. It was nice to know that there is a courteous man in the police force. I will be all right. I will call a friend to come and get me." She gave a smile to the officer, then turned and glared at the detective.

"I will make that call as soon as we get inside." She said bluntly.

"All right, make the call, but you have to go inside to make it." The detective was directing her towards the well-lit house.

She glanced back at the officer that was still standing there, showing sympathy, with the strobe lights flashing over him. He was unable to leave in good conscience. Then Chrissy had to look where she was going because the detective was brooking no further resistance from her.

Officer Hanley wanted to run after her and drag her away. They had gone into the house and closed the door. It was over for him. He was not happy in his job tonight.

Chrissy demanded to make her call as soon as they were inside. Detective Delaney took her to the kitchen, avoiding the living room where the body was still lying.

"Make your call. One call," he said firmly.

Chrissy dialed her sister Selma's number. It rang and rang. Just as the answering machine was kicking in, she heard her sister's voice. "Selma, it is Chrissy. Can I speak with Dave? But first, can you call Nancy Marshall 555-7724. She has Jared, tell her I am delayed. Dave will explain. Just let me talk to him."

"Dave, can you come to be with me? The police are holding me because of a homicide. They think I am involved. The address is 721 Langley Street over near Jensen. Please hurry," she broke the connection as her voice cracked with near tears. The overbearing detective and the day's criminal activities being just too much for her.

The detective led her over to a chair, plunking her down roughly. He started grilling her so fast she couldn't think, let alone answer. Chrissy burst into tears. Her crying was a reaction to his abusive questioning, sobbing uncontrollably.

Detective Delaney was starting to feel sorry for his rough manner. She was a pretty lady that had fatigue written all over her. The detective saw some tissues on the counter and pulled a few and offered them to her. In a gentler voice, he asked, "Mrs. Lambert, will you explain what you were doing here this afternoon?"

She was not about to stop crying. It was just too much for her. Tears to wash away her dread of this nightmare that would never end.

Chrissy was not able to lift her hand or her head, feeling wrung out. The detective took some more Kleenex and wiped the tears off her face. Then her head fell forward. She would have fallen off the chair if the detective hadn't caught her. He lifted her in his arms, walking down into the guest bedroom and laid her on the bed. He reached for a blanket off the trunk at the bottom of the bed and covered her.

Detective Delaney now knew what Officer Hanley had been trying to tell him about his macho attitude that he had ignored.

She was lying there with her eyes staring but unfocused. Her stature was of a person that had endured too much. Delaney stood there, watching. What should he do? Call dispatch or a doctor? He decided on a doctor friend of his. He went back into the kitchen and made the call. Then he went into the living room to see how they were progressing. The coroner looked finished, and the photographer was packing his camera. The fingerprinting crew was still dusting the place for prints.

"Are you about wrapped up here, guys?"

"Yes, just that desk, and we are finished."

"Let's get this body out of here." Then Delaney turned to the coroner. "Well, George, what have you got to say?"

"Well, he was slashed three times, but he bought the biscuit with the second one in the heart. The third jab was for good measure or due to his natural momentum. There is no sign of a struggle. There is a slight abrasion on the back of his head, so I would say he was knocked out enough that he was groggy and couldn't resist. The killer held him from behind and stabbed him three times. The stab wounds indicate he was a strong, tall man. I would say by the way Frank Doherty was lying, someone threw him down that way or the killer was interrupted, or he was angry. The time of death is between 1:30 to 3:30 pm by the condition of the body. That is the best I can do until the full autopsy results."

"Thanks, George. Get the information to me as soon as possible."

Delaney was berating himself for not getting a report from Officer Hanley. Why hadn't he? The woman seemed to be in shock now. He doubted he would get much out of her. He scolded himself for resenting the young officer's attraction to the woman, which was evident at first glance, which clouded his thinking.

So, he had come down too hard on them both. When the light first hit the lady, he saw her as helpless. He had surmised that was an act on her part for the young cop's benefit. Especially when she gave that one burst of anger at him for maltreating her. But now he realized he had gone too far. He would have to backpedal and contact Hanley for his report.

He looked in on the woman first. She lay there unmoving, staring into space. He would have to make the call for sure now to Hanley. "Damn, damn." He called the dispatch to patch him through to the 89th precinct. "I'm trying to locate Officer Hanley. This is Detective Delaney."

"Just a minute."

"Officer Hanley speaking."

"Detective Delany here. Can you give me your report of what happened to Mrs. Lambert, as you have it?" He made it sound like he was confirming her story, but Hanley didn't buy it.

"How is Mrs. Lambert? What did you do to her? She went into shock earlier today. You drove her into shock again, didn't you? You know you are a real asshole!! I don't care if you pull rank on me about this. But I am refusing to give you my report. If my Captain passes it on, I can't stop him. You will get nothing out of me tonight." Officer Hanley plunked down the receiver. Was Chrissy okay? Could he go to her? Poor Mrs. Lambert. He should never have left her to that idiot.

Chapter Three

Mac, I have to go and find the lady I mentioned to you. Cover for me, will you until I get back?"

"Sure, Hanley."

Hanley got in his car, engaging the lights and siren and took off, arriving at 721 Langley in 15 minutes. Most of the police cars had left, except one.

Hanley headed across the lawn at a fast pace as two other cars pulled up. He didn't wait around, continuing into the house. Delaney met him as he reached the kitchen.

"Where is she?" he was ready to take Delaney on even though he outranked him.

"In the bedroom," Delaney said as a knock came on the door.

Hanley went down the hall to the first bedroom. Looking in, Chrissy was lying there wide-eyed and unfocused. He went over to the bed and pulled her into his arms. "Chrissy? Chrissy?" she didn't respond.

Delaney entered the bedroom with two men in tow.

"This is a doctor, and the other one is her brother-in-law, a lawyer," Delaney said in explanation.

Hanley didn't want to let go of her, but he wanted the doctor to examine her. He put Chrissy gently down on the bed.

The doctor ordered everyone out of the room. "Close the door on your way out." Even though he was here at Delaney's request, he could see open animosity here. He wanted it removed from the room.

Outside the bedroom, the brother-in-law introduced himself as Dave Lomax. "What exactly is going on here?" The young cop looked like he wanted to tear Delaney apart.

Officer Hanley glared at Delaney. "Your sister-in-law hit her head on the iron gatepost outside, rendering her unconscious. She was kidnapped, released, and then went into shock and taken to the hospital. I was driving her home when this idiot manhandled her away from me against my better judgment. Now it appears she is in shock again," giving an abridged version, so Delaney didn't get any details.

"Is that correct, Delaney?"

"The only thing I know is that they showed up here during a homicide investigation. Naturally, I was interested in detaining Mrs. Lambert to get her story. Perhaps I came down a little too hard on her in her fragile state. But I didn't know about the kidnapping or the trip to the hospital."

"Didn't you ask Officer Hanley why he was driving my sister-in-law home?" Dave asked sarcastically. He didn't like Delaney either.

"No, he didn't. But I did mention the hospital was where I picked her up. I told him she wasn't involved but kidnapped and released. He dismissed me and forced Mrs. Lambert into the house." Hanley had stepped in before Delaney could answer.

Dave whipped around on Delaney. "You did what?"

"Well, I knew she had been here earlier. I am in charge of the investigation, and I dismissed Hanley," said Delaney lamely, which was unusual for him. He was usually the driving force in all of his investigations. But that was before Mrs. Lambert went into shock because of his abusive treatment. He knew he had better keep his cool around this lawyer.

They were interrupted by the doctor.

"Hal, you better get an ambulance over here for this young lady. I want her in the hospital right away." Dr. Noble was worried about her lack of response to him.

Hal Delaney looked at Ted Noble with concern. "I'll get right on it," He pulled out his radio to call dispatch, requesting an ambulance be sent to 721 Langley.

Dispatch enquired. "I thought there was only one body there?"

"This ambulance is for a young lady that may or may not be involved. She is conscious, but in shock, I believe."

Dave was glaring at Delaney as he continued. "She was kidnapped, released, and taken into the hospital already today for the shock."

"That explains it," said Dr. Noble, looking enquiringly at his friend. He walked back into the bedroom, leaving the three men to talk.

"Delaney, you are in big trouble. If anything serious happens to Chrissy, as a result of this, I will sue you up to the hilt."

"I'm sorry I didn't mean her any harm. I didn't realize she came from the hospital after being treated for shock."

"Fine for you to say that now. You wouldn't listen to me when I tried to tell you. I will include this in my report that I give to the Captain," Hanley said, anger still evident in his voice. He asked Dave to call him from the hospital. My name is Joel Hanley. My phone number is 555-7667. I will be interested in hearing about Chrissy." Dave took down the number and thanked him for his concern.

Joel entered the bedroom. Chrissy's eyes were closed now. She seemed to be shivering, although the doctor had piled more blankets on her. He walked over to the bed, where the doctor was looking on with some concern.

"I noticed you were upset with Hal."

"You bet. I wished I had never brought Mrs. Lambert back here. I should have taken her home, but she was upset about losing her purse."

"Did you find it?"

"No, but I haven't asked Delaney yet. You know she is a nice lady. She didn't deserve this. She came here to change an appointment time with Mrs. Doherty, and someone nabbed her. I assume it was the murderer."

"Well, these things happen. You know Hal isn't all that bad. I've known him for many years. It is unfortunate he pulled rank on you and didn't allow you to speak out."

Two paramedics arrived with the stretcher, so Joel left the room. He approached Delaney and Dave. They were arguing about Delaney's part in Chrissy's condition. Delaney looked at Joel.

Joel asked, "did you or your men find a lady's purse outside on the lawn?"

"Yes, my men took it down to the precinct. Who does it belong to?"

"It belongs to Mrs. Lambert. That's why we came here instead of driving directly home. She lost it here when someone kidnapped her. Also, that is her car parked at the curb."

Dave chimed in. "I'll arrange to have the car picked up, and I will be down to your precinct Delaney, to pick up her purse. Where is your precinct?"

"Over on Mill Avenue, it's the 76th precinct. When you come back to get the car, there will be a police officer here. We will have surveillance here if the murderer didn't get what he was after, or Mrs. Doherty shows up. So, get a release form from the precinct for the car. I will let them know you are coming."

Delaney was using his authority again. He looked over at the stretcher as it went by. Chrissy had her eyes closed. He regretted that he had maltreated her.

Dave looked at her as she lay there in the serenity of the sedated. She was a good person. Why had the detective mistreated her?

Since Selma and he had married, Chrissy had been a big part of their family life. She was a happy, carefree girl that made a person feel good just being near her.

The doctor broke the silence.

"Well, I am heading over to the hospital. Hal, I will let you know more when I get her settled in there. Do you know who she is?"

Dave chimed in. "Her name is Chrissy Lambert. I am her brother-in-law, Dave Lomax," he handed the doctor his card. "I will come to the hospital before I go to the police station. I want all the details on her condition before I speak to my wife."

"Dave, I will see you at the hospital then. Hal, I will be in touch." The doctor walked out after the stretcher.

"Thank you, Ted, for coming when I called," Delaney said. It had been a long day. He still had to prepare reports before he could head home.

"Hanley, hadn't you better get back to your precinct. You are still on duty, aren't you?" Dismissing him and looking pointedly at Dave, indicating that it was time for him to leave too.

"Yeah, I better get going. Do you want to walk out with me, Dave?" Officer Hanley turned away from Delaney. He knew Delaney could report him for being out of his district while on duty.

Dave barely acknowledged Delaney as he left. It was better to walk away until he had all the facts. Joel filled Dave in on the information Chrissy had divulged to him, and what had happened since the hospital.

Dave understood now why Chrissy was in such a state. He also recognized that the animosity between the two officers was over his sister-in-law. Joel Hanley obviously was attracted to Chrissy from the reflection in his voice every time he said her name. Dave wanted his hands around Delaney's throat, but he would have his day in court instead.

Hanley implored Dave to let him know Chrissy's condition as soon as possible.

"Will you get in trouble for coming back here? I appreciate your concern for Chrissy." Dave asked.

"I doubt Delaney will report me as he knows my report could cause him a lot of trouble. So, we'll all have to downplay the situation, which I wished I didn't have to. But I need and love my job."

"That's too bad. I would have liked a report cataloging Delaney's behavior with Chrissy. Delaney needs reprimanding on this," Dave's lawyer mode had kicked in.

"You're right. I will report all of the details for Chrissy's sake. She certainly didn't deserve that kind of treatment. He still will be pressuring her for her explanation of today's events at a later time. You can be sure about that."

Dave thanked him as they both headed for their cars.

* * *

Chrissy woke up in the hospital to the murmur of voices. Why was Selma whispering? When Chrissy looked around, she realized that she was back in the hospital. There was an intravenous drip above the bed. Why was she here? What had happened to her? Think Chrissy.

Then the floodgates opened, a bad feeling ran through her body. The nightmare of details came to the forefront of her mind. "Selma?"

Selma's face quickly came into view.

"Selma, am I hurt?"

"No, you were in shock. You lived through quite a trauma yesterday. Are you feeling okay now?"

"I feel like a steamroller ran over me from the top of my head to my feet. Who are you talking to?" Chrissy tried to raise her head, but she was weak and fell back against the pillow.

A young man came into view. He looked familiar, but she couldn't place him.

"Hello, Chrissy. I am Joel Hanley. You might not recognize me out of uniform. I was the police officer that came to the hospital yesterday to interview you." He gave her a huge smile.

"What are you doing here?" said the dazed Chrissy.

"I am off duty. I wanted to see if you were okay. Do you mind?"

"I don't think so. I mean, it is nice that you took the time to come."

Joel grinned deeply. "I don't mind. I just wanted to see for myself you were okay. I'll be running along. You and your sister will want to talk."

"Joel, my mind is still so chaotic. Please stay for a minute while my head clears a bit more."

"I'll stay." I'll stay forever if you let me. Surprised, he had never felt that way before. Although he had dated over the years, his full energy and emotions had centered on his career.

Chrissy turned to Selma. "What happened to me? How did I get here? I remember leaving yesterday."

"Do you remember going to Langley Street?"

Chrissy shook her head as if to clear her mind. "Yes, I went to tell Mrs. Doherty I couldn't make my evening appointment." Then her expression changed from wondering to horror. Memories flooded in. She seemed to sink into the bed as if a heavyweight had come over her.

Joel leaped forward. "Chrissy, you are all right now. You don't have to speak to Delaney unless your brother-in-law is with you. He'll stop Delaney's highhanded attitude," picking up her hand, squeezing it as if to reassure her. Chrissy clasped his hand and felt the pressure inside her lift.

Selma stood watching them. Could this be a budding romance? They certainly look good together. Chrissy needed someone in her life.

"Chrissy, the doctor said you need to rest until you get over the trauma of yesterday. He wants to keep you here a couple of days," Selma said in a soothing voice. She had always been more of a mother to Chrissy than a sister since their mother had died. She and Dave liked having her around because of her cheerful attitude. On the arrival of the baby, she would make a wonderful aunt and godmother.

"Selma, I can't stay here. What about Jared? He must be worried about me."

"Jared is fine with Nancy. I will pick him up when I leave here and take him to my place. He understands that you couldn't make the concert. He doesn't know all the details, but he knows you were in trouble yesterday and ended up in the hospital."

Selma patted her hand. She hated to see Chrissy looking so defeated when she had always been a bubbly, fun-loving sister. How could things change so fast? Dave had been furious when he came home with the news that Chrissy was in the hospital. He had ranted about a detective he would like to plow into the ground. Dave wasn't the physical type. He usually did his fighting with words.

But according to Dave, this detective had needed a thrashing for his treatment of Chrissy.

"Chrissy, did you know anyone involved in the kidnapping?" Selma inquired.

"No, I don't even know why they kidnapped me, only that Mrs. Doherty's husband was stabbed. But I never went into the house or even knocked. Someone assaulted me before I reached the door. Then I ran away, only to trip and hit my head on the iron gatepost knocking myself out," she paused, looking from Selma to Joel.

"I don't feel up to talking about it. Maybe Joel can fill you in." Chrissy closed her eyes.

In a whispery voice, Joel filled Selma in on what he knew of the kidnapping and her release. He mentioned how he took her back to Langley Street to find her purse and experienced Delaney's brutish tactics. Joel was hoping that she was truly asleep. He didn't want her to relive the drama again.

Selma knew some of it from Dave, but Joel's account seemed so much more real. She understood now why her vibrant sister was suffering this breakdown of her senses. It was hard to see her this way. The bright, outgoing girl was not the defeated woman that lay almost cowering in this bed.

Joel was looking at Chrissy too, wanting to pick her up in his arms. He had only known her for such a short time, which astonished him that he wanted to help her forget the trauma as soon as possible.

Selma looked at Joel to say something about Chrissy. Only to be astonished by the expression of gentle caring on his face as he watched her sleep. It is strange to see how tense situations can make strong bonds between perfect strangers.

Joel finely looked at Selma. "She seems to be sleeping, so I'd better go. Do you think she would mind if I came back?"

"No, Joel, I think Chrissy would like that very much. Thank you for coming, and thank you for trying to protect her against Detective Delaney."

"After all Chrissy has been through, she certainly didn't need his overbearing attitude."

"I agree."

Joel turned away and left the room after gently touching Chrissy's hand.

Chapter Four

John Taylor remembered the events of yesterday. What happened to Chrissy? She wasn't looking too good when forced out of the limo. Why had she picked that time to call at the Doherty's house? If she had kept her night appointment, the kidnapping would never have happened. He would have gone after his target and not been around to be kidnapped either. But then he wouldn't have met Chrissy.

Who was she? Chrissy had said her last name was Lambert, and she was an Interior Decorator. She must be in the telephone book.

John knew he had to find her again to see if she was okay. He pulled out his telephone book to the L's for Lambert, Bill, Bonnie, Chrissy. That is easy fives and sevens.

He picked up the phone and called her. The phone rang and rang. Finally, her voice came on the line. "You have reached 555-7777. I am not able to take your call right now. Please leave your name and number, and I will call you soon."

He left a message. "Chrissy, this is John Taylor. I hope you are fine? I feel bad that I involved you yesterday. Please give me a call as I would like to apologize in person. My number is 555-8889. I hope you are all right?" John signed off.

She was a bit of sunshine in his murky life as a P I.

His mind flicked to Mr. Hammond. Why would he want Frank Doherty killed? He had always thought Hammond was an honest politician. Why did he need a bodyguard? There was just something not quite kosher with this picture.

He had met Mr. Hammond at a benefit dinner for the widow and orphans fund for the firefighters that had died in a big warehouse fire on Clinton. Six of them had perished when the fire reached some stored chemicals. The explosion caused the roof to collapse. The fire department had been unaware of the chemicals' existence on the premises. It was supposed to be dry goods only.

Alan Hammond had been going around shaking hands and being 'Mr. Nice Guy,' encouraging people to dig deep into their pockets for these worthy fallen heroes and the families they left behind. He was impressed with Hammond's sincerity, asking John to accompany him around the room as he shook hands with everyone. John's role was to backup Alan's pleas for generosity. Then John had a drink with him after being impressed with his manner and sincerity, and now John wasn't so sure.

I think I will do a little checking into Hammond's background. He picked up the phone and called a few friends, some legal, some not so legal, but part of his network of information. As the calls progressed, he was getting two completely different pictures of Alan. So, it would appear that Hammond was leading a double life. Interesting!!

When he finished his investigation, he decided this was not the man Alan projected to him the night of the fundraising. The sincere, caring, benevolent man was indeed a facade. Hammond apparently had money invested as one of the owners in the warehouse that had burned. Well, that was indeed interesting. Well, Mr. Hammond, I think I will do some more research into your business interests.

Now back to Chrissy. Do I call her again, or do I go to see her? Why wasn't she home? Has something happened to her? That wasn't a pleasant district Geoffrey released her in. "If anything happened to Chrissy, I can guarantee I will be camped on your doorstep Mr. Hammond, and I assure you it won't be a social call."

John got up from the chair and looked out into the night. Where are you, Chrissy Lambert? What happened to you? He stood, staring into the darkness. His condo was on the fifth floor with an obstructed view by other condos of equal height. He looked up into the sky. It was a clear night with a sprinkling of stars.

John walked to the phone and called Chrissy again, but the answering machine kicked in. His hopes dashed. Then he recalled her abundant loud, almost yelling conversations. She had been mad at him, really mad.

But regardless, at this moment, he wanted to hear her voice, to know she was alright. He was a loner as most P I's are, but tonight he wanted that female voice in his life.

* * *

Chrissy was still in the hospital when she had a visitor. She hoped it would be the doctor saying that she could go home. She felt recovered enough to leave, but she had lost something of her usual bubbly self. She tried to put the unpleasant events out of her mind. She wanted her everyday life back.

But the smiling Detective Delaney was not about to let that happen. She wasn't about to return his fake smile.

"Mrs. Lambert, you are looking quite bright this morning."

"I was until you arrived," Chrissy said pointedly.

Delaney lost his smile promptly. She was not pleased to see him, which did not bode well for him.

"Mrs. Lambert, I need to ask you some questions."

"Detective Delaney, I already told the police everything except for your treatment of me. Don't you file reports that are accessible to everyone in the police force?"

"Yes, but there may be something you missed the first time when you were in shock. I should apologize for my behavior. I didn't realize at the time why you had been in the hospital."

"Did you ask? Did you let Joel fill you in? No, you just ordered him to go away."

"Joel? I take it you are referring to Officer Hanley. I didn't know you were on first name terms?"

"Joel loves his profession. He thought I might get the wrong impression because of your overbearing attitude. He wanted to explain that not all policemen were like you."

"Mrs. Lambert, I was only doing my job. I was conducting a homicide investigation, and Officer Hanley was out of his district."

"Joel is a nice gentleman. He was driving me home. I was upset about losing my purse, so Joel was assisting me in finding it. Otherwise, I wouldn't have gone back there for love nor money."

"I know that now, and I am sorry." Delaney wasn't faring well. Should he leave and come back later or persevere? He straightened his shoulders and started again.

"Mrs. Lambert, I need to ask you some questions, and you are required by law to answer them."

"Detective Delaney, after what I have been through, I don't care a sweet damn about your investigation, so arrest me," Chrissy promptly closed her eyes and lips, keeping them sealed tightly.

Delaney stood there watching her. She was a sweet little thing even if she was obstinate. Under the circumstances, he didn't blame her. But that didn't solve his problem, sweetness or not. Chrissy didn't open her eyes. She laid there listening and wondering if he would arrest her?

He shifted his feet. "Well, Miss Lambert, maybe next time you will answer my questions because I will be back. I guarantee that."

Chrissy's eyes sprung open. She gave him a hard stare and pressed her lips more tightly.

Delaney turned and walked out calmly, trying not to let his body language show his defeat. This woman had been the first one to bring him down a peg. Even though he admitted it, the truth was he probably wouldn't change his ways. He loved the power his job gave him.

* * *

When Dr. Noble arrived, he told Chrissy she could go home, but she was to take it easy for a few days.

"Your overtaxed emotions are beyond anything that you have previously had to deal with. So, you will feel slightly wrung out for a few days or a week. Take care of yourself and don't be walking into any more unpleasant situations," squeezing her hand, he smiled sincerely. "I know Detective Delaney was partly to blame for your condition that landed you here. I think deep down that he wishes it hadn't occurred. Delaney is my friend. He isn't all bad, only a bit overzealous."

Dr. Noble smiled at Chrissy and left the room, and her eyes

followed him out. He was a kind person. He probably saw the best in everyone.

She picked up the phone and called Selma to come and pick her up. Her sister had brought in fresh clothes the night before in preparation for her departure.

Chrissy showered and dressed. She wanted out of there as quickly as possible. She wanted to forget everything to do with the last few days except Joel. He had popped in a couple of times but didn't stay long. He was a pleasant guy. So, she gave him her phone number and Selma's, where she would be staying for a few days.

Would Joel call now that she was leaving the hospital? The thought surprised her. What about her all-consuming career? She wasn't enthusiastic about it now. She thought she would reschedule her workload to take a week off to be with Jared, Selma, and Dave. Her priorities had changed.

Chrissy was all ready when Selma arrived. She was glad to have a wheelchair to take her downstairs as she felt weak after her shower and dressing. Dr. Noble had been right. She did feel washed out. But she had a big smile for Jared and Selma. Jared ran to his mother. "Mommy, are you all right? Why are you in that wheelchair?" His face showed his concern. Jared missed his mommy very much.

"Jared, I am fine. I am just feeling a bit weak. But I am certainly strong enough to hug my wee boy." She gathered him into her arms, squeezing him tightly. Tears were coursing down her cheeks.

Selma quickly stepped in. She thanked the nurse and said, "Jared, come help me push your mother out of here,"

Jared quickly complied. Chrissy tried to recover, wiping her eyes with a tissue the nurse handed to her. The nurse had learned the girl's plight in the last few days and understood why she was crying, holding her son.

The sunlight hit Chrissy's face. She breathed in the outside air. Chrissy was walking, holding onto Selma and Jared's hand with a firm grasp. She was free now. She was going to try to put this all behind her.

Except that didn't happen. At Selma's, Jared had gone out to play with a neighbor's boy Sam. Chrissy's thoughts caromed towards the fear of finding herself tied to a strange male. John . . . what was his name? Hammond, no, that was the kidnapper. Taylor, John Taylor, that was it. The helpless situation and the anger against him for his male behavior while roped so firmly together. Then later abandoned in the night.

Chrissy broke down and cried and cried. Selma tried to get her stopped. Worry set in. The dam had broken at last. It was long overdue. Selma figured if she had done this sooner, she wouldn't have ended up in the hospital twice.

Chrissy always took pride in the fact that she never cried, even as a child. She always seemed to be able to laugh the hurt away that was her nature. But this had been the straw that broke the camel's back. The events that were beyond anything that Chrissy could imagine except in the movies.

The phone rang. Selma didn't want to leave Chrissy, but she thought it might be Dave. He would worry if she didn't answer the phone.

When she picked up the phone, she said, "Hello, Dave."

"No, it isn't Dave. You don't know me. I am John Taylor. I am looking for your sister, Chrissy."

"How did you get my number?"

"I have ways and means. I am not phoning to hurt Chrissy in any way. I just want to know if she is okay? Do you know who I am?"

"Yes, you are the P I that Chrissy was kidnapped and tied to. She told my husband your name but not the police. Chrissy said something about not telling last names because she doesn't want to get involved. She also said you were a friend of the kidnapper. That is why they let you go. Mr. Taylor, I don't think you should call here anymore. Chrissy is having a terrible time ever since that man released her. She has been in the hospital twice. Now she is crying, and I can't get her to stop."

"Please, I want to come and see her. I will help her get over this. I will explain everything to her. By the way, I am not friends with the kidnapper. I only met him once before. We had an activity that brought us together one night."

"I don't care if he is your friend or not. I will not expose Chrissy to you or anyone like you ever again. So quit calling," Selma started to hang up, but she could hear him yelling.

"Wait! Wait! I have to see her. It is because of me she hit her head. I want to make amends for what happened."

"I am sorry, Mr. Taylor. Chrissy is in no shape to see anyone, particularly you," Selma did hang up this time.

She went back to Chrissy. Selma found her in the spare bedroom, curled up asleep. Selma got a comforter and covered her, noticing her face was still wet with tears. But Selma left because sleep was the best medicine for her.

She heard the back door and raced out to ward off Jared's yell for his mother. He ran around but couldn't find her in the kitchen, living room, or family room.

Jared must've heard her coming curbing his yell. Jared asked worriedly. "Where is my Mommy? I can't find her?"

"Jared, your mother is okay. I have just put her to bed. I need you to be very quiet and not wake her up. Can you do that for me?"

"Yes, but I want to see her."

"Okay, we'll creep up there. But you mustn't make a sound or wake her up, promise."

Jared put his finger up to his mouth and made a shushing sound. They crept up to the guestroom. It had twin beds, one for Chrissy and one for Jared when they spent the night.

Jared went on tiptoe to the bed. He could see his mother had been crying. His Mommy never cried or not that he had ever seen. He placed a finger gently on her cheek, barely touching her. Jared wiped away a tear, lifting his finger and looking at the tear. He didn't say anything, just stood there staring. Selma placed her hand on his shoulder and guided him out of the room, closing the door behind her.

"Come down to the kitchen, and we will bake some cookies. Would you like that?" Selma whispered.

"Yes," Jared whispered back.

When they reached the kitchen, Jared stood looking at the tear on his finger. He seemed to be mesmerized by it. "My Mommy was crying. Why was she crying, Auntie Selma?"

"Well, Jared, your mother had something happen to her. She

thought she wouldn't see you again. She loves you very much, and such a sad thought hurt her."

"But Mommy never cries," Jared said firmly.

"But, Jared, she has never been separated from you the way she was this time. It upset her very much, but you have her here now. Everything will be all right. Now let's make those cookies for your mother and Uncle Dave, shall we?"

Jared went to get a chair to stand on. He had made cookies with Aunt Selma before.

"Hold it, young man." Stopping the drag of the chair over to the island counter. "You have to wash your hands first." Jared scooted to the washroom off the family room. Selma followed to make sure his hands got the proper cleaning needed for rolling the cookies into a ball. He had fun making cookies.

Dave came home before Chrissy awakened.

"Where is Chrissy?"

"She is sleeping. Oh, Dave, she broke down when she came home. I couldn't get her to stop crying. It was awful, poor Chrissy. She went up to her room to lay down and went to sleep. Then that man called, the private investigator."

"Who called?"

"The P I, John Taylor."

"How did he get our number?"

"He said he has ways."

"I'm going to look into John Taylor and find out exactly who he is. What did he want?"

"Dave, he wanted to see Chrissy, to explain things to her. He said he was concerned about her."

"Concerned or not, he is not to come anywhere near her if he is friends with a person that murders and kidnaps people."

"I know, Dave. I told him that, but he wasn't happy about it. I have a feeling he will show up here sometime. He didn't sound like the kind of man deterred from getting his way for long."

Jared came into the kitchen to greet his uncle. He was hungry for more cookies and milk. "Hi, Uncle Dave."

"Hi, Jared. What's my little man been doing today?"

"Watching cartoons, and I made cookies with Auntie Selma. Uncle Dave, my mommy, was crying, and I took a tear off her cheek. It stayed on my finger until I washed it off." with wonderment in his voice.

"Yes, Aunt Selma was telling me. Well, Jared, you will just have to understand that sometimes things happen that are unexpected, and your mom couldn't cope."

"Auntie Selma said it was because she thought she wouldn't see me again."

Dave's look swung to Selma. She raised her shoulders in a shrug but didn't say anything.

"You know, Jared, if that happened, it would upset her." Dave left it at that. He went over and kissed his wife and put his hand on her stomach. "How is the baby today?"

"Fine, Daddy. I think I felt him move today for the first time. Maybe I will get over my morning sickness now."

"I hope so for your sake. You know I love you, darling," he gave Selma a tender kiss. Jared was looking on with wide eyes.

"Auntie Selma, why is Uncle Dave patting your stomach?"

"Well, Jared, when you were born, you were in your mommy's tummy. Now, I am having a baby." Jared came over to her tummy and placed his hand beside Dave's. "I can't feel anything," looking up into their faces.

"Sometime when the baby is kicking, I will let you feel it, okay?"

"Okay, Auntie Selma."

"What's for dinner? It smells good in here." Dave quizzed.

"Dinner is ready. Steak and kidney pie with mashed potatoes, broccoli, and cauliflower."

"Sounds good to me. Just give me a minute to shed this monkey suit. I'll be right back."

Chapter Five

Dave headed up the stairs two at a time, continuing to his bedroom. Dave came into the hall after changing as Chrissy came out of her room, rubbing her eyes.

"Hi, Chrissy. Feeling better?"

"Hi, Dave. A little but not much. I don't know what's the matter with me?" Chrissy said. She burst into tears.

Dave pulled her into his arms. "You need some time, that is all. You need to get a proper perspective on what happened to you."

"But, Dave, I never cry, and today I can't stop."

"I know Chrissy, but this is a different situation for you. Your life has changed. Your emotions strained beyond your ability to cope." Dave was rubbing her back gently. Her tears finally dissipated, and she pulled out of his arms.

"Chrissy, let's go downstairs. Selma has dinner ready."

She was reaching in her pocket for a tissue, but there was none. "I'll be right down."

Dave didn't like leaving her, but he continued down the stairs.

"Is she okay?" Selma inquired.

"No, she was crying again. It is sad to see her this way, like someone has beaten the stuffing out of her emotionally. I would like to wring Delaney's neck."

"Delaney?"

"Yes, the overzealous detective that caused Chrissy to break down the second time."

"Me too." Selma stops talking as Chrissy entered the kitchen.

"Can I help, Selma?"

"No, Chrissy, everything is ready. I just have to put the vegetables in bowls. You sit down in the breakfast nook with Dave as it is cozier there."

Dave steered Chrissy over to the breakfast nook, carrying drinks. "I have a brandy for you. We are going to enjoy our drinks while Selma gets things on the table." She sat down, taking a brandy from him, giving it a little sip. She felt a warm feeling as the brandy went down.

"Cheers," Lightly clinking glasses, they both took a drink. It went down easier this time.

Selma came over to the table carrying the bowls and set them down. She stuck her head into the family room, calling Jared to come for dinner.

Jared ran to do her bidding, entering in the breakfast nook. Selma arrived at the table with the steak and kidney pie.

"Hi, Mommy. Are you feeling better?" looking at his mother with worry.

"Yes, Jared, I am fine now," Chrissy gave Jared a weak smile.

With all three looking at her with such concern, she couldn't eat much. Not that she wanted to eat anyway. She finally gave up the pretext and excused herself from the table.

After she left the room, everyone started talking at once, all expressing concern but nobody with an answer. Jared finished with, "I want my mommy back?" He got up and ran out of the room.

Dave and Selma were in full agreement. They both knew that wasn't about to happen, at least not in this first week after the life-changing incident.

* * *

Chrissy wouldn't leave the house. It took another week before Selma talked her into going home for more clothes. In response, she indicated needing to make the trip alone. Selma had been taking Jared back and forth to playschool. While Selma did that, Chrissy got brave enough to pick up her car keys and head out to her car. She drove directly to her place only to find someone parked on her veranda swing.

He had his body scrunched down so his head was resting on the cushion at the back and he was sound asleep. The man was John Taylor. Rather than wake him, she opened the door and went inside. There was a lot of mail strewn all over the floor. They were in an area where the door to door mail still prevailed.

Retrieving the letters and junk mail, she went through to the study to check for messages. There were several messages, and most customers wanted to know where she was and why she didn't keep her appointments. Some others wanted her to call because they wanted to hire her. There were several calls from John Taylor. General inquiries at first as to how she was faring. Then later, the messages were, "Where the hell are you?" The final call. "I am coming over there, and I'm going to park on your doorstep until you get home."

Apparently, John was a man of his word. But he hadn't been there that long from his appearance.

She listened to each message again, writing down names and numbers. It was then that she picked up on a rather odd call. She hadn't noticed it the first time she had listened to the messages.

It started with heavy breathing, then music and a voice saying. "If you give any details to the cops, then that death march will be for you."

Chrissy sat up straight. How come she hadn't noticed it the first time? That must've been playing while she went to the washroom. She pressed the replay, and the message came on again. Only this time, it sounded more sinister. What had she told the police she didn't remember exactly?

She sat with her head down, eyeing the floor, concentrating on what she had told the police when a hand touched her shoulder. Chrissy jumped and screamed in terror. A male voice said, "Chrissy, it is me, John Taylor."

"John, what are you doing in here?"

"You left your front door open. Where have you been? I have been calling and calling."

"Yes, I got your messages a few minutes ago," indicating the voice. Callers were expounding names and numbers which Chrissy had missed during her time out of the room. Now she would have to listen to it again. The voices finally stopped. Chrissy sat staring at the grey answering machine as though it was a gigantic spider that wouldn't crawl away.

"Chrissy, are you all right?" John put his hand on her shoulder and shook it slightly. "Chrissy, what is the matter?" John sat down beside her on the couch and pulled her into his arms. She resisted at first. Then Chrissy gave in and practically climbed inside him. She was clinging so fiercely.

"Chrissy, talk to me. What is going on here?" John wasn't about to get an answer as she started to cry. He dreaded women that wept. They took away his tough veneer. Rubbing her back, he whispered phrases of concern. He apologized for bringing her into this mess. He knew how this woman was not the same woman he spent time tied to. Not that fighting girl that was taking verbal pot-shots at him and later Hammond. He wondered what had happened to her after her release from the limo.

The phone rang, and she visibly jumped then cowered more into John's arms. "Why are you acting like this? Aren't you going to answer the phone?" Chrissy was shaking her head back and forth in a frantic 'no.'

John reached out and grabbed the phone. "Hello."

"You are not to say anything to the cops, or you will be sorry," the line went dead. John knew now what was the matter with Chrissy. He stood up, easing her up with him. John led her in the general direction of the bedrooms. They appeared to be upstairs, so he took her up there. The first room held toy soldiers and racing cars. The bed had a Batman bedspread, so it must belong to her little boy.

He continued until he reached a room that looked like it might be hers. Chrissy wasn't saying anything, letting him lead her around. He laid her on the bed and pulled a comforter over her. Then he went into the bathroom and came back with aspirins and a glass of water. She didn't respond, so he sat down, lifted her and helped her with the water and aspirins. Lying her back down, he covered her again and left the room after closing the blinds.

He went back to the study. He pressed the replay. He listened to several messages relating to Chrissy's Interior Decorating, noticing the names and numbers on the notepad. When he got to the last name and number on the pad Chrissy had written, the next message started with heavy breathing, then music, then the voice. 'If you tell the cops anything, that death march will be for you.'

John knew this was the message that had upset Chrissy. The voices continued, and John continued writing down names and numbers that Chrissy would be needing. He listened to all his own messages, which weren't strictly the calls of a friend but rather blunt. Then one came from Joel, and John wondered who he was?

After the tape finished, John pushed the erase button removing all of them. Making sure Chrissy never heard it again. It looks like he would have to pay Mr. Boots a visit.

John made some calls obtaining more information on Alan Hammond from his underground contacts and past cop friends. Of course, they wanted to know John's interest in Hammond. John skipped around the truth, mentioning the benefit fundraiser association. It didn't quite ring true to them, as they knew him too well.

He went up to peek at Chrissy. She was out like a light. She didn't look like she would wake up anytime soon. But he couldn't leave her here. Her sister would have a fit if she came home looking so upset. So, he rolled her into the comforter and grabbed a pillow, and carried Chrissy out to his car, which he had parked partway down the block.

When he laid her in the back seat, she moaned a bit but never opened her eyes. He pressed his lips on her forehead, "Sleep, Chrissy, sleep." Opening the front car door, he slipped inside and headed out to Hammond's country place. He had learned the location from his cop buddies. He worried about the fact that Chrissy was with him, but he had to put a stop to those eerie phone calls to her.

He hid his car in the woods near Hammond's. He left a message for her to wait there if she woke up. He eased out, silently closing the door, hoping she would stay asleep until he got back.

He crept through the woods to the big house. It was an impressive estate home with well-manicured lawns and landscaping. It was a home with colonial flair, with white pillars going up to the top floor and a portico roof. It would be classed as a mansion by most people.

But he was not impressed. He was here for one reason only, so he circled the house observing the place. There didn't seem to be any guards, just a Doberman dog that John calmed down with a piercing whistle. Something he had learned in a guard dog training school that a friend of his ran.

John didn't know if anyone was in residence. Approaching the far side of the house, he observed some movement in one of the rooms. Now how do I get Geoffrey outside?

John remembered a trick he and his brother used to do when they were kids. They took a bunch of stones, and then they wrapped them in leaves. Then threw them towards the front door. The leaves would open up, and the stones would spurt out, releasing them with a rat-a-tat-tat against the door. Then they would run and hide. It worked still as the pebbles hit the door.

He crouched down behind a convenient large shrub not far from the front door. His only hope was for Geoffrey to come out and start looking around so John could get behind him. An element of surprise was needed as Geoffrey was big and muscular. John didn't relish going toe to toe with him.

The door sprang open Geoffrey leaped out looked around. John was silently coaxing come out further.

Geoffrey started to go back in but looked down and saw the stones. Turning around, he came forward and looked more carefully this time. Still, he couldn't see anything, so he walked out further. John managed to get up behind him and press his knife into Geoffrey's back.

"Step around the side of the house and into the trees. We're going to have a little talk." Geoffrey started walking.

"Keep your hands away from your body. No, into the trees," prodding Geoffrey with the knife for emphasis. "That's right." When they got in a bit, John whipped him around, throwing Geoffrey off-balance, landing him against a tree. John grabbed him by the throat and put the knife to his temple. "Put your hands on the top of your head. Up, up, that's right," now he started squeezing his throat with his fingers, flexing them, then tightening them, repeating it several times, each time constricting a little firmer. "Now, Geoffrey, I want it understood there'll be no more calls to Chrissy, have you got that?" squeezing him for effect. "Okay? Geoffrey, speak to me."

Geoffrey was having trouble breathing. He wasn't able to talk, only make weird sounds.

"You can do better than that. No more phone calls to Chrissy repeat that."

"No more . . . phone . . . calls to . . . Chrissy."

"Now that was easy, wasn't it, Geoffrey? If I hear you have bothered Chrissy again, I will take your head off. Is that clear?" Pushing the knife harder against his temple.

"Chrissy had nothing to do with any of this. She just happened to be in the wrong place at the wrong time. She knows nothing. She probably wants no dealings with the police either, so she won't be talking to anyone. Do I make myself clear?" He squeezed Geoffrey's neck. Geoffrey gave a strangled 'yes.'

"Good, now you can return to the house, and if you so much as turn a bit, I will have no choice but to throw my knife at you." John released him. Geoffrey strode towards the house and went inside, closing the door.

John hightailed it out of there, leaping into his car, gunning the motor, he backed out onto the road. Then put it into drive and was up to 90 in a few seconds.

Chrissy was stirring on the back seat. The screeching of the tires probably woke her. She felt the momentum of the car, and she started to scream. The kidnappers had her again. Tightly bound in the comforter, Chrissy screams were turning to hysteria. John was yelling at her, trying to calm her down. But Chrissy's mind had gone into overdrive. She knew the kidnappers had her again, and nothing John said penetrated her mind.

John had to keep driving until he got back to the city or somewhere, far away. He couldn't risk being caught if Geoffrey had gone for a car as soon as he went back into the house. There was not much in the way of traffic, although it was midday. That meant it wouldn't be easy to hide from Geoffrey. John's car was not a race car. In fact, he had intended to get a new car with more power. But he was somewhat faithful to this old clunker. He had it from its inception in 1979 and now was its 20th anniversary. But he had to get off the highway and hide. Chrissy was in a bad way now. She was in full bloom hysterics.

No matter what, John was taking the next interchange off-ramp. He had to help her calm down. Why was I so stupid as to bring her with me? Why didn't I just leave her in the house? At least she would have woken in her bed.

The car took the off-ramp with Chrissy still screaming. He saw a motel sign and headed in that direction. When he pulled into the parking lot, he hid the car behind a truck.

John climbed into the back seat. She had managed to get her arms free and was flailing out at him. He couldn't think of anything else to do but plant his lips on hers and let nature do the rest.

What started out being a kiss of necessity became a kiss of need for John. Somehow his embrace had penetrated her mind. Her eyes took in his features, and she calmed right down. Her arms went around his neck in relief.

He pulled back slowly, ready to cover her mouth again if she started screaming. But she was laying boneless in his embrace. Her arms fell from his shoulders.

"Chrissy, I am sorry I took advantage of you, but it is the only thing I could think of to stop you from screaming. You were beyond reasoning with. Do you understand?"

She was quiet now, staring up at John. Her mind had calmed down, but her heart was still pounding. She wasn't sure if it was because of the terror or the demanding kiss.

"John, why am I wrapped up in a blanket in the back of your car?" She was surprised she could speak so calmly because that wasn't how she was feeling inside.

"Don't you remember we were at your place, and you started to cry?" He wasn't about to mention the threatening phone calls he wanted her to forget.

"Yes."

"Well, I put you to bed, and you fell into a deep sleep. I was afraid to leave you there alone, so I brought you with me. Unfortunately, I had to take care of something, and I hoped you wouldn't awaken until it was all over. So that I could explain. But you did wake up, and now you are more frightened than ever." He kissed her forehead gently. "I didn't mean for that to happen. Please forgive me, Chrissy. I don't want to hurt you ever. Do you believe me?" He was still holding Chrissy, blanket and all, in his arms.

She lay there a moment, just looking at him. Her heart had settled down at last. But after that earth-shattering kiss, she didn't know what to think. She had never received kisses like that in her whole life.

"Chrissy, say something, please?" He was getting desperate. He didn't know which way this was going to go.

"John, you know you are the first man I have truly hated. Now take your hands off me and unwrap me." Her voice sounded hard. Chrissy really meant the opposite, but she wasn't about to make a fool of herself with this man and his stupid, meaningless kisses.

John pulled back quickly like she was a hot potato. "All right, but I have to touch you to unwrap you." How could she switch so fast to this hard-voiced woman when she was screaming hysterically five minutes ago? He wasn't sure which he preferred.

"Just unwrap me, but don't touch me. I mean that, John."

He unwrapped her, then quickly pulled his hands away. "Chrissy, I didn't mean to hurt you. I brought you along because I wanted to look after you. I couldn't just walk out on you, leaving you sleeping. You were crying so hard. You wouldn't talk to me."

Chrissy was pushing the comforter away from the rest of her body. "Get out of my way. I am going to call my sister to come and get me. Where are we anyway?" Looking frantically around, which belayed her stern voice.

"Chrissy, we are off highway 21 at a motel outside of Orca Falls. I was going to take you inside in the hopes of calming you down." He didn't want her to know that Geoffrey may be following them. "Chrissy, please let me take you into the restaurant next door? Then I will explain everything over coffee. Please, Chrissy?" John was backing out of the car. Chrissy stepped out and pushed past him and walked into the restaurant. He trailed after her.

She asked the waitress for the washroom without looking around. The waitress pointed to the back. John had picked up her purse before following her. He now shoved it into her hand. Thank heavens he had thought to bring it with him.

She walked to the restrooms. The first door had a picture with a little blond girl on the door and went in. Not a classy place but very clean. She set about repairing herself, putting water on her face, and bathing her eyes. After doing her hair and fixing her makeup, she headed for the door.

Did she call Selma, or did she listen to what John had to say?

"Well, I don't know what happened since leaving my place, so I had best listen to John. I am talking to a mirror. What next?" She straightened her shoulders. She was back in control again. It was as though this latest bout of hysteria brought her back into her normal self. She didn't know how, but it had.

John was watching the back of the restaurant with watchful eyes. He didn't want Chrissy to leave without him. If she didn't come out soon, he was going in after her. He waited one more moment. Then he half rose to go after her. But the door opened, and Chrissy walked out. Her features were like when he had first seen her, makeup and hair done to perfection. She was back. He gave a sigh of relief and plunked himself down and waited.

Chapter Six

Chrissy sauntered towards John with a slight sway to her hips. His eyes focused on her. She sure had a sexy walk. She stopped at the table and slipped onto the bench opposite him.

The waitress came right behind her. "What can I get you, fine folks? Do you want a menu?"

John looked at Chrissy enquiringly. She looked at the waitress. "Earl Grey tea, please." John indicated coffee was okay for him. The waitress walked off.

He looked at Chrissy, waiting for her to say something. She sat looking at him, waiting. Stalemate came into John's mind. She looked calm now and in control.

"Chrissy, I don't know what has happened to you since I last saw you. Please tell me. You were crying so hard, back at the house. I was afraid to leave you."

"John, you owe me an explanation. I am waiting."

"I have been worried about you ever since Geoffrey put you out of the limo. I phoned and phoned, but you were never there." He paused. But she just waited for him to continue.

"I don't know why the kidnapping happened. I caught up to the man I was following, but he denied killing Doherty. Plus, he denied ever being there, even though I had followed him. I am off the case, paid in full." Chrissy still wasn't saying anything.

"Chrissy, I was in the wrong place at the wrong time, just like you. I was only trying to warn you away. You have to believe me. Now tell me what happened to you?"

"That wasn't what you told me before, John. You said you were working for the government, and Canada doesn't have an Uncle Sam. Where were you going when you got to the house where you saw the body?"

"All right. Yes, I was working for the police, and yes, I was following a parolee for Uncle S . . . the local cops. Uncle Sam is just a personal joke, okay? But, honest, my parolee wasn't involved in the murder. Besides, I didn't lie to you. I evaded the truth. Now about you?"

"John, I don't believe you. How's that?"

"Chrissy, I have a letter of thanks in my pocket that will confirm what I am saying." He delved in his pocket and pulled out the envelope. CPD was on the corner of the envelope with a Calgary address.

Chrissy pulled out the letter. 'Thanks, John, for helping us out with the parolee. Enclosed is the fee I promised you, signed Uncle Sam.' She folded the letter and gave it back to him. Looking across at him, she slowly started to talk.

"After letting me out of the limo, a truck driver came along and helped me. By this time, I was slightly disoriented, so he took me to the hospital. I must have babbled about being kidnapped because the police showed up and took a statement."

John's heart sank, but he didn't let on.

Chrissy continued, "I gave them the details of the kidnapping except I didn't mention any last names, only first names." She stopped talking, a puzzled look on her face. "Why didn't I tell them who you were and Mr. Hammond? I just don't know." She paused again.

John waited for his heart to return to normal.

She got a dreamy look on her face. "The police officer, whose name was Joel Hanley, was there when the doctor released me. He offered to drive me home, but my purse was missing. I remember not having it during the kidnapping, so I asked Joel to take me back to the Doherty's house."

So, the message was from Joel, a police officer. Now, why would she be getting private calls from him?

"When we got to the house, there were police cars everywhere, an ambulance and my car. We looked around, but we didn't find my purse. We were just about to leave when this police detective ordered Joel to leave, detaining me. He ordered me into the house. Joel tried to argue with him, but that detective pulled rank and ordered him back to his police station and his nightly duties."

Drawing a deep breath, she continued, "Detective Delaney started throwing his weight around ordering me into the house, dragging me to make his point. He was very offensive. I broke down. He called a friend who was a doctor, as Delaney knew I was pretty well out of it. The doctor called an ambulance to cart me off to the hospital. While they were waiting, Joel showed up. He told me later that he reamed Detective Delaney out for his behavior. He told the doctor that I had been in the hospital already that day with shock."

"The next thing I remember was Selma was at my bedside. The police officer, Joel Hanley, I mentioned, was there too, but he wasn't in uniform this time. He said it was a personal visit. They kept me in the hospital for a couple of days. Then my sister took me to her place because I wasn't back to my usual self yet. Then the crying spell happened, causing Jared, my son, to be frightened. I never cry. Finally, today I was able to attempt the trip to my place on my own. I was still pretty numb, but that threatening call shook me up beyond my endurance. You know the rest. Now, where are we?"

"I told you outside of Calgary at a motel."

"What are we doing here?"

"Well, you were screaming," The waitress arrived with the drinks. John hoped she hadn't heard what they were saying. Evidently, she had because the waitress gave them a strange look, putting the coffee, tea, and creamers on the table. She walked away but only to the next table. She was straightening the salt and pepper shakers and sugar unnecessarily.

John hoped Chrissy wouldn't say anything until the waitress moved away. He lowered his voice. "You were screaming, so I came in here to calm you down."

"You call kissing me, calming me down."

"Well, you stopped screaming. didn't you?" He picked up his coffee and took a big swallow, and it burned all the way down. "Damn, that was hot." He grabbed a couple of creamers and doctored the coffee.

She was pouring her tea, not bothering with creamers.

"Yes, I stopped screaming, but why was I screaming?"

"Well, you woke up while I was making a getaway. I guess wrapped up the way you were frightened you."

"I thought another kidnapping was occurring. Getaway? From what?" Chrissy was now yelling. The waitress was heading their way.

John stood up, leaning over the table, grasping Chrissy's head with both hands, kissing her full on the lips. The way he was holding her, there was no way that she could avoid him. Kissing her deeply until John felt her relaxing, then he continued with a second kiss for good measure. She was responding against her will but responding fully.

The waitress observed the kisses and decided it was just a lover's spat and turned away with a smile on her lips. *Why didn't Ben ever kiss her like that?*

Chrissy was sitting observing John quietly. *Why did she keep responding to his kisses?*

"John, you can't keep kissing me when you want to silence me. It isn't proper. I don't even know you," she said indignantly.

"Chrissy, I don't want to be arrested, and it is the only way I can think of to stop you." He wasn't going to get over this woman very quickly. She was so delectable to kiss. Where had his policy of love them and leave them gone?

"John, what getaway?" Chrissy reminded him angrily.

"Well, I went out to talk with Geoffrey. To tell him not to threaten you by telephone anymore. I was rather persuasive, and I thought we had better get out of there after I delivered my speech."

"But if you were that persuasive, why did you need to make a getaway? Why, John?"

"Well, I wasn't sure how well it sunk in. Chrissy, I just didn't want to involve you anymore. Don't you understand?"

"I understand all right. John, you are a coward."

John was horrified at the reasoning of that conclusion. No one had ever spoken to him like that. Known as 'Mr. Mean Guy' by all the people he usually dealt with, especially when he was on the police force. Only in Chrissy's presence did he come off as pathetic. Why didn't he just walk away while he was still ahead?

"Chrissy, you won't be getting any more phone calls, I guarantee it. Now, why don't I get you back home and we will call it a day."

He got up and walked over to the cash register to pay for the drinks. He turned around to see if Chrissy was coming. She sailed past him with her head held high, ignoring him. He wanted to grab her and shake her. Instead, he would take her home and walk away from her forever.

Dead silence prevailed during the ride to Calgary. He drove to her house, parked behind her car, waiting for her to jump out.

"John, I won't be seeing you again. I think that is best. I need to get my life back to normal." She got out without looking at him, but his voice followed her.

"Goodbye, Chrissy. Have a good life." He backed out of the driveway and sped off down the street, letting her know this was the end of him.

Chrissy took her comforter and pillow into the house and went up to her bedroom. She deposited it back on the bed and sat down. She just sat there for the longest time, not thinking, just sitting.

Finally, a tear cascaded down her cheek. One tear was all she shed for John. Then she grabbed her purse went into the study to pick up the list of names and phone numbers of the customers she had to call. She noted some of them were in masculine handwriting. John must've completed her list.

The answering machine was still winking. Chrissy pressed the play button. It was Selma asking where she was. He must have erased all the other messages.

She called her sister. "Hi, it's Chrissy."

"Chrissy, where are you? Are you all right? I was worried about you. You were away for a long time." Chrissy could hear how frantic Selma was. If only she knew the actual story, she would be even more upset, but she didn't intend to tell her.

"I am all right. I just fell asleep on my bed. I am sorry I upset you. How is Jared?"

"Jared is here anxiously awaiting your return. He is upset that you are missing again."

"Selma, tell him I'm not missing. I am just at our house."

"Why didn't you answer the phone when I called? I was giving you another fifteen minutes. Then I was phoning the police." Selma's voice was concerned.

"I didn't hear the phone. I guess I was too deeply asleep. I had taken a couple of aspirins. I am coming back right now. Tell Jared I'll be there soon."

She had not lied at any time during her conversation. Just avoided giving pertinent information as to the afternoon's events. Four hours that she couldn't tell anyone about.

Chrissy closed up the house, but before she could get into her car. A man walked towards her. It was Detective Delaney, the last person she wanted to see.

"Mrs. Lambert, I want to speak to you. Can we go back inside?"

"No, detective. I need to get back to my son. He is upset that I was away from him for so long."

"I could take you into the police station if you would rather." Delaney was demanding so that she would answer his questions.

"Am I guilty of a crime? Is that why you are taking me in?"

"No, but you have never answered any of my questions, and you were involved in a homicide. I can legally take you in for questioning."

"Well, Detective, my boy is more important. I didn't have anything to do with the murder of Mr. Doherty, or whoever it was." Chrissy got into her car.

"Hold on, Mrs. Lambert. I'll tell my man to follow us, then I will ride with you, and you will answer my questions. Wait here for me." Delaney went back to the police car and told Fred to follow them. Then he got into the car with Chrissy. He should have hauled her downtown, but he figured he owed her that much. His mistreatment caused her second trip to the hospital.

Chrissy backed out of the driveway and took off for Selma's. The police car pulled in behind.

"Mrs. Lambert, why were you out at Mr. Doherty's house?"

"To cancel an appointment with his wife for that night. I was supposed to go see my son's concert."

"Why didn't you just phone?"

"Because I was in the area on another assignment when I stopped in, figuring it was much easier. Boy, was I ever wrong?"

"What happened when you got there?"

"I was heading towards the veranda to ring the bell, but before I could get there, a man came up behind me. I was frightened, so I ducked under his arm and ran. He chased me, and I stumbled near the gate. I fell, hitting my head on the iron gate post."

"What happened then?"

"When I came to, a man and I were tied together on the floor of a garage. There were some cars in the garage, one of them a limo."

"Who was the man?"

"I don't know. He said his name was John. He was the man that chased me when I fell."

"What happened then?" Delaney inquired.

"We were taken into the house to see another man by Mr. Boots."

"Who was the man you went inside to see?"

"His name was Alan. John seemed to know him. Then we were untied and released. During the trip back, Mr. Boots released me first in the industrial district. It was late at night, and there was no one around. Due to the blindfold, I had no idea where I was. My injured head was bothering me also, and I felt disoriented. A truck driver found me and took me to the hospital."

"What happened then?" Delaney felt this woman was reluctant to talk, the way he had to keep prodding her.

"Officer Hanley came to take my story of the kidnapping. I told him exactly what I've told you now. The doctor came to release me. Officer Hanley gave me a ride home when I realized my purse and keys were back at the Doherty's. Officer Hanley took me back to the house on Langley Street, and you know the rest."

"You have given me the first names only. Why?"

"That is all I know. I didn't hear any others."

"Can you describe them, Mrs. Lambert?"

"Not really. The man I was tied to was taller than me, dark hair. I don't remember much else."

"You must've been appallingly close to him if you were tied together. Think, Mrs. Lambert."

"We were unconscious most of the time, both of us. His eyes were brown or gray. His features were not outstanding in any way."

"Mr. Boots, can you describe him?" Delaney figured she was jerking him around even though her story was the same as told to Officer Hanley. Maybe the blow on the head had affected her.

"He was a big man, muscular like a bodybuilder. He was ugly and had on these big boots. He kept pushing us around because we were tied together."

"And this Alan guy?"

"Distinguished man, probably a successful businessman, was my impression. He seemed to know John and ordered our release saying that there had been a mistake, and we left blindfolded."

"Your hands were untied. Why didn't you remove the blindfolds?"

"Mr. Boots had a gun, and I was confused enough without getting shot in the bargain."

They arrived at Selma's, and Jared came flying out of the house. Chrissy leaped from the car and gathered him in her arms and hugged him tightly. Jared had a stranglehold on her.

Delaney stood watching the two of them. They looked very close, especially when the sister joined in hugging both of them.

Mrs. Lambert was lying, but how could he prove that? Delaney knew it was time to leave for now. He got into the cruiser, still watching the three-hugging people. He signaled for the driver to drive on, never removing his eyes from Mrs. Lambert. She was one pretty lady, but she knew more than she was admitting.

Chrissy was still hugging Jared and Selma. It disturbed her that Delaney was watching them. Afraid he would insist on coming in. But he must have decided against it as he got into the police cruiser and drove away.

She let out a sigh of relief. "Come on, let's go inside, shall we?"

Selma broke her hold. Chrissy carried Jared into the house, following her sister. When they were inside, Selma said, "you look different, more like your old self. What happened?"

"Nothing. I went to my place, looked through my mail and

listened to my phone messages. Then I didn't feel well, so I took a couple of aspirin and fell asleep on the bed. When I awoke, I listened to more messages. That is when I realized you had phoned and I came home. Detective Delaney arrived as I was leaving, but I still insisted on coming home. So, he rode along with me, asking the same questions I'd already answered for Joel Hanley."

"Speaking of Joel. He has called a couple of times. He seems to be worried about you being out on your own. He seems to care for you, Chrissy." Selma teased.

Chrissy was glad her sister had been distracted. Even to her ears, there was a discrepancy in time. More had happened to her in those four hours. She wanted to keep to herself. She didn't want to worry her sister, nor mention John. He was gone, and that was the end of the story.

Jared occupied her with funny stories of playschool. He had lots of friends there that he loved to talk about.

Dave came in. The conversation turned to his day in court, and the case he was presently on.

He noticed as dinner progressed that Chrissy seemed to be back to her usual self. So different from her behavior of the past two weeks. She was even saying it was time to return home and recover her career before losing all her clients. Selma, the protective sister, tried to deter her, but Dave agreed with Chrissy.

Over coffee in the family room, Chrissy announced she was going home the next day when she drove Jared to playschool. Selma again protested, but Dave gave her a warning look to drop it.

Chrissy was deep in thought for the balance of the evening. To Selma's question of what was bothering her, she replied, "just planning my week with the calls I received."

Selma accepted that but didn't believe that Chrissy had got better just from sleeping at her place. Something happened to her while she was away. Maybe it was seeing Detective Delaney again, looking for a logical reason. Chrissy didn't like the detective, so she was still skeptical.

Chrissy was thinking of John and his kisses in particular. How could she respond to a perfect stranger? Those kisses that started to shut her up but soon developed into full-blown lust. John certainly wasn't her type in any shape or form. Besides, there was Joel, and he was more her type, caring, trustworthy, and kind. Chrissy liked him a lot.

The evening had progressed enough for Chrissy to excuse herself, without comment. She would have to spend more time with Jared. He was the one needing attention now. Jared was becoming clingy and fearful every time she disappeared from his sight. So, she had made a special occasion of putting him to bed that evening. Selma had been doing that chore while she hadn't been herself.

"Goodnight, Selma, Dave. Thank you for all you have done for me. I will be taking Jared to playschool and continue on my way home. I don't know how I could have gotten through all this without you both." She went over and kissed her sister, then Dave.

Dave cautioned. "Remember, no more answering questions with Detective Delaney without me there for you." She dutifully replied, yes. She headed up to bed with a jaunty step of old but inside a heavy heart. When she was out of earshot, Selma whispered.

"Dave, something happened to Chrissy today. She is back to her normal self, but different too. She didn't get that way by sleeping the afternoon away. She didn't even answer the phone when I called. By that time, she had to have slept for about four hours."

"Selma, aren't you reading more into her returning to herself than you should? Why would Chrissy lie to you?"

"But that is the very point. I don't think Chrissy lied. She did sleep some, but there was more going on. She lied by being evasive."

"Selma, a person, doesn't lie if they are evasive. They just don't tell the whole truth. You don't like that, and neither do I. We have to wait until she is ready to tell us, if ever."

Dave took his wife into his embrace and kissed her soundly while his hand lovingly traced the baby in her tummy. The kisses were so breathtaking that Chrissy's problems disappeared.

However, Chrissy was dealing with those problems and unable to sleep. What if the calls didn't stop coming? What if they found out that she had spoken to the police not once but twice? Granted, she didn't give them much information, but the message said, not at all.

Even though John had gone back and threatened them, they could come after her again. She had sent John out of her life for good, and no way of finding him if she needed him.

Unless she could find Uncle Sam, whoever he was. She knew he worked with the Calgary Police. It was ridiculous she couldn't go around asking every cop if he was Uncle Sam. John must have an office. When she got home, she would look for his number in the phone book.

Her thoughts turned to Joel. He had called again tonight, but he was on duty. So, he hadn't been able to come over. Joel was unhappy that Delaney had been back harassing her, but she assured him he was more congenial. He ended the call by making a date with her for Saturday night.

Her last thought as she drifted off to sleep was John and his lust-filled kisses.

Chrissy was warm all over, burning up with his kisses. After shedding her clothes, his hands were all over her body. But then Mr. Boots walked in. Chrissy was trying to cover herself. Then she woke up. She had all the blankets screwed up on top of her. Rearranging the covers, she punched the pillow and went back to sleep.

When she awoke, Jared was jumping on the bed. She was happy the night was finally over because she woke up again during the night moaning, her skin tingling from John's kisses and his profound passion. After that, she had been afraid to go back to sleep for the longest time. How could she forget John if she kept dreaming these torrid love scenes?

Chapter Seven

Chrissy left Selma's with her belongings and a positive attitude. She was going to resume her life. Jared was excited about going home, so Chrissy let him skip playschool. She spent an hour setting up appointments, along with giving her apologies to the disappointed clients during the past two weeks.

She wondered where Mrs. Doherty was when she came across her name on the calendar. Mrs. Doherty had not put in an appearance, to her knowledge. Chrissy thought this was strange. Had she killed her husband? No, it was Geoffrey, wasn't it? She did not know for sure, but she was going to put all that behind her.

She took Jared shopping as the fridge was bare. On returning home, lunch became a picnic in the backyard. She played with Jared on the swing set and monkey bars. They built sandcastles in the sandbox. She then suggested he go for a nap or quietly play in his room, as she had to do some phoning.

When she went into the study, the light was blinking on her answering machine. The first call was a cancellation of an appointment she had made that morning. Chrissy was looking in her client book to obtain the number when the next message started with a female voice. It was muffled and afraid. She was asking Chrissy to come to an address on the westside of Calgary. The female voice yelped like someone was hurting her. Then the line went dead.

She didn't know what to make of it. Did she ignore it, or did she go? She sat hashing this over when the phone rang again. It was John.

"I thought you were not going to call me again?"

"Well, Chrissy, although I intended to call our relationship quits, I am still fearful that Geoffrey might contact you, so I had to call. Did you?"

"Did I what?" Chrissy's mind was still on the strange message.

"Did you hear from Geoffrey?"

"No, he never called again." Chrissy's voice held puzzlement.

"Chrissy, what is the matter? Did something happen to you?"

"No, nothing happened to me."

"You don't sound okay. Tell me what is going on?"

"I got a strange phone call," Chrissy said hesitantly.

"What do you mean, a strange phone call? You said Geoffrey didn't phone."

"Geoffrey didn't call. This was from a woman."

"What was strange about it?"

"It was asking me to come to an address on the westside of Calgary. No explanation, only the address. Then the woman yelped, crying with pain as if someone was torturing her."

"Chrissy, you are not to go there or anywhere near there, is that understood? Now give me the address." She gave him the address.

So much for getting John out of her life. "John, will you call me when you find out what is going on?"

"Yes, Chrissy, I will call you. I don't suppose I could talk you into staying home for a few days until I figure out what is happening?"

"No, John, I can't cancel my appointments again. My business is my only means of support, so I can't afford to lose any more clients."

"Chrissy, be careful, won't you? Be aware of your surroundings."

"Yes, John, I'll be careful. What if I don't show up. They may kill that woman. I wouldn't be able to live with myself if they did."

"Chrissy, what if you go and you end up dead. What then? Besides, she may be dead already for all, you know. I got you into this nightmare. Let me get you out, okay? Promise."

"All right, I promise, but promise me you will call as soon as you find out anything?"

"I will, but you stay put." John rang off before any more comments.

When will this nightmare end? She sat there, staring at the phone when the doorbell rang. She went to the front door. It was Detective Delaney.

"Can I come in, Mrs. Lambert?" Chrissy hesitated. He continued. "We can do this downtown if you prefer?"

She stepped back, and Delaney marched in. She showed him into the study.

"Mrs. Lambert, have you heard from Mrs. Doherty?"

"No."

"Did you have any other contact number other than the house?"

"No."

"Did you go into the house?"

"No, John stopped me before I went in."

Delaney noticed the way she said John so easily as though she knew him.

"Wait, yes, I went in. You dragged me, remember." Her voice was slightly bitter.

"Mrs. Lambert, who is John?"

"John is the man I was tied to when kidnapped."

"You gave me a vague description. Can you recall anything more now that you have had some time?"

"I don't think so other than he was solidly built but not a muscleman like Mr. Boots. He had a gruff voice like he could be tough." She paused. "Yes, most people would call him tough, I guess." There was doubt in her voice.

"But he didn't come across to you that way?"

"Yes, he did when he chased me. I was very fearful of him." Chrissy still had a note of doubt in her voice but not as obvious this time. Detective Delaney missed it.

"Mrs. Lambert, can you describe the house where they held you?"

"We were in a garage. It had room for four cars, but there were only three in there. Two were antique cars, but I don't know their vintage and a limousine."

"But, Mrs. Lambert, you said you went into the house." Delaney had been flipping back in his note pad. He was writing notes in it as they talked.

"Yes, but John and I were tied together. It was difficult to walk.

We were concentrating on walking as Mr. Boots had a gun."

Again, Delaney flipped through his notepad. "Mrs. Lambert, you said you were untied when . . ." Delaney flipped through his note pad again. "after Alan recognized John."

"Yes, we were in a room like a study." Chrissy looked around. "About two or three times bigger than this, with lots of books on shelves. There were French doors to a terrace." She stopped as though that was all she remembered.

"Anything else?"

"No, my head was still hurting. I was upset over the gun, so I don't remember anything more."

"What about the outside of the house?"

"We were blindfolded, so I don't know anything else, other than it was a limousine that we were in."

"What happened to John?"

"Mr. Boots took John with him."

"Hasn't John been in contact with you?"

"Detective Delaney, I have been staying with my sister Selma. I just got home this morning. My son, Jared, stayed home from playschool. We had a picnic lunch. Now I am getting caught up on my business calls."

"What business are you in, Mrs. Lambert?" Delaney's voice held sarcasm.

"I am quite a successful Interior Decorator." Chrissy's chin went higher.

Delaney glanced around. "Did you do this room?" He liked what he saw, comfortable leather furniture in a burgundy color with the carpet shot through with burgundy, orange, and bright blue on a beige background. The design was eye-catching, with similar designed tall vases and a world globe with the same colors as the carpet placed strategically in the setting. How had she been able to match these pieces so that they blended in so well?

"Where did you get the vases and the world globe? Did you have them made special?"

"No, I found them at an estate sale. That is how I get a lot of my antiques and decor accents."

"Very nice." Delaney paid her a compliment because this room appealed to him. Now he was sorry about his sarcasm.

"Mrs. Lambert, how old would you say John is?"

"I am no good with people's ages." She said evasively. She had to get rid of Delaney in case John phoned.

"Try, Mrs. Lambert."

"About 30 or 35."

"Anything else you could add about him?"

"No detective, you have already asked me that." Chrissy's voice was showing her impatience. Delaney jumped to the conclusion that she didn't want to discuss John when her wish was to get rid of Delaney.

Closing his book, he got up but didn't leave. He walked over to the world globe, twirling it easily on its axis. The structure was of an intricately patterned wood. With his lack of knowledge in this area, he still knew it was a valuable piece.

"You must have a lucrative business, Mrs. Lambert." Flipping the globe once again.

"I do." Her personal information was not part of this questioning. She wasn't about to tell him her father's inheritance purchased this room.

Delaney knew he wouldn't get any more from her, so we headed for the door. The phone started ringing, but Chrissy made no effort to go back for it.

She mumbled, "the answering machine is on." She ushered him out the door, watching him drive away.

She quickly went back to the study. She punched the replay button. There were three messages. She noted their names and numbers impatiently, wanting to get the latest call, only to find out that it was just the client that had canceled that morning had reworked her schedule. She was now free.

Is it too soon to return to work? She remembered her panic because Detective Delaney was here and that John might call. Her problems were still with her. The call from the frightened woman confirmed that.

Jared appeared in the doorway. "Who was here, Mommy?"

"Just a man, wanting to talk to me for a minute, but he has gone now."

"Are you finished working?"

"Yes, darling, I have finished for today. What do you say we go to the park?" As soon as the words were out of her mouth, she wanted to retract them. What if John phoned? She wanted to be here. But it was too late. Jared was bouncing around like a jack in the box. Chrissy knew she had to follow through.

After a short time, she prodded Jared to leave the park, but he had joined up with two other boys. They were enjoying themselves on the monkey bars. Jared was laughing and having a good time. So, she gave up trying to get him to leave. He deserved to have this happy playtime after her disappearance had disturbed him so much. Jared had no idea what was going on with this latest phone request. She intended to keep it that way.

When Chrissy arrived home, she went into the kitchen to start supper. "Jared, wash your hands and face, then change your clothes. You are filthy from playing in the dirt." On the way down the hall, the phone rang. Jared was passing the study, so he leaped inside and grabbed up the phone. "Hello."

"Who are you?" A male voice asked.

"Jared, my mommy is in the kitchen, making supper." By this time, Chrissy was beside him, her hand out.

"Jared, how old are you?"

"I am four years old. Who are you?"

"My name is John. Is your mommy coming to the phone?" John could hear Chrissy asking for the phone in the background.

"Yes." Jared finally relinquished the phone to his mother, inquiring, "who is John?"

She ignored Jared and told him to continue to get changed.

"Hello, John." Her voice hesitant, fearing his message.

"Jared sounds like a cute boy, but I don't think you should let him answer the phone right now. I went to that address you gave me. It was an empty lot. I didn't see anybody around. But you can be sure there was someone nearby waiting for you. So, this hasn't ended after all. Sorry, Chrissy."

"John, I want this to go away. I had no involvement in the killing. Why am I getting these calls? Who are they?"

"I thought it was Geoffrey, but now I am not so sure. There seems to be more going on than I originally figured. Maybe you should go back to your sister's place."

"John, I can't hide indefinitely at Selma's place. Why do they want me?"

"They must think you know more than you do, but I don't see how. You never went into the house. Maybe they saw Geoffrey kidnap us. If so, they may have been the ones that did the killing. They want to know what you know or if you spoke to the police."

"Are they after you too, John?"

"I haven't received any phone calls of that nature that you have been getting if that is what you mean."

"Why me, John? I didn't see anything. I didn't tell the police your last names, and the descriptions were very vague." Chrissy was biting her lip in worry.

"All right, I believe you. Are you going to be seeing the police officer?"

"You mean Joel Hanley?"

"Yes, Joel."

"Yes, we are going out Saturday night."

"Chrissy, maybe you should tell Joel you are getting strange phone calls. He can let his Captain know. They can come and monitor your calls. Detective Delaney doesn't have to be involved. I know you don't like him."

"John, I just want this to go away."

"Chrissy, this isn't going away. I am afraid I won't be able to protect you. There is more involved now."

"John, I don't want the police at my house. Whoever's doing this may find out. They said no police."

"The police won't come. They will send undercover guys in to tap your phone. His outfit will be as a telephone repairman."

"I can't have someone listening in on my calls. I run a business out of my home. John, I am scared for Jared."

"That is why I am suggesting going to your sister's place."

"But, John, if they want me, they may go after me there too. Then Selma will be in danger. John, give me back my life. I was getting along just fine until you chased me."

"I know Chrissy, and I am sorry."

"You should be."

"Chrissy, I just need some time to start digging around. I would rather the police monitor your calls, maybe for a little while. I'll try to find out who and what is involved in this. These men aren't playing games. Something serious is going on. In fact, call Joel right now. Don't wait until tomorrow night."

"I don't know his phone number."

"Do you know the station where he works?"

"Yes."

"Well, call him there. They will put you in touch with him if you tell them who you are. Let them believe it has something to do with your date with Joel. That's important. They will give you a number then."

"John, I can't do that."

"Why not? Chrissy, this is not a game. You are in serious trouble. Call Joel now." John hung up.

She got out the telephone book. Joel had said his station was on Petersen Street. She found the number and dialed. Not hearing what the voice precisely alleged, she asked, "have you an Officer Hanley there?"

"Yes, do you want to speak to him? He is right here." Calling out. "Joel, it's for you."

Chrissy waited.

"Officer Hanley here. Can I help you?"

"Joel, it is Chrissy Lambert."

Joel figured she was calling to cancel their date. He felt let down.

"Chrissy, is something the matter?"

"Joel, I need some help. I believe it is a police matter. Can you come here to my home?"

"Chrissy, it is out of my jurisdiction. You are in another district. You will have to call the station near you. What is the matter, Chrissy?" Concern in his voice.

"Joel, I need you to come. You know already what is going on. I am in trouble." Chrissy's voice was rising in a frantic state.

"All right, Chrissy, I'll be right there."

"Thanks, Joel." Chrissy hung up.

She went back into the kitchen and continued making supper. She had put it on hold when John phoned. Jared came into the kitchen. "Mommy, who is John?"

"Just a man I met a couple of times." She didn't expand any further. She was formulating what she would tell Joel.

"Help me set the table, sport, put the knife and forks out, please."

She had just served the supper onto plates when the doorbell rang. Jared went running to the door with Chrissy hot on his heels. "Jared, don't open the door until I look to see who's there."

Chrissy peeked out through the side window. It was Joel. "Okay, Jared, open the door."

He pulled the door open to find a policeman standing there.

"Hi, Jared, I am Joel, a friend of your mom," lifting his eyes to look into Chrissy's agitated face.

She held the door open. "Come on in, Joel. Jared, you go into the kitchen and eat your supper. When finished, you can put the TV on and watch cartoons. But you must finish all your dinner first," she directed.

"But, Mommy, I want to speak to Joel. I haven't talked to a policeman before."

"Jared, your dinner first." Chrissy was pointing toward the kitchen. "Go."

Joel piped up. "Jared, I will come and talk to you before I leave. That's a promise." Jared headed for the kitchen at a run.

Chrissy took Joel into the study and closed the door. Joel stood waiting.

"Joel, I have been getting strange phone calls since I came home. They are threatening calls."

She spoke so fast she was breathless or agitated. Joel didn't know which.

"Chrissy, what calls? Chrissy, relax, take a deep breath, now tell me about the phone calls."

"The first one was on my answering machine when I got home from my sister's. It said, or rather it is started with heavy breathing then weird music, then this voice said, 'if you tell the cops anything, this death march is for you.' Joel, it was awful."

"You said there was more than one call."

"Yes, the second call was on the answering machine too. It was a woman's voice this time. It said to come to an address on the westside of Calgary. Then the woman yelped like someone was hurting her."

"Did you go?"

"No, but John did. He said it was a vacant lot."

"John?"

"Yes, the kidnapped man I was with, he called me here after I received the second call, so I told him. I also told him about the first call."

"What happened then, Chrissy?"

"John said he would take care of both calls."

"And?" Joel was now concerned more than ever. John, who was he?

"The first call John went back and threatening the guy. John figured it was Mr. Boots. He said he shouldn't bother me again, but then the second call came a day later. John insisted I call you when I said I wouldn't call the police because I didn't want Detective Delaney to come here again."

"Who is this, John? What is his interest in all this?"

"John's name is John Taylor. The man tied to me. He is a Private Investigator and an ex-cop. He is worried about Jared and me. He thinks the police should monitor my calls until we know who is involved."

Joel went to the phone and called into the station. He got a hold of his Captain and gave him a quick rundown on Chrissy. The kidnapping, the murder, and the phone calls, along with Chrissy's address.

"I know, sir, it is out of our jurisdiction, but Mrs. Lambert called me because I took the first call when she was in the hospital in our area." "Yes, I told her, she should call the police in her area, but she was too distraught. I felt it was my duty to come and help her. Can you do something to help her?" "Yes, sir, I will return to my precinct. I just want to know. Can you help her?" "Thank you, sir." He put down the phone.

"Chrissy, I have to get back to my station right now, or I will go up on charges of abandoning my duties. But Max Kelsey will be here to help you shortly."

"Thanks, Joel. I am sorry I caused you trouble. If there are any repercussions because of this, I'm sorry. Will I still see you tomorrow night?"

"Yes, Chrissy, I still want to be with you. Tomorrow night at 7:30, okay?"

"That will be fine."

"Listen, apologize to Jared for me, but I have to go right now. I promise to make it up to him another time." Joel left quickly, racing to his cruiser.

Chrissy went in to talk to Jared about Joel leaving so suddenly. Jared took it okay because she assured him Joel would come tomorrow night, off duty.

She played with Jared and then got him ready for bed. She read him a story before the doorbell rang again.

Chapter Eight

There was a blond giant of a man at the door, looking like a football hero. Chrissy didn't feel intimidated by his height or build as she had with Mr. Boots. This man radiated confidence and goodwill.

"Mrs. Lambert, I am Max Kelsey. Joel mentioned me to you."

"Yes, come in, Mr. Kelsey." Chrissy took him into the study.

Going over her story once again, except this time, she used proper names. That was how scared she was becoming. She mentioned going to Mrs. Doherty's house to cancel her appointment for the night and being chased by a man before she reached the front door. Then how, she escaped from him only to trip and hit her head on the iron gate post, which knocked her unconscious.

"When I awoke, I was roped to the man that chased me. We were in a car garage. A big bruiser of a man came eventually. Geoffrey kept prodding us with a knife even though the ropes were too tight. It made it difficult to walk. John finally talked him into untying our legs so we could manipulate steps."

"John who?" Max put in.

"John Taylor, a P I and an ex-cop." Chrissy was thinking so hard. She didn't notice Max Kelsey's reaction to John Taylor's name. Max knew John really well. "Go on, Mrs. Lambert."

"We entered a room. There was a man who recognized John. He told Geoffrey that he was to untie us. Apparently, the man knew John from some charity affair."

"This man's name?"

"Mr. Hammond, Alan Hammond."

"The senator?"

"Yes, that is what John called him. Mr. Hammond told Geoffrey to let us go. Geoffrey blindfolded us and released us separately. I became disoriented after my ordeal and head injury. A truck driver found me and took me to the hospital." Chrissy paused to draw a breath.

"Go on, Mrs. Lambert." Max Kelsey knew about this because he had reviewed Joel's report.

"That is when Joel showed up and took my statement in the hospital about the kidnapping. I told him that John had chased me to keep me out of the house, where there was a dead man. He phoned that information into the police station. I understand the police didn't know about the killing until then."

"I was released from the hospital. Officer Hanley offered me a ride home. I didn't know him by his first name until later." Chrissy added in Joel's defense, realizing she shouldn't be calling him by his first name. Joel had been very professional until off duty.

"Go on."

"I asked him to drive me to pick up my purse, my keys, and my car, which was back at Mrs. Doherty's. He didn't want to take me there, but I insisted. When we arrived, there was an ambulance and lots of police cars. We didn't find the purse."

Kelsey noted her expression change. "A man came out of the house and ordered me inside and told Joel to leave. Every time Joel tried to say something, he would cut Joel off and dismiss him. Joel finally left. The man harshly prodded me inside. He said his name was Detective Delaney. He did not have a nice manner about him. After all that had happened, I broke down. The doctor said it was a combination of shock and my head injury. They sent me off to the hospital in an ambulance." Kelsey now knew what caused her facial change.

"I was in for a couple of days. Then I went to my sisters for two weeks." Chrissy was not happy to have to repeat the story and relive the ordeal.

"Go on, Mrs. Lambert."

"When I finally went home, there were a lot of messages on my answering machine. One message frightened me. It was heavy breathing, then the death march music, I believe. Then I heard a voice, 'If I went to the police that death march would be for me.' I was glad now I hadn't revealed any last names." Max noted the telephone message was new to her story.

"I can't remember what happened next, other than at some point, John showed up and heard the message. He said he would take care of it. And I believed him, but there was another message today from a lady. She told me to go to an address on the westside of Calgary. Then she yelped as if someone injured her."

"Did you go?"

"No, I was too afraid. At some point in time, John phoned, and he said he would go instead. Phoning back, he said it was a vacant lot. Someone was trying to get me. He did not feel it was Mr. Hammond or Geoffrey this time, but someone else. John ordered me not to go out but to call the police. I was afraid I would get Detective Delaney. John finally convinced me to call Joel, and you know the rest because you are here."

"Mrs. Lambert, do you usually go to clients houses to cancel appointments?"

"No, I usually phone, but I had another appointment nearby and decided it would be nicer under the circumstances to drop in. I was canceling because I had mixed up my appointments with my son's playschool concert. I promised my son that I would be there. I never made it." Chrissy ended sadly.

Chrissy uttered, "wrong place at the wrong time. Life's unexpected moments when you wish you could turn back the clock. If I hadn't gone to that house, none of this would've happened, and now, I am fearful for myself and my son."

"Mrs. Lambert, how well do you know John Taylor?"

"Not at all. He just seems to be appearing every once in a while, mostly when I need him. Which is quite odd."

"I notice you call Officer Hanley Joel?"

"Yes, Joel was upset with Detective Delaney's treatment of me. He paid me a few calls since, in his off-duty time. We have a date set for tomorrow night."

So, this woman drew Joel's awareness. Max didn't blame him as Chrissy was one sweet lady.

"Mrs. Lambert, we will set up a telephone tap to monitor your calls for a couple of weeks. I think you should stay close to home."

"I can't. My business is Interior Decorating. I need to keep my appointments, or I will lose them."

"Well, we will have to tail you for a week. We will see what happens. Now, Mrs. Lambert, why didn't you reveal who Mr. Hammond was?"

"I was terrified after the kidnapping and Geoffrey's threats when he released me."

"What about John Taylor, were you frightened of him?"

"I don't think so, but I am not sure why."

"Well, that is enough for tonight. A repairman will be here tomorrow. Give me a schedule of your appointments, so I can have a man here when you go out."

"What about my son? Will he be okay?"

"I don't think you should send him to playschool. Is there someone that looks after him for you?"

"Yes, there is a babysitter, Mrs. Marshall, a neighbor."

The phone rang, and Chrissy glanced at the clock. It was 9:30. Who could be calling this time of night? Instantly, she felt frightened. Her hand poised over the phone, but she hadn't picked it up yet. Four rings. Max Kelsey watched her, noting the emotions changing on her expressive face.

"Pick it up. If it is one of those calls, signal me." Chrissy picked up the phone.

A voice screeched. "You didn't come. Are you trying to get me killed?" A female voice yelled. Chrissy had eased the phone away from her ear and indicated to Max that it was one of those calls. He was listening in with Chrissy, which wasn't difficult the way the woman was yelling. "You have to come. You have to come alone tonight. Please help me." The line went dead.

Chrissy slowly put the phone down. "Who is this woman? Why is she calling me?"

"Chrissy, we don't know who she is, but we better comply this time. I will call in for some backup. Try to get your babysitter over here."

She was frightened, but she didn't know if it was for the woman on the phone or herself. She called Nancy to come over. Her husband was home so that he could watch their children. Chrissy only said she had to go out and that it was important.

Max made a few calls, and everything was in place. After Nancy arrived, Chrissy drove to the same address as given before.

Max had arranged for cars to be in the area. He followed Chrissy at a safe distance as he knew her destination. She entered the deserted street. According to John, it was a vacant lot, so she slowed down. She was thankful for the locked doors. When she arrived at the vacant lot, Max had told her to stop. Two men ran up to the car. They were brandishing guns.

"Open up, Mrs. Lambert." The one gunman was yelling and wrapping on the window. "I'll shoot you if you don't open up."

Chrissy released the locks. The door was pulled open. The gunman pushed her over while the other man ran around and got in the other side. Chrissy was now between the two of them. The car took off with squealing tires, the backend fishtailing.

Max was hot in pursuit. One police car tried to cut them off, but the cop got out of the way when Chrissy's car didn't slow down.

The car was speeding down back lanes, taking corners of streets on two wheels, weaving in and out of traffic as it entered the congested downtown. She was frightened, but she had to admire the young man's driving skills. He was an expert. *Where were Max Kelsey and the others?*

The driver let out a yell of success. "We lost them. I knew I could do it. How did you like that driving?"

"Yeah, you were good, kid. Now let's get where we need to be." He took a scarf out of his pocket and tied it over Chrissy's eyes.

Kidnapped again. What had Chrissy done to warrant this? Where were the police? They were supposed to protect me.

The two men never talked, so it was a silent ride except for Chrissy's crying mind. *What was to happen to her?*

Max put in a call to his friend John Taylor. When John answered, he stated. "John, they have Chrissy."

"Damn it, Uncle Sam, how did that happen? How come you are involved?"

"You told Chrissy to call Joel, and his Captain called me. She got another call while I was with her. I set everything up. We had three cars in the area, plus I was following her."

"Then how the hell did they get Chrissy?"

"There were two men. They ordered her to open up at gunpoint. They got in her car. We didn't expect that. The driver was an expert. We lost them."

"That is just great. Why did you let Chrissy go there?"

"The call indicated she had to come alone. It sounded like they were trying to kill the woman on the phone. There were four police cars, so we should have had her covered. I assumed; they would take her into a house in the area. We just didn't expect them to take off in Mrs. Lambert's car." Max finished lamely. "John, what do you know about all this?"

"Nothing much, unfortunately. I was tailing that dweeb when he took me to Doherty's house, and the tale began. The guy you had me tailing disappeared out the back door. And no, I don't think he had time to stab Doherty. After losing him at the back, I came around the house. There was Chrissy, so I tried to stop her from entering."

"John, what has Mr. Hammond got to do with this?"

"I don't know, but I feel pretty sure that he is involved somehow. I think there are other players in this besides Hammond that has Chrissy now."

"Have you found out anything yet?"

"Nothing positive, just rumors. Give me some time. I'll see what I can come up with. In the meantime, find Chrissy's car. You must have her license number if you followed her. You do have her license, don't you?"

"Well, I didn't expect them to take her car, but I did see part of it. I got 534 on it." Max said lamely, not his usual confident self.

"I will call the sister. She will have to know. We may be in for trouble. Her sister's husband is a high-profile lawyer. Maybe you have heard of him, Dave Lomax?" John's voice was stern.

"Yes, I have heard of him. You're right. We may be in trouble. I'm sorry, John, I thought we had her covered."

"Well, Uncle Sam, you better pray nothing happens to Chrissy before we find her because if her brother-in-law doesn't get you, I will." John was very angry with his friend for the first time that he could recall. John was terrified for Chrissy. Mainly because he just didn't know who had her or where to look.

John hopped in his car. He had to get out on the streets, talk to his contacts. Find out if anything was going down. He parked his car not far from the sleazy part of town. The best way to make contact with his informers was to walk.

He was out there for a couple of hours but nothing. How is that possible? Someone had to know something. He went into bars and back alleys. He was ready to call it a night when he ran into Benny. Benny tried to evade him. John was persistent.

"All right, Benny, spill it." John had him by the collar.

"I don't know anything."

"Then why have you been dodging me? It doesn't make sense." He twisted Benny's collar tighter around his neck. "Now, Benny."

"I don't know anything."

"Benny, we can do this the easy way or the hard way. What's it to be?"

"I don't know what you mean."

"Easy way you just tell me, the hard way I rough you up, which is it? Either way, you will tell me what I need to know." John twisted his collar tighter, so Benny's face was turning red.

In a half-strangled voice, "I don't know anything." Then John eased up.

John pulled out a switchblade knife. When it clicked open, the sharp blade whizzed out. Benny opened his mouth and started to sing.

"I only know that some chick was hoisted. There is talk of a gang killing, and there is to be more."

"Why were you afraid to tell me?"

"Because I heard it also involved you. I didn't want to be part of the killing."

"Not good enough, Benny." John pressed the blade against his throat.

"It is big time, but I don't know any details or names."

"Benny, don't you want to live? Give."

"Look for the car. It is over on 34th Street."

ˇIt better not be Chrissy inside, or I'll be back." Giving him a prick with a sharp blade without drawing blood.

"34th and where? It is a long street."

"34th and 57th Street."

John ran for his car. He squealed his wheels as he took off doing a U-turn. He arrived there quickly. He drove down 34th. After a couple of blocks, he saw Chrissy's car. He pulled in behind, leaping out. He ran over to her car with a failing heart, seeing an unconscious woman inside. He yanked open the unlocked door. He climbed in the back seat, but the woman there wasn't Chrissy. The woman wasn't unconscious but dead. Now he feared for Chrissy more than ever. He used his cell phone to call Max.

"Hello, Uncle Sam, this is John. I found Chrissy's car."

Uncle Sam, a joke name John had dubbed him with.

"Is Chrissy in the car?"

"No, but the other woman is dead. I assume it is the lady whose voice was on the phone."

"How was she killed?"

"She was beaten and shot."

"John, I am sorry I fouled up on Chrissy."

"Max, I am worried. These guys are playing for keeps. Don't release the information to the press until I talk to Chrissy's sister. I will call her right now. I will let you know if I reach her."

John disconnected and called information for the sister's phone number.

After he punched in the number, a man's voice answered the phone. John asked for Selma. It was after eleven, so he wasn't surprised when the male voice said. "This is her husband. Is there something I can help you with?"

"Mr. Lomax, this is John Taylor, a friend of Chrissy. I have some bad news." John paused. How do I tell him when you are personally involved? It is hard.

Dave waited.

"Mr. Lomax, Chrissy has been kidnapped again. The police have her car, but she isn't in it."

"John Taylor? I know who you are now. John was the name of the guy that got Chrissy kidnapped in the first place. What did you do now?" Dave was yelling into the phone. "Where is she?"

"I don't know, and neither do the police. I have to tell you there is a dead woman in Chrissy's car, but it is not Chrissy."

"Woman, what woman?" yelled Dave again.

"We don't know yet. We haven't identified her. The police are looking into it as I speak." He looked over at Chrissy's car, which was surrounded by police. Max Kelsey was walking towards him.

"I am coming down there. Where are you?" Lomax indicated.

John gave him directions and hung up. He stepped out of the car. "Lomax is on his way. What do you know, if anything?"

"She was taken out with a 45. No identification, but I saw a picture of Mrs. Doherty when I was looking into the case before seeing Mrs. Lambert, and that photo matches the dead person. So that has to be Mrs. Doherty. That is not good, John."

John's heart dropped. Things did not look good for Chrissy. "Why do they want Chrissy?"

"Maybe they want to find out how much she knows. Somehow, they must know she was at the Doherty house." Max answered.

"Benny said gangland killings, so who are the players? My guess is Hammond. Who's the other? Any ideas?"

"Only Delvietti. Do you think Hammond is in on this? I always thought he was straight." Max was guiltily thinking of Chrissy.

"So did I, until I ended up at his country place. Unless there are more rats in the woodpile, we will have to go along with Delvietti. What do you know about him?"

"Not enough to raid his place. So, I can't get a search warrant."

"Well, I guess it is up to me." John wasn't about to sit around while Chrissy ended up like Mrs. Doherty. "Any hint why a gangland slaying?

"A message or a takeover, take your pick. I didn't even know about Hammond." Max replied.

"Me neither, but I guess we're about to find out." Just then, a car came to a screeching halt. Dave Lomax had arrived.

"Damn you both, you had to play games, didn't you? Chrissy would never go off on her own. She never takes chances, not with her son losing his mother. You goaded her into it, didn't you? Now Chrissy is missing. You have a dead woman in place of her, haven't you? Wasn't once enough for you guys? How do you sleep nights playing with other people's lives? Who has her?"

"We don't know. It seems to be gangland related."

"Just fine. Chrissy has nothing to do with the mob, so they probably think she is expendable like the dead woman. What are you going to do about it?"

"We have a name. I'm going to check it out through my sources." John said.

"Oh, yes, the P I with despicable friends. What are you doing here? Why aren't you out canvassing your underworld snitches? You better get Chrissy back in one piece, or I will personally nail you to the wall and use you for target practice. I am not that good with a gun, but I am a quick learner."

"I am very sorry, Dave. I would never hurt Chrissy. She means too much to me." John looked over at Max. "I am out of here."

Dave yelled after him. "You better find her quick and bring her back safely. Then you're out of her life for good. Got that, P I?" Dave said sarcastically.

John got in his car and took off. Dave turned to Max Kelsey. "Okay, tell me. How did Chrissy get into their hands? You used her as bait, didn't you?"

"Not intentionally. We had four cars on her. What we didn't expect was that they used Chrissy's car. The driver was a pro. He lost us. We thought they would drag her out of the car and take her into a nearby house. But that didn't happen." He looked disturbed. "They threatened to shoot her if she didn't open the car door. When she did, they pushed her into the middle and took off with a man each side of her."

Dave gave him an angry look, waiting for him to continue.

"The guy obviously knew the district like the back of his hand because he was quickly navigating back alleys and streets so fast, we just couldn't keep up. Once we tried to block him off, but he drove directly at our man, so he had to move or be killed."

"Do you have a name?"

"We think it is Delvietti."

"Oh, fine. The worst gangster in the city. Why aren't you raiding his place?"

"We don't have anything on him, at least not enough to get a search warrant. John will find him with the excellent network he has. John cares for Chrissy. I can tell by the way he talks about her."

"Chrissy doesn't need a deadbeat P I sniffing around her. When he gets her back here, this all ends? You can tell him that, do you hear me?"

"Loud and clear the way you're yelling. We will cross that bridge when we get to it."

Dave got back into his car and drove home. Max returned to Chrissy's car. The coroner had arrived. The estimated time of death was about 10:00 pm, about the time they kidnapped Chrissy. The first thought through Max Kelsey's mind was Chrissy witnessed the brutal slaying. It was good that Dave and John had left, or they both would have torn another strip off him. Max did not get a good feeling about ever seeing Chrissy alive again. He would have trouble sleeping tonight.

Max gathered up some men. They drove to the area believed to be Delvietti's territory to see what they could come up with.

John had been pounding the pavement for a while, asking questions, and gleaning information. He was mainly looking for Benny, but he seemed to have disappeared. John found out that Delvietti had several places of operation. They moved around at a moment's notice, shutting down one spot and opening at another. John needed to know where he was now.

Benny must have known he would come back for more information because he wasn't at any of his usual haunts. He had made himself scarce.

John was just about ready to give up when a blond streetwalker overheard him asking for Benny. She walked over to John. "What's in it for me if I tell you?" John whipped out some bills. When he got to sixty dollars, she said. "Benny got worked over earlier tonight. Apparently, he ran into some information he wasn't supposed to share. He is holed up in his lair, licking his wounds, so to speak."

"Where is his lair?"

The blond held out her hand. John put a twenty in it. "The back of the old burlesque hall is converted into lowlife housing over on Grange."

John quickly found the place because they had never removed the canopy from the front of the building. He opened the door and walked through to the back. There were two doors. When he knocked on the first, a woman answered with a baby on her hip. She gave John the four-letter word when he murmured. "Sorry, wrong door."

He went to the other door but didn't bother to knock. He just put his weight to the door and shoved. The old wood gave way with just a little splintering. He was inside. A small table littered with dirty dishes, empty cans of beer, and an overflowing ashtray with a butt that was still curling smoke. He looked past the table to a bed. There Benny was sprawled out only half-conscious. They had done a pretty good job of making him forget. John went to the sink in the corner. There was a small jug there, and he filled it with cold water. Walking back to the bed, he poured the water in Benny's face. Benny lifted off the mattress in shock. Then he dropped back down and closed his eyes when he saw John.

"Benny, talk to me?"

"No, go away. You are the reason I look like this."

"Benny, you're going to feel much worse if I don't get my answers." John pulled his knife, letting the blade snap out quickly like a gunshot. Benny eyed the knife, but he also knew that he would be dead meat if he squealed on them again. So, he tried to ignore John's knife.

"Benny, an innocent young woman is in their hands. She will die if you don't tell me what I need to know. Then you will die too. I will see to that, start singing."

Benny kept his eyes closed. But he felt the knife cut through his shirt, exposing his chest.

"Why did you do that? It is my best shirt, and now look at it,"

Benny wailed.

"Benny, you won't need a shirt when I get finished with you if you don't give me the answers I need," digging the tip of the knife in for effect. John hated this part of his job. Most often, the site of the honed blade of his knife was sufficient. But not this time. Benny was more afraid of the bad guys. Drops of blood came to the surface of his skin and trickled down his side.

"More, Benny." Placing the knife closer to the heart. John was silently begging 'give in, Benny.'

"Old warehouse on Johnson street, three blocks over from here." The blade had earned it's keep again without drawing more blood. He quickly retracted the knife and threw forty dollars at Benny and told him to see a doctor. Then he left.

Making Johnson Street in record time, he found three warehouses. The boarded-up warehouse was too obvious, so John discounted that one. The next had a name sign swinging in the breeze Manson's Textiles. The last one only had a number evident above the entrance.

Chapter Nine

Chrissy was tied and gagged. She had been too mouthy. She had kicked and scratched as soon as they dragged her out of the car and inside the warehouse. The blindfold had slipped down, and she could see. She had aimed her nails into their eyes. Chrissy had just honed her curved pointed nails the day before, and they were like weapons. Two guys showed evidence of her action.

One guy's eye was swollen, almost shut. The other had bleeding streaks down his cheeks. They got her flailing arms and claws tied behind her back after two other men had pounced on her from behind. The two guys she injured took turns hitting her across the face. Chrissy now had at least one black eye that she could feel. But it was still worth it to savor the damage she had inflicted on them. They wouldn't forget her anytime soon.

Chrissy was scared after she heard them talking. They had killed the woman that had been the voice on the phone. She would probably be next. Why did they want her anyway? She didn't understand their persistence.

They had moved out of ear range so that she couldn't make out any definite conversation, only the occasional word. Something about 'zero hour' 'retaliation,' and 'no holds barred.'

Chrissy, missing dinner, was hungry and thirsty. She was hurting from the whacks on the head. Worse, she didn't know if anyone was looking for her. Surely, Max Kelsey would continue to look for her. She knew the driver had driven in and out and around buildings as

Chrissy had a good sense of direction even though she couldn't see. They probably lost the police easily.

The young driver was the one who had given her the black eye after she had attacked his eyes. He was that angry with her. He had raised his foot to kick her when somebody behind her had called a halt to the beating.

That was when they went into another part of the warehouse. Chrissy had wiggled over to the wall, leaning her aching head on it. Thank heavens the floor felt clean. She hoped there were no rats in here. The thought made her skin crawl, but she didn't hear anything scurrying around as this part of the warehouse wasn't too well lit.

Chrissy was worried about Jared. She conjured up Jared's face, seeing him on the monkey bars with those two other boys. The last real memory of him at play. Tears were falling down her face unchecked.

She didn't know how long she had been sitting there. The voices had disappeared as though they had gone into the bowels of the building. She thought she had dozed off for a while. What was going to happen to her?

It was then she heard a noise off to her left, a slight scraping sound. Was it rats? No, a rat doesn't scrape. Then she felt hands on her. She shrunk away. But then she heard a voice against her ear.

"Chrissy, it is me, John. You're going to be very quiet when I release you. You will do as I say, exactly. Then we may get out of here alive." John couldn't help himself. He planted a light kiss on Chrissy's temple, so thankful to have found her.

Then he untied her and took off the gag. Once freed, she threw her arms around John and held on tightly. He wanted to just hold on to her. But he knew there wasn't time, so he whispered. "Chrissy, we have to sneak past two guards, so you mustn't make any noise." John removed her arms from his neck but retained her hand.

He started leading her away towards the shadows on the far side of the warehouse. It was difficult to find cover because the warehouse was practically empty. Chrissy was wearing a pale lilac blouse, which almost glowed in the half-light. He slipped off his jacket to put it around her. She tried to roll up the long sleeves. John pulled them up and grabbed her hand. He put his finger to her lips to silence her as she was about to say something.

He knew only too well in this hollow warehouse that voices could carry like a megaphone. They found cover behind some boxes when John heard footsteps coming in their direction. With John's muscular shoulders, Chrissy was pinned against the wall, hardly able to breathe. She started to cough, but John covered her mouth with his, taking her cough inside him.

Once he started, he deepened the kiss even though Chrissy was trying to push him away. John was pressing heavily against her already in the small space. Chrissy was making a moaning sound. He knew he should stop and get out of there. One of the guards walked by. John raised his head, giving Chrissy a meaningful look, holding her close to his body so she couldn't move.

He was hoping that no one would check on Chrissy, as they were taking too long. Their discovery will be soon. A guard had stopped the other side of the boxes.

Why was the guard just standing there? Had he heard something? Was he standing there listening? John was fearful if they didn't get out of there in the next ten minutes, it would be game over.

A voice called out. "Leon, are you there?" The man standing near the boxes replied. "Yeah, I'm here. I thought I heard something, but I guess not." Leon moved back toward the other guard.

John breathed a sigh of relief. Leon must have heard Chrissy. Why was it that he kissed Chrissy every time to silence her, it always led to more kisses? John was usually all business when he was on the job, especially when lives were in jeopardy.

Leon and the other guard had struck up a conversation, so John dragged her behind him until he neared the window, he used coming in. Chrissy was shorter and couldn't reach. John hoisted himself up then eased around to pull Chrissy up after him. Then he dropped down to the ground. She was half lying out the window. "Chrissy, try to bring your legs up so you can turn yourself around and dropdown. I will catch you." John called to her softly.

Chrissy kept trying to hook her leg over the window sill. She wasn't as agile as John.

"Keep trying, Chrissy," John called in a louder whisper.

"John, I can't do it."

He heard loud voices within. They had discovered her. "Chrissy, drag your body up and fall forward. I will catch you. I promise."

"John, someone has a hold of my foot." John jumped up, grabbing Chrissy by the arms, trying to pull her out. Chrissy's leg was up in the air, but the guard still had her other foot. "He won't let go."

John jumped again. This time he reached her shoulders and yanked. Chrissy had kicked with her clear foot against the guard's hand. He let go. She went tumbling to the ground on top of John.

It was only a matter of time before they would be coming out after them. John quickly righted them. They began to run. He was holding Chrissy's hand, hauling her along. The guards were in hot pursuit, yelling, "stop, or we will shoot." John kept running.

They reached his car, shoving Chrissy towards the passenger side. John hopped into the car. She entered the vehicle, but there were shots fired. The back window shattered, then the side window. John finally got the car started. One of the guards was beside the car, trying to open the door behind him. When John sped away, the thug fired.

In his mirror, John saw a car escaping from the warehouse, only stopping long enough for the guards to pile in.

John kept his foot shoved to the floor. He turned the corner, then made a right turn, then a left turn. But the car was gaining on them, and he made another left. There was a police car coming towards them. John aimed his vehicle at the police car to get their attention then veered over in time. The police did a quick U-turn, lights flashing and sirens going. The thug's car was between John and the cruiser.

John was saying. "Come on, keep after us." Meaning the police as he started swerving the car into the wrong lane and back to provoke the cops more. The thugs realized they couldn't do anything with the police following them. They turned off at the next corner, shaking their fists at him.

John slowed down. The police siren blasted. Finally, John pulled over. The cops got out of the car with their guns drawn. John just sat, waiting for them to come to his window.

"Get out of the car with your hands on your head. Now!"

John eased the door open. He didn't want them to get trigger happy.

"It's okay. I am surrendering." John's hands were on his head as he stood to his full height.

The officer grabbed him and whipped him around, flattening him against the car. The officer's hand was going over John's body, looking for a gun and found the knife. The other officer was up beside Chrissy. "Get out with your hands up."

Chrissy eased the door open and got out. Her legs were shaking.

"All right." said the officer to John. "What is going on here?"

John replied, "radio to dispatch and tell them to call Max Kelsey. Tell dispatch to tell Kelsey that I have Chrissy Lambert. She was kidnapped."

The officer behind John looked over at his partner. "Do you know anything about a kidnapping?"

"No."

"All right, mister, what is your game?"

"No game. Call Max Kelsey. He will verify that Chrissy Lambert was kidnapped. I am John Taylor, a private investigator. I just recovered her from those thugs that were in the car behind us. They were the ones that shot out my windows."

The officer behind Chrissy said, "this is so farfetched he has to be telling the truth. It won't hurt to call in and verify," noting Chrissy's abrasions. He pushed Chrissy gently over to the police cruiser and placed her in the back seat. Then he got in the front seat and radioed dispatch, telling them to contact Max Kelsey. Ask him if Chrissy Lambert got kidnapped."

Dispatch said, "10 4."

The officer waited. There was a lot of crackling on the radio. Then dispatch finally came back with, "Car 369, yes, Chrissy Lambert was kidnapped, do you have her?"

"Yes, we have her and John Taylor in custody." Silence except for crackling then another message. "Car 369, bring them into your station. Max Kelsey will meet you there."

The cop said, "10 4." Easing out of the cruiser, he called. "Hey Carl, they are legit, but we have to take them to the station. Max Kelsey will meet us there."

Carl lowered his gun. "Do you want to ride with us or drive your car?"

"I'll drive my car. I don't want to leave it here." John said with relief.

Carl walked back to the cruiser and got in. He kept the flashing lights on but didn't use the siren. John eased in behind him after the police car pulled out into traffic. He didn't want to lose sight of Chrissy.

When they arrived at the station, they took them into one of the back rooms. Max Kelsey was waiting there with another officer.

"Congratulations, John, for recovering Mrs. Lambert, well done. Mrs. Lambert, are you okay?" Max looked closely at Chrissy. He could see that they had bashed around her face and head. Her eye was black and blue with yellow and green intermingling.

"Other than needing a washroom, I guess I am okay." With John's jacket on her, she looked smaller than Max remembered.

"John, this is Captain Todd Kramer." John acknowledged the introduction but quickly switched his eyes back to Chrissy. He was assessing the damage in the bright light of the room. His body physically flinched, seeing the swelling of Chrissy's bruised face and a black eye.

Captain Kramer thanked the officers for bringing them in. "Carl, send Tracy in." The two officers left with a nod of acknowledgment to the thanks from their superior.

A few seconds later, a woman officer arrived. "Show, Mrs. Lambert, to the ladies' room, please. Then arrange for some coffee. How about you, Mrs. Lambert, would you prefer tea?"

"No, mineral water, please." Chrissy followed Tracy out of the room.

When the door closed, Max Kelsey whipped around to John. "All right, buddy, how did you manage to steal her away?"

"I found Benny, my contact. By the way, they beat him for talking to me earlier about Chrissy's car and the body. I persuaded him with a threat. I would make him feel worse than he already did. He gave me the approximate location of the warehouse, and I managed to get in. Fortunately, they had finished with Chrissy and had left her alone with two guards near the back doors. So, I cautiously crawled through the window. I didn't know what to expect."

"I found her tied up and gagged. After freeing her, I got her out of there. But they chased us, after shooting out a few windows of our car. I think I took a hit." John, who had been standing, plunked down on the nearest chair.

Max reached his side. He could then see a crust of blood down the side of John's head and on his shirt. "You were lucky, buddy. The bullet just grazed your head above the ear. It's not too deep with some blood.

John let his head fall back, closing his eyes. His adrenaline was gone. The reaction set in from his tension. The worry that Chrissy wouldn't survive the rescue because he didn't wait for police help.

Max had his hand on his friend's shoulder. "Do you need to go to the hospital, John?"

"No, just give me a minute." John still had his eyes closed. His body slumped.

The door opened. John shot erect, shaking off Max's hand. John turned to look at Chrissy, who was looking a bit better. Someone must have lent her a comb or brush. Her face must've been cleaned with cold water because it wasn't looking quite so abused. He turned his head away from Chrissy so she couldn't see the blood when he looked directly at her.

Max could see John was playing the macho man for Chrissy. She was carrying John's jacket over her arm. Her blouse had a couple of tears, but they were near the shoulder. She walked with her head held high, indicating she was surviving better than most women would have. Max was sure these two were putting on a show of bravery for each other.

Chrissy was steered to a chair by Max's hand, placing her on John's right side so she couldn't see the blood. "Mrs. Lambert, do you know why they grabbed you?"

"No, they never said."

"Do you know why they killed the other woman?"

"They said, 'they didn't need her anymore' was what I overheard."

"Is there anything else you can tell us?"

"They talked in a different area. I only managed to catch a few words 'zero hour – retaliation – no holds barred' or something like that."

"Why did they rough you up? What were they trying to get you to say?"

"That was retaliation for my trying to fight them off before I was tied and gagged."

John's fist clenched. The thought of Chrissy's harassment was upsetting to him, even though he was proud of her courage to fight them. He wanted to plant his fist in their faces. Maybe he would get the chance yet."

The drinks arrived, and Chrissy drank thirstily. When she had finished, they asked if she was hungry?

"No, but I would like to talk to my son. Does my sister know about this last kidnapping?" Genuine concern in her voice.

"Yes, but we have also let them know you are safe. I'm surprised your sister isn't here yet. They said they were coming." Max Kelsey offered.

They heard loud voices in the hall. The door was thrust open, and Dave strolled in, not waiting to be announced. Tracy was trailing behind him with an annoyed look on her face.

"Chrissy, are you all right? What did they do to you?" Dave looked at her in horror. Then whipped around to Max Kelsey. "You are to blame for this, using her as bait."

"Bait, what are you talking about? Chrissy, oh my god, are you all right?" Selma had pushed past Tracy too.

Chrissy got up and went into her sister's arms. "I'm all right, really I am. It looks worse than it feels." Selma was holding her tightly.

Dave whipped around to John. "So, you're here too. I should have known. You have meant trouble for Chrissy ever since this started."

Max interrupted. "Mr. Lomax, that is enough. John was the one who saved her, so lay off. I was the one who persuaded Chrissy to go."

Chrissy spoke up then. "Dave, a woman was pleading for help. I was trying to save her. It wasn't Inspector Kelsey's fault or suggestion. I did it on my own. It was the woman's voice on the phone, sounding like they were torturing her that made me go. John tried to stop me from going." Looking back at her sister, Chrissy said, "they killed her anyway."

Selma was patting Chrissy's beat-up face. "It looks like they were trying to kill you too."

"I don't care why you went, Chrissy. It was up to the police to protect you. They failed. I am going to sue them. You can bet on that." Dave was still so angry at everyone, especially when he looked at Chrissy's face.

"Look, Dave, Chrissy thought she had a good reason for doing what she did. I commend her for that, and you should too." Kelsey replied.

"That's fine for you to say. Chrissy is the one injured here, not you." The way Chrissy was now standing near the door with Selma. She could see John's head. "John, you were hit." She separated from Selma, going over to John, as he sat at the table facing an angry Dave.

John reached up to cover his head as Chrissy put her hand out to touch him. Her hand touched his. He pulled away like he had felt an electric shock. "It's all right, Chrissy. It is only a scratch."

"John, that is more than a scratch by the amount of blood. That thug shot at you, hitting your head. You should go to the hospital for attention." Now Chrissy had her fingers on the wound. John pulled away quickly.

"Chrissy, I am all right. Please, sit down, and we will try to straighten this out, and that goes for you too, Dave. We don't know why they want Chrissy, so she is still in trouble."

Max Kelsey stepped in. "Yes, everyone sit down. We will discuss this rationally. Both John and Chrissy have been through enough without listening to accusations and threats."

Dave sat, but he was still glaring from Max to John and back. Chrissy sat beside John, and Selma sat beside Chrissy and held her hand.

"Chrissy, I know you have been through a lot. I commend you for trying to save Mrs. Doherty. But the problem we are facing is that they may try to get you again. Both John and I believe this. We don't know why they want you in the first place, so they may keep trying."

"Oh no, Chrissy isn't going to be bait again," Dave yelled.

"Calm down, Lomax. We don't want her to be bait either. But

we are going to have to figure out a way to protect her from being recaptured." John's voice was like steel. "We don't know why Delvietti wants her. But she is still in danger until we do find out." John stopped talking and turned to Chrissy to see how she was taking that comment.

She looked at John in horror as the implication of his statement set in. She was shaking her head 'no.'

"Yes, Chrissy, you are still vulnerable until we find out why Delvietti wants you."

Dave stated. "Just pick up Delvietti on a kidnapping charge and question him."

Max interjected. "It isn't that simple. You just don't drag someone of Mr. Delvietti's power in for questioning. You have to have something more positive. Even if we did, they could still grab Chrissy again to use her as a bargaining tool. So, we are back to square one. Until we know why they kidnapped her, she is still in danger."

"Well, you can bet I will be looking in on Delvietti's business interests to see what I can find," Dave replied. He knew that he couldn't protect Chrissy. But, as a lawyer, he was good at finding out information.

John answered. "Go ahead. I'm sure Max will appreciate anything you can dig up. But the point here is Chrissy." John reached over and took her hand. Chrissy understood all that was said, but not happy about any of it. She wanted to pull her hand away and hit him for causing her to be involved in the first place. But her hand in his felt like a lifeline of security.

Max was saying, "Chrissy, we can put you and your son in protective custody. But these men have far-reaching networks. They could locate you, so I think your best bet is to stay with Dave and your sister."

"No." Chrissy leaped in. "I am not putting them at risk. That is out of the question." She was steadfast about that.

John offered. "Max, I think the best thing would be for Chrissy and her son, Jared, to have protection in her own home. I will move in to protect her inside. You post others outside."

"You live with Chrissy, no way. It is your fault that she was kidnapped in the first place." Dave lamented.

"Dave, I don't want John in my house either, but I think we have no choice. I want to stay there and have Jared with me. I am just going to have to put my life on hold until this is all cleared up." She looked from Dave to Selma, hoping and wanting their understanding.

"Now, if there isn't anything more, I would like to go home to my son." Chrissy stood up, removing her hands from both Selma and John. She was animated by the bickering and threats. This problem wasn't going away. She had to gather strength to see this through.

Max stood also. "Mrs. Lambert, there are a few more questions, but they can keep for now. We will have men around you, as well as John protecting you and your son. You should go home now and try to get some sleep. You have had quite a night. I am sorry that they grabbed you. Unfortunately, they took us off guard when they used your car to get away."

Chrissy remembered how fast it had happened. How expert a driver the young man had been. It was no wonder he had lost the police cars. She dipped her head in acknowledgment and walked to the door, ready to leave. The rest struggled in haste to their feet to follow her.

John was right on her heels as she exited the door. He had almost keeled over again when he rose quickly from the chair. His head was aching, causing a king-size headache, but he wasn't letting Chrissy out of his sight.

Dave and Selma were right behind them. Dave was calling. "Chrissy, wait for us." She kept going until she was out of the police station. She stood on the broad steps taking deep breaths. She had found the tension in the room stifling.

Chapter Ten

John stated in panic. "Chrissy, you can't run off like this if we are going to protect you properly."

Dave agreed with John on this, at least.

"I couldn't breathe with all the animosity in that the small space. I just had to get some fresh air." Chrissy looked at each of them pleadingly, wanting them to understand.

John sort of teetered, feeling a bit dizzy.

Chrissy grabbed his arm. "You are going to the hospital before you go anywhere else." She turned to Dave and Selma. "I'll be all right now. Thanks for coming and giving me your support so promptly. But I have to see that John gets to the hospital. I know you don't like him, but he did save me from those criminals. I heard shots, but I didn't know a bullet hit him. So, I have to get him to the hospital. Dave, can you go back and tell Inspector Kelsey where we are going first." Chrissy reached out and hugged Selma then Dave. "Thanks."

Taking John's arm, Chrissy steered him towards his car. He was amused at the way she had taken over, directing everyone. He wasn't feeling good, so he went along with her. When they got to the car, she put out her hand for the keys. He didn't want to give them up. Her expression indicated she wasn't budging until he gave in. Gone was the girl that had been in that warehouse, numb and feeling helpless and scared. She wasn't the victim any longer.

John didn't know whether that was good or bad. But he did finally hand over the keys. Her bruised face showed that she was the one needing first aid. She drove the car expertly. Every time she looked in the rear-view mirror at the smashed windows, her insides turned over.

Arriving at the hospital, she parked the car as close as she could to the emergency door. She took John's arm and went inside. John's stomach wasn't feeling too good.

"Chrissy, I'm going to be sick, so we need to find the restroom first. But you are staying with me."

"John, I can't go into the men's washroom."

"Fine, then we will go to the lady's washroom instead." John was walking in that direction.

"John, you can't do that."

"Just watch me. I'm going to stay with you like a leech, so get used to it." He pushed open the lady's washroom door dragging her in with him. Once inside, he said. "Don't leave" as he darted into the nearest cubicle.

Chrissy stood waiting as John was retching into the toilet. She felt sorry for him. She wished she had her purse so she could give him a *Cloret* when he came out. But she had lost her purse along the way and had no idea where.

Perhaps she had left it in the car. Trying to think back, yes, when those men were pushing her around, she didn't have her purse. Where was her car now? John flushed the toilet and stood, leaning against the cubicle's side, trying to regain his energy.

"John, are you all right?"

At Chrissy's voice, he straightened up and came out. He went to wash his hands and rinse his mouth. He was drying his hands when a woman walked in saw John then went to walk out again. Looking at the door, realizing it was the lady's room. She whipped around and said. "What are you doing in here? You can't come in here. You're a man."

Brilliant observation, thought John. "My wife felt ill, so I didn't want her to come in alone." The woman looked at Chrissy and noted the bruising and black eye and whipped back to John. "You should be arrested, beating your wife. You should be put away for good."

John couldn't resist. "Come on, my darling, or I will have to beat you again." Taking Chrissy's arm roughly.

Chrissy laughed. "Cut it out, John." It was the first time that he had heard her laugh. She had a nice laugh.

"Yes, dear, I promise I won't beat you again." He cast a massive smile in her direction.

They could hear the woman mumbling about 'beastly cruel men' as they exited the lady's room, only to get another dirty look from another lady wanting to go in.

Chrissy was trying to keep a straight face as though John had a perfect right to be there. He still didn't feel good, so leaned on her. Chrissy went over to sign in with the desk. John's turned head hid his injury. The nurse said, "your name and address, please?"

Chrissy responded, "not me. He is the one needing attention because he is wounded. His name is John Taylor. Where do you live, John?"

"742 Sussex Boulevard Calgary S.E."

"Age? When were you born?"

John looked at Chrissy as if waiting for her to respond. "John, when were you born?" Chrissy prompted.

"August 4th, 1960. I am 39. Can I sit down now? I don't feel too good."

"Yes, Mr. Taylor, your wife signed for you." Looking strangely at Chrissy's face.

Chrissy figured she was thinking John beat her, and she had retaliated by shooting him. She didn't bother to straighten things out. She followed John over to the free chairs near the window. Nearly all the chairs had patients or loved ones occupying them. Chrissy knew by the looks. There was no doubt that they thought John was an abusive husband, like the woman in the lady's room.

They sat for three hours until it was their turn. Fighting sleep for the first hour or so, they fell asleep. Chrissy's head on John's shoulder and his head was leaning on hers. John had mostly been resting his eyes to help ease the ache in his head. John's fingers moved naturally over Chrissy's arm in an intimate way. The people looking on were re-evaluating their opinion. His fingers were too gentle in their caress.

"John? John Taylor?" Their eyes popped open. They finally

managed to stand up awkwardly as they were both still exhausted.

"Chrissy, you are coming too." John made it a statement of fact.

"She can't do that," the nurse said.

John turned away. "Then I am out of here."

"Okay, she can come." The frantic nurse said, knowing she would get in trouble if he left.

The doctor arrived within minutes of their entering the examining room. John was sitting up on the edge of the examining table. Chrissy was on the chair. The doctor looked from one to the other.

"What is going on here?" His first observation wandered over Chrissy. Her battered face had drawn his eyes. John's uninjured side was showing to the doctor while he talked.

"Well, doc, it is a matter of a bullet wound that has long ago stopped bleeding. My head hurts like the devil."

The doctor walked over to him. He turned John's head. Then he saw the blood on his face, ear, and clothes.

"I see a bullet has creased the side of your head. Nurse, clean up the wound with an antiseptic so I can get a closer look." Stepping back. "Who shot you?"

"An unhappy man who was objecting to me taking Chrissy away from him."

"You know I have to report all gun wounds to the police."

"They already know. I just came from the police station. When you report the shooting, send the message to Max Kelsey's attention."

The nurse had finished cleaning his ear and the side of his head.

"Nurse, write that name down, will you? Max Kelsey, did you say?"

"Yes."

"So, the man that shot you was the one who beat up this young lady?"

"Yes."

"Was he her husband?"

"No, just a thug who had kidnapped her." John thought he should give the doctor more information to get out of there quicker.

The doctor returned his eyes to John's head. "Well, he just creased the side of your head. You were lucky. You will probably have a headache for a few days, which I will prescribe painkillers, but don't drive while taking them." The doctor wrapped John's head with a bandage securing it with tape.

The nurse was holding out a pen and pad for the doctor. He scribbled something and tore it off, handing it to John.

"Now hop down while she hops up. I want to look at her too. Kidnapped, you said?" John eased himself off the examining table slowly and walked over to Chrissy.

She was saying, "I'm all right."

John and the doctor were both saying. "Hop onto the table."

Two against one made it apparent that she might as well just comply.

The doctor touched her face gently. It doesn't look like any bones are broken, but that is a dousy of a shiner. You were lucky he didn't damage the eye. It seems like a ring cut right next to it. He must have worked you over pretty good."

"Not one but two brutes. I would like to get my hands on them to see how they will enjoy my fist." John said strongly.

"Do you have a headache, too?" the doctor asked Chrissy.

"No, just really tired, and my face hurts. I just want to go home to bed."

"Okay, you can get down. A cold compress on that eye should be helpful. I take it the police know about your kidnapping?"

"Yes."

"Did they hurt you anywhere else?"

"No, thank goodness. John rescued me before they could."

"I take it, John isn't your husband?"

"No." John piped up. "I am her protector from now on, isn't that right, Chrissy?"

"Yes, can we go now?" Chrissy asked anxiously.

"Yes, it doesn't look like I can help either of you except with a little advice. Take up with nicer friends." Then the doctor laughed like he had made a joke.

They both gave the doctor a withering look and headed for the door. John took her hand, turning he thanked the doctor and nurse."

Chrissy insisted on driving again, wanting to be at home so badly.

She wanted to see Jared, going straight to Nancy's house. The door opened. Jared ran to his mother, and his arms enclosed around her like locks. She bent down and lifted him into her arms. "Mommy, you are hurt."

"It looks worse than it is, honey." Squeezing him tightly.

Nancy said. "Chrissy, you don't look good. Are you all right? The police phoned and told me you had been hurt and to keep Jared in the house all the time."

"I am tired. But I will be okay once I get some sleep," easing Jared to the ground. She was too exhausted to hold him any longer. "Let's go home, sport. Thanks, Nancy."

John was by the car, watching the reunion of Chrissy and her son.

Nancy looked closely at Chrissy's face. She was telling her how to get rid of the swelling and the bruising. Jared, however, was observing John's bandaged head. Nancy was eyeing John too as Chrissy said goodbye with thanks.

"Jared, say thank you to Nancy." In the back of her mind, she wondered how she would explain John to Jared without upsetting him. She had never brought men into the house over the years. She had concentrated solely on her business.

When she and Jared reached the car, Chrissy said, "Jared, this is John. He is staying with us for a few days."

"Why?"

"I'll explain when we get home." Jared climbed into the back seat with his backpack, and John got in the front.

Jared spied the broken windows. "Mommy, what happened to the windows?" John had spread a blanket on the back seat to cover the glass while Chrissy talked to Nancy. "Is there any glass on the seat, Jared?" asked Chrissy in a shocked voice.

John quickly said, "no, I covered it with a thick blanket."

"Good. Jared, we had a bit of an accident. I'll explain when we get home." She was still trying to decide how she would handle the conversation.

John was thinking, *Yeah, Chrissy, how are you going to explain me?*

"Mommy, are you going out tonight with Joel?"

"Oh, my gosh! Honey, I forgot about Joel. I can't go out looking like this." She sent John a sharp look.

"Joel? Your boyfriend?" John eyed her questioningly.

"Just a friend," Chrissy said weakly.

"He is a policeman." Jared sang out proudly.

"A cop, that is interesting. Chrissy, I am not letting you out of my sight. Jared and I will have to go along." John said positively.

"You can't do that. Joel can protect me. He is a cop."

John was adamant. "Chrissy, you don't get out of my sight until we resolve this."

His remark got Chrissy's independent back up. She intended to cancel Joel because of her face, but now she didn't know if she wanted to. "We will discuss this further when we get home," she said through gritted teeth.

"How come everything is when we get home, Mommy?" Jared asked in wonderment.

"Jared, mommy has a headache. I will discuss things later." She turned onto her street. There was a police car parked outside her house. It had started. She would never be alone again, at least for a while. She pulled into the driveway. John got out and went to talk to the police.

Chrissy hurried Jared into the house. When they were inside, she took him on her lap. "Jared, mommy met some bad men that hurt my face. Until they catch them, John will be staying with us."

"Is he going to sleep here?"

"Yes, Jared, he is going to sleep in the spare bedroom."

"Will he eat with us?"

"Yes, of course, he will eat with us. I will be staying home from work. You will be staying at home with me for a while."

Jared grinned, having his mother's full attention was great. He hadn't seen much of her lately. She seemed to keep disappearing. He hugged her tightly. "Good, I like being with you, Mommy."

John locked the door behind him. "Is everything all set here?" Evidently, he had missed the explanation between them, by the looks of their faces. He was wondering what she had said.

"Jared, go get your hands and face washed, and I'll make lunch."

Looking at John curiously. She knew John wanted to talk about ground rules and Joel.

"John, I can't live in your pocket. I have to breathe a little." Jared being the obedient child had run to comply with her wishes.

"Chrissy, you have been kidnapped twice. We don't know why. Until this is over, you will live in my pocket. Your wording, not mine. Except at night, of course, when you sleep," he said with a cheeky grin.

"Where are you sleeping outside my bedroom door?"

"I would like to, but I will be in a bedroom near you. I am a light sleeper, and I will hear any strange noises. Now, Joel, who is he?"

"Joel was the cop that interviewed me after the first kidnapping. I mentioned him before."

"Do you always go out with strangers that interview you?" John's headache was playing havoc with his memory.

"No, Joel was worried about me. When I ended up in the hospital the second time, he came to see me when he was off-duty. We talked several times on the phone as well. He asked me for a date, which is tonight."

"Chrissy, phone him and cancel. You can't go out with him tonight." John was firm.

"John, I will be safe with Joel. He is a police officer."

"Chrissy, I don't care if he is the King. You will not go out with him unless Jared and I are tagging along. So, Joel had better pick a place for all of us."

Chrissy stomped her foot. "John, you are unreasonable."

"No, Chrissy, you are unreasonable. I am trying to protect you. Whoever is after you is not going to stop because you got away. These men are serious. They will find you again, for sure."

Jared walked in. "Why are you and my mommy fighting?"

"Because I want to protect your mommy, and she won't let me. Jared, you would like to go out with Joel and your mother, wouldn't you?"

"Oh, yes. Mommy, can I go with you?" Jared was jumping up and down.

Chrissy was throwing daggers at John. She turned her back and strode off to the kitchen to make lunch.

John was saying. "You and I are going to be great buddies. Do you know that, Jared?"

"Yes, sir."

"No, Jared, call me John. Now, let's go see what your mother is making for lunch." He held out his hand, and Jared put his hand in John's trustingly and grinned.

Chrissy was talking to herself as she was plying the bread with mayonnaise, pieces of luncheon meat, lettuce, and tomato. She was unaware that Jared and John were standing behind her.

"Chrissy, we have to come to an understanding before Joel gets here. It won't be so bad."

"John, I know I agreed to this, but I hadn't thought it out. I can't have someone living with us. I like my independence. It just won't work for me. I need space." Tears were piercing her voice. She cut the last sandwich and piled it on the plate.

"Jared, you carry these over to the table for mommy. I'll get the drinks." Jared carried the plate over to the table with John following. He was giving her space. Chrissy headed out of the room.

While eating their sandwiches, John asked Jared questions about his home life. Jared answered eagerly. John was cementing their relationship by telling him tales of his childhood, which had been full of his dad's stories.

"I don't remember my daddy. He died in a car accident when I was a baby. Mommy showed me pictures of him, but that is not the same as a real daddy, is it?"

"No, Jared, it is not. Well, shall we clean up here? Then we will go to find your mother." Jared stood on his chair and washed the dishes while John dried and put them away. John finished tiding the kitchen and wrapped Chrissy's sandwich in plastic wrap. Looking around, John saw a cozy kitchen with gleaming counters and modern appliances. The cabinets looked new.

"Well, everything's sparkling. Let's go find your mom." John allowed Jared to run ahead of him. Jared headed up the stairs to the bedrooms. John's head still throbbed, causing him to amble slowly.

"This one is mine." John looked in. It was a typical boy's room with toy soldiers, racing cars, and stuffed animals. The dresser held some models of antique cars.

"They were my daddy's cars. Mommy, let me have them for my room."

John realized Chrissy was trying to give Jared a sense of a father in his life.

Jared went to the next door. Here is where you are sleeping. We have it for Selma when she stays here. I don't have a grandma or a grandpa," he said, moving on past the next door.

John looked in the door leading into the bathroom, which was quite large for a small house. The shiny tub was huge and made to languish in with armrests and a rubber pillow. The motif was three shades of leafy green.

"The next door is my mommy's room," Jared whispered. John knocked lightly. No answer. John put his finger to his lips, then gently opened the door. No sound came from within. They crept inside. Chrissy was lying on her side, her hair falling around her on the pillow. Her cheeks looked wet like she had cried herself to sleep. John looked around for a blanket. There was a rocking chair by the window with a colorful Afghan on it. He went over and retrieved it to cover Chrissy.

Her eye looked darker. The bruise was blackish-blue with tinges of green and yellow. He wanted to treat the swelling, but sleep was more important for her right now. He placed the colorful afghan around her, signaling Jared that they were leaving the room.

Hopefully, their talk would go better after she had some sleep. John spent the time on the phone while Jared watched cartoons. Jared stated that he was too old for the afternoon naps now.

John was shocked to find out that they killed Benny. He felt a pang of regret knowing he was probably to blame for forcing information from him. This was not a pleasant world at times. John completed his calls. He hadn't learned anything new other than about Benny's death. He found out that from Uncle Sam. Benny's body was found in a dumpster in an alley by a store owner, depositing his garbage behind his place. He called the police, stating positively 'hearing nothing and seeing nothing.'

Benny wouldn't have to worry about his next meal or where to bed down now. The city's 'powers that be' had been clamping down on the homeless before winter set in. The winters were always too severe for the homeless. His wandering mind came back to his problem. What now? How could he be with Chrissy every minute and be out there looking at the same time? An impossible situation.

When he was getting nowhere, a solution came, why not take Chrissy with him. She would probably balk at the idea. But sitting around here wasn't the answer by a long shot. He knew Chrissy would fight this tooth and nail, but he couldn't sit here. Not knowing was irritating him more than anything. Why did they want Chrissy?

John went in to see Jared. He was half asleep but fighting it. He walked over and sat down quite near him but not touching. Jared looked up at him and grinned. John immediately thought that this boy was looking for a male he could relate to. He wanted to say, not me. I am a loner. Instead, John pulled Jared into his side and said, "what are you watching?"

Jared curved right in tightly. "I am watching the Land Beyond Time. It is a cartoon about dinosaurs. They aren't big and mean like Jurassic Park. Mommy said I could see this one because the dinosaurs were nice."

"Jurassic Park, no, that picture isn't for you. This cartoon looks like fun," concentrating on the TV screen.

"Why does mommy have to have a guard? Did she do something bad?"

"No, Jared, your mommy is a good person. There is a bad person out there who wants to get a hold of your mother. I am here to stop him."

"Why doesn't Joel arrest him? He said he was a policeman."

"Because Joel doesn't know who the bad man is either or he would, I am sure."

"Will mommy be guarded long?"

"Jared, as soon as we find him, your mommy will be safe. We will lock him up. Then she won't need me to guard her anymore."

Jared looked at the TV for a while.

"John, my mommy needs a man, and so do I," he said in a sleepy voice. He closed his eyes and went to sleep. John sat, looking down at him. No kids should be part of his world, as events of late indicated.

John watched the cartoon, holding the boy close to him. This little boy was creeping into his heart. It wasn't long before John's head fell back against the couch. The night without sleep finally caught up with him.

Chapter Eleven

The next thing he heard was the doorbell. He eased away from Jared. Then he went to the door, rubbing the sleep from his eyes and massaging his face awake.

He opened the door gingerly. There stood a young man about five years younger than him. John knew this had to be Joel. He looked at his watch seven o'clock. He slept longer than he thought.

"Joel? Come in, come in. Sorry, we were all sleeping."

"What do you mean you were all sleeping. Who are you? Where is Chrissy? The police stopped me, asking questions, indicating someone kidnapped Chrissy again. What is going on here?"

"Come in, Joel, and I'll explain." John led Joel into Chrissy's study away from Jared and Chrissy.

"You better start explaining. From what I hear, Chrissy was bait."

"Chrissy was kidnapped again. But I . . ."

Before he could finish, Joel yelled. "Yes, and I want to know why?"

"Hold it, Joel, let me finish and keep your voice down. Chrissy and Jared are sleeping." John paced back and forth. "Chrissy is upstairs. She is okay. I am here to protect her. We need to find out who and why the kidnapping was necessary? We don't have any idea yet. They didn't tell Chrissy either."

Joel was not happy with this explanation. "Why are you here? What do you have to do with all of this? Who are you anyway?"

"I am John Taylor. I am a former cop. I'm a Private Investigator. I was the one who rescued Chrissy. I am here to see that she isn't retaken."

"If you rescued Chrissy, who had her? You must know that? Was it Mr. Hammond again?"

"No, this time it was Delvietti."

"Delvietti, I have heard of him. Why did he want Chrissy?"

"That is the problem. We don't know. We don't have enough on Delvietti to arrest him and his thugs."

"How did you get involved?" Joel inquired.

"Because I found out from a police buddy of mine that someone had taken her."

"But that doesn't explain how you know Chrissy."

"I was the one kidnapped with Chrissy by Senator Hammond."

"Your John, Chrissy talked about." Joel grabbed him. "You chased her, and then they kidnapped her, you creep." John easily broke Joel's grip because Joel was puzzled and didn't have a firm grip.

"You're right. It was me. Believe me. I am truly sorry, getting Chrissy involved in the first place."

"You're sorry. That is just fine. One word and you want to be absolved from all that Chrissy has been through, kidnapped twice, and harassed by Detective Delaney. Also, in the hospital twice and since beaten up. Sorry isn't good enough."

Joel observed Chrissy's face as she appeared at the door. He raced to her side. "Chrissy, are you all right?"

"Yes, Joel, it looks bad, I know. I tried to dissolve some of the puffiness, but it didn't help much. Joel, I am sorry. I meant to phone you and cancel our date, but I must have fallen asleep." She smiled at Joel.

"Cancel? I would have come immediately if I had known." Joel glared at John.

"Let's go into the kitchen. I'll make some coffee and something to eat." She swung towards the door then back to John. "Where is Jared?"

"He is sleeping in front of the TV."

"You'd better go wake him up, or I will never get him to sleep tonight." John knew Chrissy was trying to get rid of him while she talked to Joel in private. He raced into the family room, picked up

Jared, and headed for the kitchen, not even breaking stride.

Jared woke up, amazed John was carrying him. "John, is something the matter?"

"No, Jared. Your mother wants you in the kitchen, that is all."

Chrissy was saying. "Joel, John has to be here. I don't want him here. But I am afraid they will retake me. I don't know why this is happening to me." Joel was touching her face tenderly with the tips of his fingers. John could read it in her eyes that she was enjoying his touch.

"Here is Jared. He is ready for dinner, aren't you, sport?" John put Jared down. "Perhaps you should go and wash your hands first." Giving Jared a little push then turning to Chrissy, John said brightly, "is there anything I can do to help you with dinner?" Pulling Chrissy away from Joel. She was so amazed. She let him lead her across the kitchen to the fridge.

She recovered and looked back at Joel beseechingly for understanding.

Joel decided the best thing to do was get dinner over with so Chrissy and he could talk. He asked, "is there anything I can do? Maybe order pizza or Chinese or help here?"

She didn't want to play Susie homemaker, especially with these two males. "Pizza will be good. I'll give you the number. Jared likes a small cheese and pepperoni. I like their meat deluxe."

She never ordered meat deluxe, but she thought the men might prefer it. She wanted to keep them eating to keep conversation to a minimum. "Extra-large." She added, handing Joel the number. She started making coffee.

John pulled out a chair, turning it around and straddling it. He leaned on the back so he could observe Chrissy and Joel, both busy with their tasks. He wasn't about to go away.

She was feeling so uncomfortable under John's eagle eye that she spilled the coffee. *Why was John being so annoying?*

Joel got off the phone and walked over to Chrissy. "Let me do that. You are still too shook up. You sit down. I'll make the coffee," Joel said lovingly. Chrissy gave him a big smile of relief. She stood close to Joel and watched him. He cast her a returning smile.

Jared returned at a run. "What's for supper, Mommy?"

"Pizza." put in John, Jared yelled. "Yeah." Then he went over to John. "Why are you sitting like that? Mommy always makes me sit in chairs property."

"I think you mean properly." Ruffling his hair but not explaining for his chair's ethics. Jared grinned up at him, liking this man's attention. Having seen Joel once fleetingly, Jared didn't react to his being here.

John realized Jared didn't know Joel, so that meant he had not been around much. Maybe this was their first date.

"Jared, you remember Joel? He came to see us once." Chrissy put in as though reading John's mind.

"You are the policeman. I remember you." Jared clarified. Joel had finished putting the coffee to brew, and reached out to shake Jared's hand.

"Yes, I am the policeman. Nice to see you again, Jared."

She watched the two men. They seemed to be taking each other's measure. What was going on here? "Joel, I'm glad now that I didn't cancel our date. I need your company tonight. I have been through a lot lately. I could use some male companionship to take my mind off things." she gave Joel a charming smile.

Joel came over to her, caressing her face lightly. "I hate seeing you all beat up this way. I wish I could find the guys that did this to you." Joel continued stroking her face. Chrissy was responding by closing her eyes and leaning into him.

John jumped up. "Come on, Jared, you show me what's to drink, and we'll set the table."

Chrissy leaped away from Joel. The moment broken. She turned to John, glaring at him as she swept out of the room.

"Yes, Jared, show us where everything is." Joel was ready to help with the table setting. Jared directed the two men in different directions while standing, watching them jump to his bidding. He liked this attention, not understanding what was going on, only that these men were doing what he said.

Chrissy had gone to her room. She was furious with John. She went to fix up her face and change her clothes. She would have liked to take a shower but didn't feel she had time.

Chrissy tried to cover her bruises, but it was too painful. Joel had already seen them, so she gave up. She put her hair up in a ponytail with a matching ribbon to her pink sweater. She had on form-fitting black jeans that clung to her hips and legs. She was satisfied with the look but not the face that made her frown. She headed for the stairs as the front doorbell rang.

Joel yelled. "I'll get it. Come help me, Jared." Whipping bills out of his pocket on the way to the door, Jared running behind.

John had walked out into the hall. He stopped at the bottom of the stairs looking up to see Chrissy walking down. His eyes were going from her soft pink slippers to her tight-fitting jeans. His eyes paused there for a bit, watching the motion of her legs and hips. Then his eyes lifted to the pink sweater, enjoying the look of that soft clinging cashmere. His eyes finally traveled up to her face and her furious glower. Her ponytail swung back and forth as she stomped down each step quickly to end John's gaze. He gave her a sassy grin, knowing full well that she did not appreciate his scrutiny.

Joel had returned from the door carrying the small pizza while Jared brought the extra-large. Joel stood there, giving Chrissy an appreciative look. Chrissy responded with a smile.

John said coyly. "Shall we eat?" Then he led her in the kitchen, gallantly seating her, for which he earned another glare.

Joel took the big pizza from Jared. "Climb up on the chair, buddy. Your pizza is in front of you." Joel didn't acknowledge John's byplay. He opened the larger pizza and served each of them a piece. Sitting down, Joel sent Chrissy a smile saying, "Chrissy, you look lovely. I like the pink ribbon. It matches your pretty sweater."

"Thank you, Joel," she smiled charmingly.

John said with a mischievous grin, "I like the way your black jeans hug your hips and legs. I hardly noticed the ribbon." Chrissy's head turned to John with another scowl. Joel was looking from one to the other. Apparently, she didn't care for this man. He remembered her anger at John when she had related the first kidnapping. Joel felt sorry for Chrissy having to put up with John as her protector.

She must have decided for Jared's sake to put this animosity towards John aside. The meal proceeded with general conversation and some bantering between the two men. Being cops, they shared some of the antics that were part of a cop's life. The pizza disappeared. They had been sitting there for two hours, much to Chrissy's surprise when she finally looked at the clock.

"Jared, time for bed."

"Ah, Mommy, do I have to. I had a sleep."

John had decided to give Joel a break. "Come on, Jared. I'll supervise your bath and the bedtime ritual tonight."

Chrissy looked at John with shock.

He cast her a sweet smile as he headed out of the kitchen, behind Jared's jumping leaps all the way. He was a typically exuberance four-year-old. They headed upstairs. John was tickling his sides, causing Jared to giggle gleefully. John and Jared were playing battleships and submarines in the foam from the bubbles. It was indeed fun having this man around, making bathing an enormous success.

Chrissy had taken Joel into the living room after the kitchen was clean at Joel's insistence. He was easy to talk to, and there was much laughter, which was an excellent tonic, after her experiences of the past two weeks. Chrissy put the thought away and just enjoyed Joel.

The doorbell rang. Chrissy got up to answer it. John was coming down the stairs after tucking Jared in for the night. His hand stopped Chrissy as he passed her on the way to the door.

"I'll get it." She stood back, waiting to see who it was. John had taken out a knife, unbeknown to Chrissy. He eased the door open.

"Yes." John looked at the man enquiringly. He had the look of a cop, although he was in a suit. Detective Delaney had expected Chrissy to open the door. His look of surprise rendered him speechless.

"Well, what do you want?" John queried.

Delaney fumbled for his wallet, enclosing his badge. "Detective Delaney, to see Mrs. Lambert."

"Why?" John wasn't about to comply too easily. He had heard about this detective's highhanded methods.

"I have a few questions for her regarding an investigation I am conducting. Who are you?"

John still didn't invite him in. "I am John Taylor. I am here for

Chrissy." John did not elaborate.

"Well, I need to speak to Mrs. Lambert." Delaney persisted.

But John closed the door and turned to Chrissy. "Do you want to speak to this guy?"

Joel was behind her now. "You don't have to talk to him, Chrissy. Not this late at night." Joel put in. John rationalized Joel didn't like the detective either.

She didn't know what to say, looking from John to Joel, knowing Detective Delaney wouldn't get past either man.

"Joel, maybe I should talk to him, but I don't want to. Not tonight anyway."

That is all John needed to hear. He opened the door and said. "Mrs. Lambert isn't available to answer questions tonight. Come back tomorrow."

Delaney looked from John to Joel, as Joel had pushed Chrissy back into the living room. Delaney knew it was a lost cause. Neither of these men intended to let him speak to her. So, he backed off saying. "I'll be back tomorrow morning. I will speak to her then," Delaney said firmly.

John just said. "You do that," closing the door in Detective Delaney's face again.

Joel had walked back into the living room and had pulled Chrissy into his arms. Not liking the defeated look on her face. She relaxed against him. Not even moving away when John appeared.

"What does Detective Delaney want?" John was asking the room in general.

Joel answered. "He was the Detective handling the first homicide that started all this. His rash attitude was what put Chrissy in the hospital the second time." Tightening his arm around her, Joel put his chin on her hair.

John thought they made a pretty picture of a couple in love. They looked to be about the same age. She seemed to fit nicely into his arms as Joel was shorter by a couple of inches then John.

"Did he ever question Chrissy after she came out of the hospital the second time?"

Joel lifted his head and looked down at Chrissy with her head buried into his neck. Her eyes were closed as though she was enjoying the closeness. Joel inquired. "Did he, Chrissy?"

She leaned back. "Yes. The Detective came here one time, but I thought I had answered all his questions," she said lamely. "I don't like that man, and he knows it."

Joel kissed her forehead, and she seemed to melt into him more.

"Chrissy, would you mind getting fresh coffee?" John asked innocently.

Joel stepped away from her. "You sit down, Chrissy. I'll get fresh coffee." Joel walked out of the room.

Chrissy sat down on the couch. John sat in the chair across from her, separated by a coffee table.

"Chrissy, do you know something that I am unaware of?"

"No, you were there. You stopped me before I even reached the door. When I went in later with Detective Delaney, I never went near the room where it occurred. I don't remember much, only that I started crying and couldn't stop. He must have called a doctor. Because the doctor put me in the hospital."

When Joel arrived with fresh coffee, the two of them seemed to be sitting there deep in their thoughts. While making coffee, it had occurred to Joel that maybe John had wanted to get Chrissy alone. But they weren't even talking.

Joel sat down beside Chrissy on the couch. They drank for a minute in silence. All seemed lost in their own thoughts.

Then Jared appeared at the door. He ran to his mother.

"What are you doing up?" Chrissy asked, pulling Jared onto her lap.

"I dreamed you were gone again," Jared said with a sob in his voice.

"Honey, I am right here. No one is going to separate us again."

John clarified. "Jared, that is why I am staying here. The police are outside. We are here to protect your mom."

Jared looked at Joel. "You are a policeman. Are you staying here too?"

"No, Jared, I have to work at my station, so I can't stay. But I am here tonight, so your mother is safe." Joel answered.

Chrissy hugged Jared lovingly. "Mommy is safe, and so are you. I won't leave you again. You won't be going to playschool for a few days. So, we will have lots of time together."

John had not broached the subject yet of Chrissy coming with him on his investigation. That was what he had been contemplating while Joel was making coffee. How best to put it to Chrissy without her retreating at the thought. He certainly didn't think now was the time either, not with Joel here to protest. That was another reason why he hesitated to tell her.

Chrissy was stroking Jared's hair. He snuggled in tightly, enjoying his mom's closeness.

John was watching them with envious eyes. Would he ever have a boy to snuggle up to him like this?

Joel reached over and patted Jared's back. "Your mother is safe now. You don't have to separate anymore. You should be dreaming happy dreams about being with your friends and having fun with your mom. Maybe I should get you a puppy to keep you and your mom company." Joel looked at Chrissy.

Jared sat up. "Would you really get me a puppy, Joel?" His nightmare forgotten. "Mommy, can I keep it if Joel gives me a puppy?"

Chrissy hesitated. "Yes, I guess a puppy would be company for us."

"Won't that be fun, John? Joel is getting me a puppy."

"Yes, buddy, that will be great. You will be able to romp in the park with a puppy as well as your backyard." John replied.

Jared got off his mother's knee and walked around the coffee table to John. He took John's hand. "I think I can go to sleep now."

"All right, let's go." John stood up, retaining Jared's hand. "Say goodnight to Joel and your mom first."

Jared went over to his mom and gave her a smacking kiss, then said. "Good night, Joel." Then he turned around, grabbing John's hand again. "John, that will be neat having a puppy." Jared's voice was all excited as they headed up to his bedroom.

Chrissy watched her son leave the room with John. Just like it was his dad putting him to bed. She wasn't sure she liked that picture.

Why did Jared trust him so much? Chrissy sat, staring at the doorway. They disappeared through.

Joel broke in. "I hope you don't mind my suggesting a puppy? I know that it will be extra work for you. But I do think Jared will enjoy a puppy. I always had a dog when I was young. Maybe I could help train it," Joel said wistfully.

"That would be nice. I know very little about dogs. We never had animals when we were young. My mother was allergic to them. We had goldfish, my sister and me. We soon tired of them because they were in such a small bowl and swam in circles."

"Do you prefer a certain kind of dog?"

"No, something that won't grow too big. I think that would be best."

"I know someone whose dog just had pups. Fred works at the station. I don't know what kind they are. But he said there were six pups, two females and four males.

"I think a female would be best, aren't they supposed to be more placid?"

"Well, that all depends on the breed, I think. Some male dogs can be good-natured too." Joel said hopefully, in case the two females were already given away.

John came back into the room. "Well, Jared is all settled in. His dream will be about puppies now. He is so excited by the thought."

Looking at Joel, John said. "You better come across with a puppy now that you have his hopes up."

"Yeah, Fred, at the station, his dog just had pups. I'm sure I can get one from him if they aren't too big a breed." Looking at Christie reassuringly, he stood up. "Well, I think I had better be going. You should be in bed after all you have been through." Looking admiringly at Chrissy.

John, who was still standing, said, "I'll see him to the door, Chrissy. It has been an eventful day for you after last night."

Chrissy sent John a withering look before turning a brilliant smile on Joel and thanked him for coming and making it an enjoyable evening.

John headed for the door hoping Joel would follow.

Joel patted Chrissy's hand on the way by. "Have a good sleep.

I'll arrange that puppy in the next few days. If they are old enough to leave their mother, that is."

John stood by the front door, ready to open it. Joel didn't delay. He was almost right behind John.

"Goodnight, Joel." John pulled the door open.

"Goodnight, John" then he looked back at Chrissy, who had entered the hallway, and he winked.

Chrissy gave Joel a warm smile, which turned to a scowl as soon as the door closed behind Joel.

"How dare you order people around in my house," said Chrissy angrily.

"Chrissy, you are beat. Go to bed. I did it for your own good."

John was fast approaching her. So, she turned, heading upstairs quickly. She was too exhausted to stand her ground tonight, although she didn't want to retreat. Chrissy had a shower. After, she put cold face cloths on her face. The swelling was still quite evident. Would her face look better tomorrow?

Chapter Twelve

This just wasn't working having John in her home. He has a domineering personality. She kept bowing to his directions, but this was her home. It should not always be his way. Chrissy got tired of giving concessions. Her face was reflecting her anger, which her attire did not complement.

She was in a pink nylon nightie that barely came to her hips. Chrissy walked over to the bed and pulled back the covers.

The bedroom door opened without a knock, and John came in, carrying a mug. He advanced to the bed with his hand cupped containing pills. Chrissy was standing dumbfounded. "What are you doing in my bedroom? You never even knocked," she accused.

"I thought you were in the shower, and you wouldn't hear me." John's eyes were roaming over Chrissy liberally. "I was going to leave the milk and aspirins. Then I was going to remove myself." John's eyes were mischievous. She was frozen in place by her fury. He was enjoying the pink nightgown that revealed her breasts.

Chrissy stiffened when she noticed that John was enjoying the sight. But it only made her breasts jut out further. She dived under the covers.

But he didn't apologize, repeating instead, "I brought you some warm milk and some aspirin." He walked towards her, a grin of appreciation on his lips.

"Wipe that look off your face and get out. Don't you ever come into my bedroom again. I will have to arrange with Max Kelsey for someone else to guard me."

John ignored what Chrissy was saying and sat down on the bed. She tried to scoot away, but he was pinning the covers down, hampered by the other side tucked under still.

"Get off my bed." She was shocked that he would actually dare sit down.

"Chrissy, drink your warm milk and take your aspirins," he said soothingly, holding out the mug and pills. John was having trouble keeping a straight face.

"We will talk tomorrow when you have had a good sleep." John was leaning over her. She was still trying to release the bed covers from being trapped under John. He wasn't moving.

She took the mug and pills, drinking the milk after the aspirins went down, her face screwed up in distaste. "I hate warm milk," shoving the cup back at him.

He took it but kept his position leaning into her. "Chrissy, relax, and have a nice sleep. We will discuss things in the morning. Goodnight, dear."

His lips dropped a light kiss on her forehead. "Pleasant dreams, Chrissy." He got up, quickly vacated the room. He started to whistle as he closed the door.

She was too tired. She would get angry tomorrow.

She burrowed down under the covers and put out the light. She started thinking about the evening with Joel and John. Two different men but in almost the same occupation. John would be about five years older than Joel. His attitude towards Joel was that he liked him. Although at times, John seemed to be jealous of Joel or was that her imagination? She drifted off to sleep.

It was sometime during the night that she started thrashing about, crying out. "No! No!" Her body was flinching. "No! No! Stop"

The overhead light went on. John was moving towards the bed.

"Chrissy, wake up. You're having a nightmare." He grabbed her and pulled her into his arms, tangled covers and all. Her eyes flew open, looking into his. "John, they were hitting me," she answered in a hurt voice.

"Sssh, it was just a dream. They can't get to you now. I have you.

You are safe." He was rocking her like she was a child in his arms.

"John, will it ever go away all of this, whatever this is?" Chrissy lamented.

"Sssh. We will talk in the morning, go back to sleep." He continued rocking her and patting her back gently, trying to soothe her into sleep. She was like a firecracker around him during the day, waiting to go off. But as she slipped into sleep, she was quite tranquil.

John was surprised when he gently laid her down. She had a sweet smile of pleasure, curving her lips. He went back to his bed to lie awake for an hour or more, thinking of Chrissy's dilemma.

How was he going to find the answers about who and why they wanted her? All he knew for sure was that he couldn't sit around, waiting for Uncle Sam to come up with something. He had to be out there looking for himself. Chrissy was coming with him, as he couldn't leave her behind alone that might not be wise.

His tired body took over, and he finally drifted into sleep, only to have someone crawling around on his bed. His bed? John's eyes flew open.

There was bright sunlight hitting his sleepy eyes. He closed them again with a groan. More movement on the bed and his eyes popped open, looking into blue eyes, a screwed-up nose, and a giggling mouth. Jared was leaning on John's chest, chuckling.

"Mommy told me to come to see if you were awake, but your eyes were closed," Jared said with the innocence of a child. John put his arms around Jared, hugging him and thrusting his nose at Jared's nose, tweaking it.

"Now, I am awake."

Jared giggled and giggled. John rocked him tightly.

Jared had his little hands on each side of his face. "You have a scratchy face, but I like it." Planting a kiss on John's cheek. "Mommy said to tell you breakfast is ready if you are awake." Jared was still wiggling around, enjoying the attention. An experience that was new to him as a man had never slept in his house before.

John turned Jared over and propelled himself up onto his elbows over him and preceded to tickle. Loving the sound of the little boy's laughter. John wondered what happened to Jared's father? He didn't think he should quiz the boy. No, he would ask Chrissy.

Chrissy's voice called up the stairs disrupting their play. "Breakfast is ready. Are you two coming?" She was a bit envious of all the laughter that she heard.

Today she intended to tell him that having him in the house with her wasn't working. It was bad enough having the police out on the street. She felt more like a prisoner rather than the protected.

Then she remembered her nightmare during the night. John's crooning voice was soothing her back to sleep. She recalled him holding her, rocking her and how safe she felt. She shook off the warm feeling. John would have to go.

She entered the kitchen after hearing running steps on the stairs.

Jared entered the kitchen, laughing. "John is so much fun, Mommy. I am glad he is staying here." Chrissy looked at Jared, and his face was so full of life. He seemed really happy. She had a twinge of regret that Todd had not lived to see his son. Todd had never experienced Jared's romping in bed with him as Jared had just done with John, a stranger.

Chrissy's heart was breaking with sadness. Todd had been taken so early in life, and she loved him and missed him so much. He had gone into a cold lake to save a little girl. He got tangled in the weeds and drowned along with the little girl. While Chrissy and the little girl's mother watched in horror, waiting for them to resurface. They realized too late that the lake held them prisoner. Even though another man had tried to free them, it was too late by the time he reached them. Chrissy gave a choking sob.

"Mommy, what's the matter? Why are you crying?"

"I'm not crying. Something got caught in my throat." She gave Jared a weak smile. Someday she would have to explain Todd's death to Jared. She had told him God needed him in heaven. It hurt too much to speak about Todd's death.

Todd had been so excited about having a baby, but he never saw him. She had not wanted a baby that soon. But after Todd was taken from her so early in their marriage, she was glad now to have Jared.

* * *

John's steps entering the kitchen brought Chrissy out of her memories. "Good morning, Chrissy. Sleep well?" John asked with a twinkle in his eyes.

"Err, yes, I slept well, did you?" Chrissy sort of stuttered.

"Yes, very well, although I seemed to have had a nice dream about holding you in my arms. You were very cuddly." John couldn't help teasing her. She blushed redder than the crimson top she was wearing with black hip-huggers. He had seen them advertised on TV. They looked so much better on Chrissy.

John sat down opposite Jared and gave him a wink. Jared tried to wink back but kept closing both eyes. John laughed. "You need a little practice, but you'll get it. Close only one eye like this," he winked at Chrissy as she sat down next to Jared.

Jared was looking at him with eyes wide open and then closed them both. John laughed. "We'll work on it, buddy. Eat your cereal."

Jared dug in and happily complied. Chrissy could see that Jared had taken to John. Why couldn't it have been Joel who was to be my protector? Chrissy liked Joel. The first man she had thought of that way since losing Todd. She glared across at John. He gave her another wink and smiled. He was having a good time watching the play of emotions on Chrissy's face, knowing full well that the glares were when she thought of him. But that wasn't a deterrent. He was going to be around for a long time yet.

The breakfast progressed with John complimenting Chrissy for the crisp bacon and scrambled eggs done to golden fluffiness. He liked the family picture they were projecting, despite Chrissy's glare.

Jared asked to be excused when finished. His mother granted him this, as John said okay too. Another scowl from her, but he politely asked for another coffee, as though he hadn't caught the glower. She filled both mugs and then sat down. She could hear that Jared had put on cartoons. Now she would have that talk with him.

John waylaid her by saying, "do you think Nancy will mind Jared while we go out together?"

"Yes, she would look after him, but we are not going out together. John, you are leaving here. Someone else can be assigned to protect me, or the police on my doorstep is enough." Chrissy poked her chin out in determination.

"Chrissy, I have no intention of leaving you, and you will come with me when I go out," he said firmly.

"Not in your dreams," replied Chrissy arrogantly.

"Chrissy, you can balk all you want, but it isn't going to change anything. I will be clinging to you, figuratively speaking, until the mystery of your kidnapping is solved. We will go out together. I need some clothes. I need to get my car repaired. Most importantly, I need to be out there to find out what is going on rather than sitting here having glaring contests." John had finished his coffee. "I'm going up to shower. I wish I had a change of clothes. Can I use your razor?"

"Certainly not," she said emphatically.

"You do have a razor, don't you?" John asked flippantly.

"Of course, but you aren't using it."

"Ah, come on." John leaned over and rubbed his chin on Chrissy's cheek. She jumped as though shot. She couldn't believe he would do something so blatantly.

"There is a spare razor in the third drawer of the main bathroom. Stay out of my personal bathroom." The thought of John having a shower in her shower bothered her for some reason.

John left the kitchen whistling. '*Oh, my darling, oh my darling, Clementine.*'

Chrissy flounced around the kitchen. Her talk with John had not gone the way she had planned.

* * *

John went to his place after dropping off Jared at Nancy's.

Jared was disappointed he wasn't going with them. But John told him, "We are going grown-up places. It won't be any fun for you." Jared accepted that without argument.

Chrissy was surprised at John's house. She had just assumed he lived in a bachelor pad somewhere. The house was in an upscale neighborhood. It wasn't modern but that of a substantial English country home with property. When John went to the front door, no one came and yet as she looked around the grounds and inside the house, it was immaculate. Chrissy looked at John enquiringly.

"This can't be yours. Where are the servants?"

John laughed. "Yes, it is mine. There are no servants, only a couple that comes in three times a week. Toby looks after the grounds, and Gretchen does the cleaning and cooking on those days. Today is their day off."

She was gazing around in amazement. Her eyes kept lighting on this object or that furnishings, with wonder. "John, I repeat, this can't be yours."

"I didn't buy it if that is what you mean. It was passed on to me by my parents, who moved to England. My father was English born, and my mother was Canadian. My father inherited a place back in England from his father. He decided to move back there, leaving me with this place."

Chrissy realized then that John's family must have money. She had never known anyone wealthy. Her clients didn't run to the affluent yet. Although she had a successful Interior Decorating business, she hoped someday to have one or two wealthy gems to work on as she became more successful. But the way things were going in her life, that wasn't likely to happen anytime soon.

John certainly didn't have the look of wealth in his clothes or attitude. She would never have guessed. Maybe it was his line of work that made him act the part of a middle-class male. He looked as though he knew his way around but was not a part of it.

He went into the study and sat down in a well-used chair behind the desk, not shabby but antique. He started looking through the mail. Chrissy was still not convinced. So, she blatantly walked over to the desk and picked up some envelopes. They were all addressed to John Taylor. He raised one inquiring eyebrow. "Didn't believe me, did you? I am not rich. My parents are well off, and there is a fund to keep this place in shape. Otherwise, I am middle class like you."

"How can that be possible?" She was looking around in awe.

"Because the house came from monies inherited by my dad, and he enjoyed his home. That's where he put his money. He worked in Real Estate. He enjoyed entertaining rather than going out on the town. So, when this came on the market, he bought it. The furnishings came with the house mostly. It was an estate sale that my father bought."

"Can I investigate?"

"By all means, enjoy yourself." He knew she was looking at the place from an Interior Decorator's point of view. He returned to his mail. There was an eloquent letter from his mother, begging him to visit soon. He flipped through the rest of the mail. Bills, advertisements, and charity requests. Standard everyday mail until he saw a buff envelope with bold writing.

Taking a letter opener, he slit the envelope. It was an invitation for him and a guest to a Charity Gala Dinner at the Convention Center from Senator Alan Hammond.

"Well, well?" An invitation to another charity due. His first response was no way. Then he thought he would see what Hammond was up to. Taking Chrissy would be perfect to see Alan's reaction to them coming as a couple. John grinned. Yes, he thought that should be interesting.

He piled the rest of the mail into bills and others. Then he got up to go and find Chrissy. She was out on the back terrace looking out over the manicured lawns and shrubs, which somewhat surprised him. He expected to see her looking at the upper floor. He walked over to her and watched her face. The animation of pleasure mirrored there.

"What, Chrissy?"

"You are in the heart of the city almost. Yet there is so much land attached to this house?" There was a question in her voice.

"This house was built before the city became so dense. It stayed in the family until my dad bought it fifteen years ago. The family kept the property intact, and so did my dad. Would you like to see the upstairs? I take it you covered all the downstairs?"

"Yes, and yes again." He took her hand and led her back inside through the intricately scrolled glass French doors.

"Why would anyone ever want to leave this place?" She meant John's parents.

"Because they have the real thing in England, I guess." He had never felt about the place the way Chrissy was feeling. He hadn't grown up here. John had never lived in it until his parents went to England three years ago. He debated renting it out instead of moving in, but his parents had talked him out of that idea.

He guided Chrissy up the broad oak stairs, shiny and curved. He still held her hand, so she could crane her neck, not missing any of the splendor. There were seven bedrooms and three bathrooms. Two of the bedrooms had ensuites.

John's room, she figured, was not the master bedroom that was yet to come. They had viewed six bedrooms. One in a child's motif that had been for the children until they were old enough to move on to a bigger room.

He continued down the hall, which was wide and carpeted with a brilliant red scrolled rug. Lamps lit the hall at night rather than overhead fixtures.

He stopped at an open door. The room was furnished with colossal furniture that looked reasonable in the vast space. The decor was in keeping with the furnishings. John watched Chrissy's eyes scan the room for every detail while explaining that this was his parent's room. And to her, it said it all. He was a guest in his parents' house.

He took her through to the bathroom, which was as big as Chrissy's bedroom. The monstrous tub took up most of one end. There were two pedestal sinks with gold fixtures positioned in front of separate mirrors. There were even separate his and her showers with another door into a dressing room. There were clothes still hanging there. Evidently, his parents had not taken all of their things with them. It was as though they had gone on a trip and would be coming back. John indicated that they stayed for a month each year.

He excused himself and left Chrissy to indulge her curiosity. When she went back into the hall, John was coming out of his room. He had changed his clothes, and he held a packed suitcase. He had ignored her demand for someone else to protect her.

"John, I don't think this is . . ."

He cut her off. "Chrissy, I am going to live with you until this is over," his firm voice brooking no argument.

She looked at him intently. He had changed his bandage for a gauze compress. The band he used when working out, wrapped around his forehead at a jaunty angle, contrasted in royal blue with his jet-black hair—dressed in a black ensemble. He looked like he was of foreign extraction, but he had said his father was British, so his coloring must have come from his mother.

He was trying to figure out what Chrissy was thinking. Was she planning an escape? She had never shown any interest in him at all. Chrissy had to be formulating a plan or something.

The black showed off his muscular shoulders and arms, his chest tapering to a lean torso. *Snap out of this, Chrissy. You don't want him or need him in your life.*

Chapter Thirteen

W hat do you intend to do now?" Christy inquired.
"First take my car in for repairs, then hit the streets. That is where the information is."

"I don't think I can do that."

"Chrissy, I need to find out why they need you. I am not going to find that out sitting at your place."

"But, John, I don't know anything about investigation work."

"Then act like my girlfriend. Just be with me and help remember conversations. My problem isn't you being with me, but getting information after Benny's death. That was a clear message. Now nobody wants to talk."

"Benny was the one that gave you information about me, right?"

"Yes, he was found in a dumpster shortly after."

"John, this is dangerous. Who will look after Jared if anything happens to me?"

"Chrissy, they are not going to do anything to you as long as you stick with me. I will see that Jared always has a mom, okay?"

"John, I will just hamper your search for information. I know I will."

John leaned forward and kissed her.

"Why did you do that?" She asked when he ended the kiss.

"It is the only way I have been successful in keeping you quiet," John said meaningfully. Chrissy jumped back out of his reach.

"Forewarned is forearmed. Kisses can be useful." John said with a rakish grin. "Come on, Chrissy, let's hit the streets." He headed for the door without looking to see if she was following. She decided there was no point staying here and trailed after him. He locked the door after setting the Security System.

She was already settled in the car when he got in. He looked at her inquiringly, but she wouldn't even make eye contact. She was here, but not liking the prospect.

He drove to the auto glass place. They were teasing him about jealous husbands and guns. Evidently, they had seen Chrissy's wedding ring. They knew John was single. The jokes got pretty vulgar. He called a halt by saying a lady was present. She was in the waiting room, but he felt sure that she heard because the men were using loud voices. They had tried to outdo each other with their lewd comments.

When the windows finished, he was glad. They were still making lewd remarks. John was mad at himself for not squashing it when the bantering first started.

He mumbled as he entered the car. "Sorry, Chrissy." She ignored him, looking out the window.

John concentrated on getting down to the red-light district. He parked his car in a parking lot with an attendant.

"Now we walk." She was glad she wore sensible shoes because that is what they did, walk up and down street after street. Sometimes stopping to talk but mostly just walking. The persons he was looking for wasn't available. After walking for hours or so it seemed, he directed her into a restaurant.

"Coffee, Louie, one with one without." He knew she never took milk in her coffee. He sat at the counter and indicated she should take the next stool.

"Louie, where is Ralph? I've been looking for him. Has he been in?"

"Not today. Maybe Ralph heard via the grapevine that you were around. Look what happened to Benny after you talked to him."

"All right, where is Mannie? Has he been around?"

"Sorry, John, no one wants to know you right now."

"Louie, I have a problem that needs fixing. I need the information to fix it. Do you understand?"

"Sorry, John, I would love to help, but I can't. I love my family too much."

"I appreciate that. How are Linda and the girls?"

"Fine. Angela is turning out to be quite the piano player since you provided that piano for the girls. I wish I could help you, but I can't."

"Okay, Louie. I understand."

"Are you going to introduce me to your lady friend?"

"Chrissy, meet Louie. Louie, meet Chrissy. Come on. We are leaving." He got up and threw a bill on the counter, which included a large tip.

She didn't want the coffee as it was too bitter, so she was glad to leave. He pushed her through the open door that he held. His hands stayed on her back as he stepped outside. She tried to put some space between them, but he didn't let her.

"We have to act more loving, so we look like we are just slumming. I need to make some contacts fast before everyone clams up. Now play along." He eased his hand up Chrissy's back and then let his arm encircle her shoulders as his hand snaked up into her hair, drawing her closer. This time she didn't move away. He was nuzzling her ear with his mouth. She couldn't figure out what this was accomplishing other than making her uncomfortable. They continued walking.

Next, he pushed her into a dark doorway. He started kissing her. Chrissy was trying to resist, but John was being very masterful. Then as she was about to submit, he pulled away from her. They continued down the street with John's arm wrapping Chrissy against his body. She couldn't figure out what was going on. What was John up to?

Again, John pulled Chrissy into a dark doorway and started kissing her again. This time she didn't resist, but she didn't respond to the kiss either. He was up to something. She resented him using her this way. He broke the kiss, continuing their passage down the street.

The next time when he tried to direct her into a dark doorway, she stopped. He just started kissing her in the open while propelling her into the dark entrance. Chrissy wanted to bite him, but he only deepened the kiss when she opened her mouth. She had had enough. She tried to pull his hair while she kicked his shin. He released her mouth, pinning her against the wall.

"Ralph, I know you're hiding in here, so don't move." Chrissy stiffened, but John still had her pinned to the wall with his body. He whispered in her ear. "Keep still. I need to talk to Ralph. I need you to make it look like we are necking. Chrissy, please help me, or I won't get the answers I need." She put her arms around John's neck and put her face into his neck like she was yielding to him.

He whispered. "Ralph, I need to know why they killed Benny? What did he know?"

Ralph stayed mum.

"Ralph, if you don't talk, I will drag you out into the open. Do you want that?"

"Benny knew that the girl was to be a hostage against someone. But he didn't tell me who. Honestly, I don't know who."

"Not good enough, Ralph. You know more."

"Honestly, I don't, I don't." Ralphs' voice sounded panicky.

"Ralph, I will give you one more chance." He started kissing Chrissy again. She had had enough of this. She wasn't about to cooperate anymore, so she started pulling his hair.

"They said it would happen at some charity affair. Honest, that is all I know." John reached into his pocket and pulled out some bills, and they disappeared out of his hand. He was still nuzzling Chrissy. "Okay, it's over now. Act like we are hot for each other, or you will have another person's death on your hands."

John pulled her out of the doorway. Chrissy put her mouth up to John's as though she wanted more. He said, grinning, "soon, baby, you will have all of me." John tucked her into his side as though they were heading for somewhere to make love. He whispered to her, "thanks, you did good, Chrissy."

It wasn't long before they were back at the car. He backed her up to the car and kissed her again. This time Chrissy did not cooperate, but he felt they had satisfied any curious eyes, so he helped her into the car. He went around to get in, reaching to put the key in the ignition. He got a jab from her elbow.

"Don't you ever kiss me again without my permission. No matter what the circumstances."

"Chrissy, if I told you what was going on, you wouldn't have cooperated. So, I had to do it that way."

"You are darn right. I wouldn't have agreed. You can drop me off. Then you are leaving. You will not reside in my house ever again."

"Chrissy, it is not over. They still need you. You heard Ralph. They want you as a hostage for some reason. I can't leave you now."

"Why take me hostage, for what purpose? What charity affair?"

"As to purpose, I don't know. I do know the charity affair. Mr. Hammond has invited us."

"Mr. Hammond?"

"Yes, Mr. Hammond. We will attend as I want to know what this is all about."

Chrissy gave him another jab in the ribs. "You are not to touch me again. If you hadn't chased me, I would never have been kidnapped. Then you wouldn't be kissing me at all. You degrade me with your meaningless kisses. Just because we were in the red-light district, you didn't have to make me feel like a lady of the night. It is daylight for gosh sakes."

John wondered what the daylight had to do with anything. He was rubbing his ribs, where she kept jabbing him. Her bony elbows had hurt.

"I am sorry, Chrissy. I have already apologized a couple of times. But there was no other way to get the information. You heard Louie that no one is talking. You think that was easy treating you that way. I like you and respect you too much to make you feel like a lady of the night. Honestly, that wasn't my intention. But I just knew I wouldn't get the information I needed unless I made some kind of a deceptive tactic. It worked, didn't it?"

"For you, yes, but not for me." She was still very angry with him.

"Can I suggest a truce in front of Jared? I don't want him to know what is going on." They had arrived at Nancy's house. Jared must've been watching for them because he came flying out the front door like a projectile.

"Mommy, Mommy, your back." Jared's voice showed his fear that she would disappear again. She leaped from the car, leaving the door open to catch the boy caroming in her direction. "Jared, it is okay. I am okay. I promised I wouldn't leave you again, didn't I? We said we would be back in about five hours, and here we are." She was hugging her son and glaring at John over Jared's head.

Nancy had come out on the veranda. Chrissy walked with a funny gait as Jared wasn't about to let go. "How was he?" Chrissy asked Nancy.

"He wouldn't leave the window. He even ate lunch there. Jared is feeling very insecure right now. I have never seen him act this way before." Nancy's voice held censure.

"Well, I won't be leaving him again for a while. Not until he gets over this dread, at least. Jared, go greet John while I pay Nancy. "

John had stayed down at the sidewalk. He stuck out his hand to greet Jared and tussled his hair with his other hand.

"Hi Jared, see, I brought your mom back. I said I would, didn't I? You have to trust me. I won't let anything happen to her." Jared leaned into John, so he pulled him against his side, and Jared's arms went around him.

"Okay, I trust you." But he kept his head buried in John's side. John felt terrible that they had left him so soon after Chrissy's disappearance. He should've waited a couple of days until Jared had felt more secure. But he needed that information from Ralph. Now, he knew the gala was the time of the next act. He could relax because the charity event was a week away.

Why had they grabbed Chrissy so far in advance? It didn't make sense somehow. John just had to hope Ralph knew what he was talking about.

Chrissy was standing beside him now, watching her clinging boy. Her son was getting too close to this man emotionally. She would have to work at separating them.

She put her hand on Jared's shoulder. "Come, Jared, it is time to go home." John didn't say anything. Just let Chrissy direct the boy into the car, helping him fasten his seatbelt. She closed the door, easing her body into the passenger seat. John had already started the car. Chrissy and Jared were waving at Nancy as the car pulled away.

There was no conversation on the short trip home. Chrissy was planning a way to make Jared feel more secure but not including John.

Jared was sleepy. He had been too tense too long and nodded off.

John was thinking of how-to counter Chrissy's arguments. He knew she would blow her stack when she heard. He intended taking them to his place instead of staying at hers. Police protection outside was just not good enough.

When they arrived at her place, there was no evidence of the police. John guessed they had to leave from protecting an empty house. So, that meant his plan would have to go into effect soon if he was going to guard Chrissy. He would call Uncle Sam.

He pulled into the driveway as close to the garage as he could. He told Chrissy to stay in the car and lock the doors after him, needing to check the house first.

Chrissy was glad that Jared had fallen asleep. She didn't want him more nervous about the situation than he already was. She watched the house for John to come out.

She wanted all of this over with. She wanted her life back, and it was ruining her business. She would have no clients left and have to start over. It wasn't going to get any better until this was over in a week, perhaps longer.

She was starting to get nervous. John hadn't come out. What should she do?

Then John appeared. Chrissy breathed a sigh of relief. He was signaling okay by waving his arm. The door locks clicked loudly, waking Jared.

He looked around sleepily. She was reaching for the back door when John came up beside her. "I'll get Jared."

Jared had his seatbelt off but looked groggy. John whipped him up in his arms, leaving Chrissy to lock up the car. Jared nestled into his neck and went back to sleep. John loved the sensation of the trusting boy. The sleeping Jared was a far cry from the scared boy picked up a short time ago. This boy was creeping into his heart right along with his mother. John knew that Chrissy wouldn't like that bit of information, in the least.

Chrissy was right behind him when he entered the kitchen. "Put him on the couch in the family room. I don't want him to sleep too long, or he won't sleep tonight."

She threw her purse and the keys on the table. She would have a firm talk with John. Not wanting him weaseling into her son's life. She didn't like it at all.

Chrissy set about preparing coffee. There was still an hour before she had to think about dinner. She realized she was hungry. They had missed lunch, walking the streets.

He knew as soon as he came into the kitchen that she was angry at him. Another confrontation was coming.

"John, you have to leave. You can't stay here, and that is final."

"Chrissy, I agree we can't stay here. We're going to my place but via Banff."

"Banff? What are you talking about?" Chrissy yelled.

"Keep your voice down. You'll wake Jared. He is upset enough as it is." He went over to the table and sat down, indicating with his hand that she should too. She stormed over, plopped down. She was ready to explode.

"Chrissy, before you fly off the handle, listen to me." John pleaded.

"Fly off the handle is mild compared to what I intend doing." Her stern look at him indicated a much more forceful action.

John reached for her hand. She pulled away from him as far as she could and still stay sitting. "Chrissy, listen to me. We need to leave here. Max Kelsey had to pull his men. There are another two murders, and Max needs them, unfortunately. Max thinks the murders are no connection to us in any way. It is just unfortunate it happened right now. I talked to him while I was in the house here. He says you won't get any more surveillance for a few days." She started to say something, but he continued. "They need you as a hostage for whatever they are planning. We can stay here, but it isn't wise."

"Banff? What has that to do with anything?"

"We need to make them think we have left town. Then we will double back and stay at my place. You are going by train, and I am going by car. You are getting off the stop before Banff. I will be there to pick you up. Kelsey said he would give me a man for protection until the train gets to that stop. Jared will be on the train with you. I don't like the idea of you traveling without me, but it is the only way I can think of to get you to my place, without their knowledge. Jared would love a train ride, wouldn't he? I will put you on that train early. Then

I will drive to where I will meet you."

"Promise me, Chrissy, you won't leave the train before the stop where I will be waiting. Your life and Jared's may depend on it. I very much doubt they will be on the train. They will just find out your destination, at least that is what I am hoping. We have to make this work, Chrissy."

"It is the only way I can think of to guard you for the next week without police protection." John stopped talking. He needed her to absorb it all. He got up to get the coffee. He also put some scones and jam on the table. He had seen them in the bread box when she made breakfast. He walked back to the cupboards for little plates and knives.

Chrissy was sitting there stunned. Banff, she couldn't go there. She had to stay here and make Jared feel secure again. Without John, she added in her mind.

John was still waiting. No comment had come from Chrissy. He buttered his scone and put jam on it before proceeding to eat and drink his coffee. She was taking longer to explode than he had expected. He just kept eating as though nothing untoward was happening.

Finally, she sputtered, "I just won't do it. You can't make me." Not the answer he was wanting or expecting. He patiently buttered another scone and plied it with jam, and took a bite. In her fury, she reached across, shoving the scone into his mouth.

John set down the now broken scone, licking off the jam. Then finished off with a napkin.

"Chrissy, you are acting childish."

Before he could finish, Chrissy said, "childish is that the way I'm acting? Well, let me tell you, your highhanded tactics aren't pleasing me either. Having landed a bomb on me, how can you sit there and eat?"

"I am hungry. We missed lunch, remember. I did not land a bomb on you. I just told you what was going to happen next."

"Next, Mr. Taylor, you are getting out of my house. That is what is happening."

John pushed his plate aside as it annoyed her.

"Chrissy, be realistic. I can't leave, especially now. I told you that you wouldn't have police protection. Chrissy, for some strange reason, they want you as a hostage. They will get you if you don't do as I say. They might even take Jared this time. They don't need him, so you know what that could mean." Chrissy's look of fear made him wish he could retract that statement. But she had to face the possibility.

"John, I hate you with a passion. How could you come into my life and turn it upside down? My life was good. Jared and I were getting along famously. Then you appeared. Now my life has been threatened ever since. I don't want to be part of it. I want my quiet life back."

"Chrissy, it was you that walked into this when you stopped at the Doherty house that day. I only tried to protect you."

"Yes, and you got me kidnapped not once but twice."

"No, Chrissy, only once maybe but not the second time. I told you not to go, but no, you won't listen, and you were caught all on your own."

"You won't admit that it was your fault the first time?"

"No, Chrissy, you came to the house all on your own. I didn't drag you there. I just tried to stop you from going in. You ran away and hit your head, not me."

"But you chased me. You know that if you hadn't chased me, I wouldn't have hit my head." She looked at him intently.

"We can talk in circles about the kidnapping, but it won't solve anything. I saved you both times, so give me some slack here."

"John, I can't have you around anymore. I'll go to my sister's. Jared and I will stay inside until the charity gala is over, I promise."

"Chrissy, that won't work. We talked about this before. It will only put your sister in danger too, and that means her baby also. Do you really want to do that? I don't think so." John continued.

"Chrissy, you have to do this my way. There is no other way. I need to protect you, but it has to be away from here. We want them to think you have gone away. Then I'll take you to my place where you will be safe. Please, Chrissy, think about it." John just had to convince her. She seemed to be the key to this whole mess.

She got up from the chair without touching her coffee. She stormed out of the room, anger in her body language.

His shoulders sagged as soon as she left, giving in to the pain pounding in his head. He leaned his head in his hands.

She finally came back. She stood in the doorway watching him, seeing the effects of the pain on his body. They shot him because of her. Why was she mistreating him? She was a complacent person and very caring of others.

He must have sensed her standing there because he looked up at her releasing his head and straightening up. "Chrissy, did you decide?"

She continued to the sink for water. Turning on the tap, she let it run to get it cold, as she reached for a glass to fill and some pills. She returned to the table. "John, take these pills. The doctor gave them to me for my head when they checked me at the hospital."

John took the pills and water from Chrissy, accepting them gratefully. Anything to stop the pounding. He lifted his eyes to her face. "Thanks, I needed that. But I need your cooperation more. Chrissy, please cooperate? This is the only way. Do you want Jared involved next time?"

"All right, John. There will be rules. Rule one - no more kissing. I won't be a party to your kissing no matter what the reason. Rule two - I will be responsible for Jared. It would be best if you didn't get the boy used to you in his life. You will be leaving us as soon as this is over. Rule three - no more intimate talks or dinners. I want you out of my life immediately after that charity event is over. Rule number four - you are to take your things and spend the time in any other room that Jared and I aren't occupying. Do you think I can have some peace around here without you hammering at me all the time?" This last was to support rule four, he felt sure.

Chrissy stopped and waited.

John looked at her intently. Her rules were ridiculous if he was going to protect them. Except for the kissing, he could comply with that rule, but then again, he liked using that as a tool to get her to behave the way he wanted. He finally said.

"Rule one I can accept, but the rest are under question if I am going to protect you and Jared. I can't make this work if you hold me to the last three rules."

"Take it or leave it. Those are the conditions that I will agree to your being here or at your place."

"Then you will do the train and come to my place?"

"Yes, but the rules stand as is," she said firmly.

Chapter Fourteen

John gave in about the rules only to make a move to his place. It would be easier there because of all the rooms to separate them. He would be busy in his study a great deal of the time.

"Okay, Chrissy, it is a deal. We leave tomorrow." He walked over to the coffee pot and poured himself more coffee. He went back to the table and pulled his plate back in front of him.

Chrissy stood there with her mouth open, and then she said, "John, I need you to leave the kitchen. I'm here. Rule four, remember?"

"When I finish my coffee, I will leave the kitchen. If you want to enforce Rule four, you leave. I am finishing my coffee and scone." He took another bite, jam oozing out the side of his mouth. He had been a little too liberal with the topping. He calmly wiped his mouth.

She growled and stomped out of the kitchen. She had to separate from John to get control.

John leisurely finished his coffee before going to his room. Where he laid down on the bed, promptly going to sleep. Chrissy saw John go upstairs. She immediately went into the kitchen for her coffee and scone, which now infringed on her dinner. It was so late, but she had to eat something. Hunger was why she was partly so bitchy.

Chrissy started making dinner. She would make a casserole of pork chops, rice and mushroom soup with a green salad. The easy meal could be kept warm in the oven when John had his turn in the kitchen. She set the table while she was waiting for dinner to cook, her mind on their problem.

What if somebody whisked her away, before the train station, or forced her to stay on until Banff. It could go astray the way the second kidnapping did. Chrissy decided she didn't like the idea of the train ride, which made another method necessary.

What if they went to the train, but they didn't get on? All they did was pretend to get on, then get off further down the train, and hide in the washrooms. They would leave empty cases on the train while their actual clothes would be in John's car. The train for Banff must be quite long. If they went into the back of the train and found a seat, wave to John through the window, and make a big production of it, he would leave. Chrissy would sit back for five minutes. Then head for the front of the train and descend just as it was ready to pull out. Then head for the nearest restrooms.

She reasoned that she would feel like a sitting duck if she stayed on that train. She knew John wouldn't go for this, but she just wouldn't tell him. She would hide for quite a while, reading to Jared in the restroom. Then take a taxi to John's house. John would show up eventually when she didn't get off the train. She would have to obtain a key from him ahead of time. An easy plan if she used her fourth rule.

Dinner ready, she called for Jared. Jared automatically went upstairs and woke up John.

"No. Jared, I will eat later. You go have your dinner first." John hated that Rule two more than four.

Jared was persistent. "Mommy expects me to come when called, so she will be mad if you don't show up right away."

John didn't think he should be the one to explain to Jared, so they headed for the bathroom to wash their hands. John kept making his big hands bump into Jared's while sharing his soap at the same time. Jared's smile was so huge, and his eyes were shining. The giggles he emitted warmed John's heart. Rule two had to go, even though he understood how easy it was to form a close relationship.

Chrissy's voice echoed up the stairs. "Jared, your hands are clean enough. Quit fooling around and come for dinner." Chrissy could hear giggles but not John, so she didn't realize his involvement. She went back into the kitchen to serve out Jared's and her meal.

Jared finally appeared, his face and hands washed, and his hair brushed. So, Chrissy was not surprised when John appeared right behind him.

Jared quickly sat down. "Mommy, where is John's dinner?" John's innocent look drove Chrissy crazy.

"John is eating later. Too many scones to enjoy dinner right now. You can watch TV, John, if you like." Chrissy said meaningfully.

"It is alright. I think I will enjoy dinner now."

"John, you can't possibly enjoy dinner after all those scones. You can eat later. The casserole is in the oven keeping warm." Chrissy was gritting her teeth as she talked because John was making no effort to leave.

Jared chimed in. "John, sit down beside me. You will like this dinner. It is one of my favorites." John sat down with a silly grin on his face, which he was casting in Chrissy's direction. She was ready to strangle him. For her to leave would mean leaving Jared with John breaking Rule two and four, so she strolled to the oven and prepared a plate for John. Chrissy had to explain this to Jared in private, but how?

* * *

The next day they prepared to leave. John had snuck out clothes for Chrissy and Jared during the night under cover of darkness. So, they wouldn't have to carry heavy suitcases tomorrow. When they came out, they were both carrying empty cases. John hastily took them as though they were full, putting them in the trunk.

He bought the tickets at the train station, and everything was preceding to plan, or so he thought. Chrissy had not told John what she intended to do. Jared and Chrissy entered the train after John ruffled Jared's hair and told him to look after his mother.

Chrissy stuck out her hand before John could kiss her. She just knew that was his intention. She wasn't letting that happen again. He gave her a mischievous laugh as he squeezed her hand and said goodbye.

They sat at a window on his side of the train so they could wave. John walked away before the train pulled out. Chrissy and Jared sat back out of sight for a few minutes as though settled in for the train ride.

Chrissy nudged Jared to ease up out of the seat but leave the suitcases as though they were coming back. They moved from car to car at a reasonable pace trying not to draw attention to themselves. She heard 'the all aboard' when she figured she was at the front of the train. At the next door, they got off the train. They walked towards the engine and the end of the platform. They ducked behind some people as the train moved out of the station.

She was scared Jared would refuse to be ushered around by her without explanation, but he didn't. He just held on to her hand. She applied pressure periodically on his in the hope of keeping him quiet. However, Jared was not letting go. Where she went, he was going too.

She slipped into the lady's restroom as soon as they came alongside. It was a smaller one than the washroom nearer the entrance. Chrissy was much happier with a smaller lavatory. Then they weren't likely to get as much traffic.

They went into a cubicle. Chrissy whispered into Jared's ear that they had to be quiet for a while. She held him in her arms and kissed his cheek as a reward for his silence. She leaned against the wall and closed her eyes.

John would be furious when she didn't get off the train at the stop before Banff. He would probably think she was part of another kidnapping. She should have told him her plan, but she had kept it to herself. She knew he would disagree. She felt she would be a sitting duck on the train. Why she felt like this, she didn't know.

Chrissy did manage to get a spare key off John last night when they argued about sticking to the four rules. He had given her the extra key pacifying her. But she would never need it because he would always be with her.

Jared tightened his arms around her neck. Opening her eyes, she looked at her watch. She was surprised to see that fifteen minutes had gone by since they had left the train. She flushed the toilet, opened the door. She made a production of washing their hands in case someone entered, but no one did.

She put Jared on the counter by the sink. She leaned on the wall while she read Jared a story. She explained that they had to stay there a while longer. He accepted that since she was reading one of his favorites. He loved making the noises of each animal mentioned in the book, after which he would giggle. Chrissy was starting to relax, hearing Jared's chuckle. They were infectious and got her laughing too.

"Jared, when we leave here, we are going to walk along like we have all the time in the world. We can talk, but you mustn't say anything that will draw attention to us, agreed?"

"Yes, Mommy, are we playing a game? Why did John go away and leave us? He said he was going to meet us somewhere else. But we never stayed on the train." Chrissy knew she had to say something.

"Jared, Mommy gets sick if she travels a long distance on trains. So, we are going to John's place instead, okay?" She hadn't lied. She felt sick as soon as she got on the train, knowing that she intended to change John's strategy. She just hoped he wouldn't be too upset with her.

"I want to go to John's place rather than a train ride." Jared smiled up at her.

"Okay. Jared, we need to get a taxi." Taking Jared's hand and opening the door, looking down at him rather than around, like she had nothing to fear. She looked at the window display in one of the little concessions spread out around the train station. Then she glanced at her watch nonchalantly, forty-five minutes had gone by since the train had pulled out.

"Jared, let's find a taxi and go see Grandma. She will be wondering when we will get there?" She winked at Jared. All Jared said was, "okay."

When they got into the taxi, she told the driver 'just drive' as she had to dig out the address from the bottom of her purse.

"What direction? I, at least, need to know that." He put his car into gear, heading down the road in front of the station.

"West." searching in her bag. "Oh darn, I can't find the piece of paper, but it's okay. I think I know the directions. She named a street not too far from Selma and Dave's and settled back for the ride. Jared piped up as he recognized the area. "Are we going to Auntie Selma's?"

"Oh, dear." She appeared to be looking around anxiously. "I've given you the wrong address. This is my sister's address. I meant to give you my mother's address." She gave the taxi driver John's address.

She just hoped she had enough money for the fare. She hadn't thought about that when she had planned this false trail to John's.

A block from his place, she mentioned, "it is to be a surprise. If she sees the taxi, my mother will know." Chrissy managed the fare except for the tip, but the driver said. "It is okay. I am bound to pick up a good tipper in this area on my way back downtown."

She took Jared's hand and walked along as though out for a stroll. When they got to John's street, there didn't appear to be any suspicious cars, so Chrissy approached the house, inserting the key in the lock and opening the door. She eased inside, closing and locking it.

John stepped out into the hall.

"I knew you wouldn't follow my orders." Chrissy was so shocked at seeing John. Her heart almost stopped. When she recovered enough to breathe again, she inquired. "How did you know?"

"Well, for one thing, you were a little too insistent about having the key—the second thing, why did you insist on empty suitcases. Chrissy, you saved me a long trip. Thank you."

"You aren't mad?"

"No, Chrissy, actually, your plan was better than mine. If you got here, I knew you had been successful. I was getting worried when you took so long. I didn't know what your plan was, except that you intended to come here. The spare key was an obvious tip." John let Chrissy digest that.

He bent down and whispered to Jared. "Let's go into the back yard and see the goldfish in the pond."

"Goldfish!" Jared didn't whisper, he yelled. Before Chrissy could stop them, John headed towards the back of the house, ignoring Chrissy's. "Come back here, Jared."

She still hadn't explained to Jared. That he was supposed to stay with her and ignore John. Chrissy felt sure John knew she hadn't said anything to Jared and enjoyed himself to the hilt.

Her feet came unglued from the floor, following in the same direction, looking out the big window next to the French doors. John must've hoisted Jared to his shoulders as soon as he exited the house. They had cleared the terrace. Jared perched comfortably on John's shoulders.

John was pointing at trees that would be good for climbing. He eventually stopped at a large pond quite a way down the garden.

John eased Jared off his shoulders into his arms and dipped him upside down. Jared was giggling. John pretended to drop him into the pond head first. Jared trusted him so much and just laughed loudly. John put him down, and Jared fell to his knees exclaiming over the giant colorful goldfish. They were monstrous compared to the little ones he had seen in the pet shop at the mall.

John explained, "the goldfish in the mall are babies. When they are allowed to roam free in a pond, they grow into big fish." Jared was staring transfixed at the many fish swimming around.

John looked back at the house and saw Chrissy standing at the window. His heart lurched. *Why couldn't this be his family?* John knew he could quickly settle down to married life if they were. But in the next instant, he recognized that Chrissy didn't like him. She had made that abundantly clear by wanting them in separate rooms.

He gave a huge sigh. "Come on, sport, let's get you and your mother settled in your rooms. Then maybe you can come back to see the fish."

John was holding out his hand. Jared reached up and took it trustingly. The grin on Jared's face filled John's heart.

Chrissy watched Jared and John enter the house. She couldn't show her anger in front of Jared. She would have to go along with John until she told Jared about the rules. Why was she delaying?

She knew Jared enjoyed John's attention, so she was reluctant to spoil things when they first arrived. But at the same time, she feared that Jared would be heartbroken if John disappeared from his life. Besides, a boy of four wouldn't understand why he couldn't be near John in his own house. She was waging war with herself. The end result was Rule two and four were impossible conditions.

John could see Chrissy was upset, but he had no intention of complying with her rules. They were on his turf now. Protection meant knowing where she and Jared were at all times.

John kept up a running conversation with Jared, first about the goldfish. Then a little of the history of the house and his family. Jared was a bright boy. He asked lots of questions. The conversation went from there to Jared asking personal questions about his time with the police force. John kept the conversation to exciting aspects of what police work involved.

He would look at Chrissy every so often to see if her demeanor was improving or not. She seemed to be coming to terms with everything. Her face seemed to lose the annoyance. He was hoping she would realize Rules two and four were not realistic for a four-year-old to understand.

Chrissy had switched her thinking to Joel when John was talking about his experience with the police. Joel must be trying to reach her without success. She would have to phone him and let him know where they were. She would call him as soon as they finished lunch.

She had been surprised that John's kitchen had been supplied with so much food when he never seemed to be home. He must have asked his housekeeper to stock it. Chrissy was able to whip up an excellent nutritious meal that Jared enjoyed. Thank goodness he wasn't a picky eater like some children.

Chrissy's eyes swung to Jared. John's ramblings kept his attention. Jared was beginning to relax when Chrissy wasn't in sight, which was not the case right after the second kidnapping. He would get a panicky look if he couldn't see her and would be clingy. Now she could leave the room, and he never appeared behind her like a little shadow. John had done that for him.

Their lives turned entirely upside down since Chrissy had first stopped at Mrs. Doherty's house. She had built a good life for Jared and herself. Now, she knew she couldn't go back to that life they once had. Jared was enjoying John in his life. Chrissy had to admit it was kind of nice letting someone else do the thinking for a change.

No! Chrissy, you change that way of thinking immediately. She must have said the 'no' out loud because John and Jared both sat staring at her.

Finally, John asked, "no, what?"

"Just no. Can't someone say no without having a reason?" Chrissy knew it was a dumb answer. But she wasn't about to tell John what she was thinking. She glared at John then looked down at her plate, concentrating on getting the last morsel on her fork.

John asked, "Jared, would you like ice cream for dessert? Maybe you could come with me to the freezer and pick out what kind you would like."

Jared leaped off his chair with the prospect of choices of ice cream. John sat, watching Chrissy. *Would she continue pushing her rules, or was the argument going on inside her, winding its way in his favor?*

Chrissy's face was expressionless after that last glare.

John got up, leading Jared into the pantry, where the big freezer sat. Opening the lid and propping it, he lifted Jared to see the colorful ice cream packages while listing all the flavors. Gretchen had outdone herself, stocking the pantry with supplies with enough food to withstand a siege. Gretchen must know boys better than him because he didn't recognize half the flavors displayed in the freezer. The cartons sat side by side in the removable sliding basket.

Jared picked a concoction showing a picture of nuts and chocolate syrup running through a vanilla ice cream called Bear Tracks.

John tipped Jared over so his hands could reach the ice cream of his choice. Jared clutched it in his hands and arms so that he wouldn't drop his prize, all the while making sounds like the container was freezing. After closing the freezer, John followed Jared's skipping feet to the cupboard where the dishes resided. Jared standing on tiptoes pushed the ice cream container onto the counter. Patiently, he waited until John served it.

"Jared, I don't know how much you can eat, so stop me when you think your dish is full enough." Jared was hopping from foot to foot in excitement. John started filling the dish. When it reached the point that John thought was enough, he paused.

Jared's eyes were on the spoon, waiting for it to be refilled. So, John complied with two more scoops. Jared said, "enough." Putting his hands up to receive the dish heaped with ice cream. He carefully carried it to the table.

John put some ice cream in two more bowls and followed Jared. Chrissy had been watching them. "Jared, your eyes are bigger than your stomach." Jared had put the bowl on the table, placing his hand on his tummy. "No, Mommy, my stomach is bigger," Jared said in all innocence, not understanding his mother's comment.

Jared leaped onto his chair and dug in. The ice cream disappeared while John and Chrissy watched with amusement. When Jared had finished, John asked him if he wanted more.

Before Jared could answer, "not on your life, he has already had more than enough."

John laughed, and Jared giggled. Chrissy couldn't help but join in the laughter. John's heart jolted. There was that feeling of family again.

"The last one to take the dishes off the table washes the dishes. The table has to be empty before you can stop." John got up as he was saying this and started grabbing dishes. Jared joined in quickly, so Chrissy joined in along with them. They were all laughing when John ended up the last one.

Chrissy was waving the way toward the sink and handing him an apron that must've belonged to Gretchen. John made a big production of putting on the apron to the accompaniment of Jared's giggles. John gave Chrissy a loving look and winked at her. She smiled back before she realized she was responding to his jesting. But her heart felt lighter than it had for a while.

Jared wanted to see the fish, so he dragged his mother along. He tried to introduce her to the goldfish in the pond. John watched them through the window. They made such a peaceful picture. Life could be so different if these two would stick around.

It was then that he saw movement in some shrubs off to Chrissy's left. John was out the door at a fast run. "Chrissy, Jared, come here quickly." John was yelling as he tore down the path towards them. He had removed his knife from the case attached to the belt at his back.

Chrissy saw the man as he leaped forward towards them. She grabbed Jared's hand and started pulling him back towards John. The man was closer than John. He grabbed Chrissy, yanking her off her feet with such force that she dropped Jared's hand. The man was backing away with the now kicking and screaming Chrissy.

Jared was screaming for his mother. Jared started running after them. Chrissy changed tactics when she saw Jared coming with them and started yelling for Jared to go back to John. As soon as she stopped kicking and wiggling, her captor was making better time, escaping.

John had whipped Jared up into his arms, making it difficult for him to use the knife. "Jared, go to the fish pond while I get your mommy back. You are to stay there until we return. Promise?" He pushed Jared towards the pond but didn't take the time to see if he was obeying. He had to stop the mugger from spiriting Chrissy away. Why didn't he carry a gun?

Chrissy had started kicking out again now that Jared was out of the way. The thug was big and very muscular, so she wasn't having much success breaking his hold.

John was making better speed now and was coming into range. Because she was wriggling around, he was afraid he would hit her if he threw the knife.

John changed direction, taking a shortcut to the street, where it was less hilly. The ground was steeper where the mugger was climbing, and with Chrissy's added weight would slow him down.

John hoped to get in front of the mugger near his car. Maybe then he would get a chance to get a clear path to the assailant.

Chapter Fifteen

John cleared the shrubs and hit the pavement at a run. He could see the car. The driver was vacating the auto as John appeared in front of him. He tackled the man, pushing the guy off balance against the side of the vehicle.

John swung his arm, aiming the knife for his side, but the ruffian saw the dagger coming and tried to deflect it with his arm. The knife connected with the man as John's momentum slanted the blade, leaving a sizeable cut. The man doubled over in pain.

John turned towards his property, looking through the shrubs at Chrissy's assailant. She was struggling weakly in his tight hold. John ran towards them.

The shock registered on the assailant's face when he saw John coming. He stumbled over a rock, and Chrissy spun from his grasp. He tried to save himself from tumbling. John got what he needed for a clean target. He let go of the knife, traveling as straight as an arrow into the man's chest. The man continued falling forward to hit the ground, driving the blade deeper. His screams of pain pierced the air. Lots of blood flowed onto the area.

John heard the sound of squealing tires as the other man escaped. He sprang towards Chrissy that had landed half on the pavement. John could still hear the auto's screeching tires as it fishtailed down the street.

Chrissy seemed to be unconscious or winded. He didn't know which. He fell to his knees beside her, pulling her into his arms.

"Chrissy, are you okay?"

She opened her eyes, gasping for air. John was relieved.

"You're safe. I have you," John's eyes remained on Chrissy's face watching her recover her breath. His heart was still pumping from the run and the fear that they might have been successful in grabbing her.

John gave up on his control and kissed Chrissy. The kiss of relief progressed into a deeper kiss. She responded now that she was breathing normally. He broke the kiss when he heard noises from the wounded assailant. He sat Chrissy up, then headed over to the groaning man. John managed to roll him over, releasing the pressure on the blade protruding from his chest. Blood soaked his body and ran from his mouth.

John lifted him off the ground. "Who are you working for? Why do you want this woman?" The man collapsed in John's grasp as his breath wheezed out of his body in death. He would not be giving any messages of clarification. John placed him back down on the ground, then pulled him amongst the shrubs off the street until he contacted the police.

Racing back to Chrissy, he held out his hands to help her up. She seemed recovered enough to make an effort to rise. Holding her against him, they preceded towards the garden and Jared.

When Jared saw them, he sprang from his crouched position of crying. He came running, released from the turmoil of thinking he was alone, as his mother had gone again.

"Mommy! Mommy, you're here," running full tilt into his mother. It was lucky that John was still holding her, as the force of Jared's body flew against her. Jared's forceful body would have knocked her over. Her arms encircled him. They leaned into John's body together. She felt safe for the first time since the muscleman had put in an appearance, some minutes ago. Why did they want her so badly?

Her tears flowed as shock set in. Jared joined her with his tears, letting his fears flow over him. John lifted Jared and drew Chrissy against him. His crooning words of being safe calmed them. Their crying petered out. His prime concern Chrissy and Jared. The police call delayed. The body by the roadside wasn't going anyplace.

John got Chrissy settled with a hot cup of tea and Jared with hot chocolate. Jared was in his mother's lap. She was helping him drink in between her sips of tea. John stood, watching them from the doorway. She looked smaller and very vulnerable.

He left to go into the study to call Max Kelsey and was put through right away.

"Max, Chrissy was almost kidnapped again. Two men, I think from Delvietti, but I'm not positive. One got away with a knife wound in his left arm. The other man took a knife in the chest, which probably wouldn't have been fatal except that he fell forward when he tripped, forcing the blade deeper. He is now a corpse."

"Where are you?"

"I am at home. I thought we had fooled them by putting Chrissy and Jared on a train to Banff. But she didn't arrive there because she got off again. Delvietti must have put two and two together and showed up here."

"Chrissy and Jared were in the back acreage looking at the goldfish in the pond when they snatched her. I managed to get Jared away from them. Then I took a shortcut to the street where I injured the second assailant near the car. Then Chrissy and the other man arrived on the street. The shock of seeing me, he tripped. Chrissy broke free, and the guy fell on my knife. You've already heard the rest."

"Stay put. We'll be right over."

"I won't be going anywhere. I have to look after Chrissy and Jared. They are quite shaken." John headed back to the kitchen.

Chrissy and Jared were crying again. Guilt set in. He had made the mistake of thinking that they were safe, having more time before anyone would show up here.

How could he have been so wrong in his estimation of the situation? Now, he would insist on around the clock police protection. Chrissy would have to stay inside until the night of the Charity Gala, which John had every intention of attending.

The aftermath of the frightening experience for her and Jared was telling on her. Normalcy had to return for Jared's sake. She had been so frightened when that thug grabbed her, but John had other plans for both of them, thankfully.

Just thinking of it again was causing her heart to pump faster.

Why do these men want her? What could she mean to them in their evil dealings? She didn't know any details that they could require.

She gave Jared a kiss and a big hug. Jared finally seemed to accept they were both safe because he wanted down. He ran to the door where John was standing watching them. "You didn't protect my mommy the way you were supposed to." He was hitting John. He could easily deflate Jared's punching, but he wanted Jared to get rid of his frustrations. "You were supposed to protect my mommy, and you didn't."

After he landed one more punch, Jared buried his face in John's side and started to cry. Kneeling, John pulled Jared into his chest. "I know, son. All I can say is I am truly sorry. I was wrong in believing that they wouldn't appear so fast. My thoughts clouded by wanting you and your mother to enjoy my home. I was lax in my duty, but I promise it won't happen again. Do you forgive me?"

Jared stayed buried against John's chest, taking in his words and weighing them. He drew in a deep breath and eased away. John loosened his arms to let Jared move.

Sniffing, he said, "I guess so. You saved my mommy. I don't want any bad men touching her again."

"Neither do I, Jared. I will do my very best to see that it doesn't happen again, okay?"

"Okay." Jared hiccupped, which surprised him, giving a little giggle.

John smiled. "I will stick to your mom's side. So close, no one will get near her again, and that is a promise, Jared. Now, shall we see if mommy's okay?" Jared retained eye contact between them. Finally, the decision to believe was there. Jared pulled away and ran to his mother.

Chrissy hugged him. She was surprised to see her son attack John for not protecting her.

John was standing close now. "I am truly sorry, Chrissy. I didn't do my job properly. But I just didn't expect them so soon, I'm sorry." He kept moving his hands helplessly, wanting to touch her but knew that he didn't have the right.

The ringing phone sent John to answer, expecting it would be

Max, but it wasn't. It was Joel asking for Chrissy.

"How did you know she was here?" Surprise evident in his voice

"I happen to be at the station when Max Kelsey took your call. I asked him for your phone number. He gave it to me because I told him I was a friend of the family, Chrissy's family."

"Just a minute, I'll get her." He looked over at Chrissy. "It is Joel. Do you want to talk to him?"

"Yes, of course." She eased Jared away as she got up and went to the phone.

"Joel. Yes, I am okay."

"Did they hurt you at all?"

"No, Joel, I hit my head when I fell out of the assailant's arms, but I was mostly just winded."

"Where was your bodyguard? Why didn't he stop them?"

"John was in the house, but he was there right away and stopped them."

John stood listening. He should have fielded these questions before handing the phone to Chrissy.

"Jared's okay. He was just upset to see me carried away."

"It must've been frightening for him to see that," Joel exclaimed. If only he were with her, hugging her, to give her a feeling of security.

"Yes, it was. He was terrified. I had better go now."

After talking a bit, they said their goodbyes. Chrissy replaced the receiver.

The doorbell rang. John headed for the door. Max Kelsey was standing there waiting for an invite in. John attacked him instantly.

"What do you think you were doing, giving my phone number to anyone? Kindly check with me in the future before you are free with my number," jutting his jaw out.

"Hello to you too, John. I see you are in a foul mood. Maybe I should come back later except you were the one that called me." Max grinned. "Did someone phone that shouldn't have? Don't want or need competition, buddy?" Max's grin enlarged.

"Very funny," John said meekly. Max elbowed his way in as though he was doing a football play.

"Your defenses are down." Max grinned.

"Look, Uncle Sam, I could arrange to have you deported back to where you came from in the good old USA."

"Now, John, why are you in such an uproar or are your undies in a twist?"

"No, damn you. You better watch your mouth when you're talking to Chrissy. After all, it was your brilliant idea that got her nabbed the second time, remember."

"All right, John, simmer down and let's discuss things rationally."

"Max, I want around the clock police protection for Chrissy until the Charity Gala on the 16th. And no more pulling them off for any reason. This is the third time. I won't let it happen anymore. So, get the police out there patrolling the perimeter of my property." John's voice was almost a threat. Max, who had known him a long time, knew he was serious. John was better as a friend than as an enemy.

"Okay, John, you'll get your wish, and I'll get some answers. Can we go talk to Chrissy now?"

"I can tell you everything you need to know."

"John, I would prefer to see and talk to Chrissy. I want to see how she is. You can yeah or nay anything after I hear her version."

"Chrissy, Max is here. He would like to ask you some questions. Jared, would you like to go watch TV as we will be busy talking." Holding out his hand, Jared latched on. Jared scowled at Max.

"Don't upset my mommy," Jared left the room. John quickly put on the TV and settled Jared into a cartoon that would keep him amused for a while. He wanted to get back to the kitchen and the questioning.

Chrissy must've been describing how things had gone in sequence because as he arrived, he heard her say. "When we came over the hill, my assailant was surprised to see John in front of him. He could see that John had injured the other attacker trying to get into the car to make his escape. His arm appeared to be bleeding badly. John was brandishing a knife that unnerved the ruffian carrying me after seeing his partner injured and fleeing the scene. He tripped, loosening his grip. I flung myself away from him and sailed out of his reach, falling heavily on the ground. John must have thrown the knife. I didn't see that. I had the breath knocked out of me. When I recovered, my attacker was face down. There was blood coming out from under him.

While John held me . . ."

Chrissy looked at John then continued. "We heard the attacker moving. John quickly got up and went over to lift him, but the knife appeared deeply embedded in his chest. I guess from falling on it. Blood was coming out of his mouth. John picked him up, but he seemed to cave in, releasing his breath. He collapsed in John's arms as though he was dead." Chrissy's voice ended almost in a whisper. A shudder racked her body at the memory.

"Thank you, Chrissy. May I call you Chrissy? I feel we have been through enough to be on first-name terms." Chrissy mumbled, "yes."

"John, come in." Max acted as if he had just noticed him. However, he had been aware of John behind him as soon as he had arrived there. "John, would you like to give your side of the story? Chrissy has explained her side."

John related the details almost word for word. He revealed taking a separate route to grapple with the mugger on the road. Giving the fact that he hadn't meant to injure him so severely, but the movement of the guy's arm caused the knife's descent to rip his arm open." John paused, looking at Chrissy, hoping she didn't think he was some kind of a monster.

"I heard them coming over the hill. The injured driver was trying to get into the car. Ignoring him, I watched instead for an opportunity to stop the other guy who was holding Chrissy. The attacker seemed so surprised to see me. He observed his buddy's exit into the car, arm all bloodied as he crested the hill. He tripped, losing his balance, and loosened his grip on Chrissy. She threw her body sideways, which seemed to add to his downward momentum falling on my knife, and the bruiser of a guy knocked me sideways. He continued to fall to the ground driving the knife deeper into himself."

"I ran to Chrissy. I was concerned for her because she seemed to be unconscious. I thought she had injured her head enough to knock herself out. When I reached her, I realized she was not breathing properly and must have had the breath knocked out of her because she started gasping for air. I helped her into a sitting position." Glancing at Chrissy, then continued.

"Then I heard the assailant moving. I got up to see if he was alive enough to talk. But when I picked him up, he wasn't able to speak. He just collapsed in my arms. I put him in the shrubbery off the roadside because I knew it would be a while before you got here. I had already moved him by picking him up, so I wanted him out of view from the street."

"Yes, we found him before I came in."

John was eyeing Max, wondering how he was taking their stories. Max was reviewing them in his mind. He thought it odd both Chrissy and John paused, looking at the other at the mention of her recovery from being knocked breathless. There was something unsaid, perhaps the way John had held her.

The other point of difference was that Chrissy had said John must've thrown the knife because there was blood under the face-down body. John's story was the assailant fell on the blade. "Chrissy, you said you thought John must have thrown the knife. Why?"

"Because John was lower down than us, down the hill, when I had thrown myself away from the man. However, hearing John's story, it is possible as my assaulter did stagger forward. That was how I was able to throw myself clear. My movements must have thrown him off balance more, causing him to fall forward on to John's knife."

Max looked from John to Chrissy, but neither had a reason to lie. John was usually honest. In fact, too honest if he recollected. So, he would take John's story if the coroner confirmed entry of the knife could be due to falling or stumbling down the hill.

"Now, we still have the problem of why they want you so badly? They keep trying to kidnap you, Chrissy. John, do you have any theories?"

"No, it has me buffaloed. But I do know the answer is at the Charity Gala. I intend to be there to find out. I have our invitations already."

"I will have to get an invite too. You can be sure of that." Max admonished. "This has gone too far, making us look like fools because we can't get an inkling of what this is all about. I have certainly tried. I am sure you have too, John."

A knock on the door, John went to answer it. He greeted the officer standing there.

"Yes."

"Will you let Inspector Kelsey know that the coroner is here to view the body."

"We will both be there as soon as I inform him." John closed the door.

But Max was right there behind him. "I heard. I recognize the knock."

They got to the road where the body resided on the-roadside, almost in the same spot, it initially fell. The knife was still protruding obscenely from his chest.

The coroner was on his knees, bent over the body, getting a closer look. He looked up as their feet came into his peripheral vision.

"Hi, Kelsey."

"Hi Douglas, what do you think happened here?"

Douglas looked at John. "Your knife, I presume. Nice, where did you pick that up?"

Kelsey introduced John. "John, this is Douglas. This is John Taylor."

"We've met. Let's say I picked it up in my travels." John had taken the knife off an unsavory character that had tried to use it on him. He had resented it so much that he had kept the knife. Besides, he liked the way it handled. It was a slim knife with a gleaming thin blade. The handle embellished with symbols of ancient sorcery probably came from the orient.

"What's your take on the situation?" Max inquired.

"The projection of the knife went in as though the person was in a downward fall, which made the knife go deeper. It was when the knife went deeper that the damage was most harmful. The assailant died from the piercing of the artery and bled to death. Was that his story?"

"Just about," Kelsey replied.

"Can I have my knife back?" John inquired. He didn't want to admit he felt naked without it. "It has sentimental value for me." John finished.

Both Douglas and Max looked at John skeptically. But John didn't enlarge any more on the subject.

"We have to take it in, but after we finish with it, you can claim it at the precinct. I very much doubt there will be a trial at anyone's request."

The three talked for a while longer. The body was lifted into the ambulance for transfer downtown. The three men parted with Kelsey saying, "John, I will have a police car here for 24/7. I will be in touch if we need any more information. Otherwise, see you at the gala. Oh, yes, we will see that the area is left clean." Looking at the blood clotted into the earth and sidewalk. Too nice a neighborhood for these kinds of events." Max looked around admiringly. He knew John's story and how he happened to be living in this posh neighborhood.

"Thanks, I would appreciate that. I try to keep a low profile around here. I always feel like an interloper. Perhaps that is why I avoided the place while my parents lived here.

"How are your folks?" Kelsey nodded in acceptance of John's reasoning about the neighborhood.

"Fine, the last time I heard from them. I think I am due for another letter any day now as my mother likes to keep in touch. I phone rather than write."

"Well, John, it looks like the gala will be our next meeting. Take care of Chrissy in the meantime," jabbing John's arm. "Man, that is hard work, isn't it?"

John grinned in response. "A tall order to have to sit around all day looking at a pretty lady."

"Yeah, you wish you were out on the beat again, no doubt. How long has it been? Four, five years since you drummed yourself out of the force?"

"Four coming up to five, I can't say I miss it a bit." John was happy to be away from the routine and that type of risk. John was glad to be his own boss. His career wasn't always steady, but he was busy enough. Danger wasn't usually a part of his job. So, carrying a gun wasn't necessary anymore. This particular case was unusual and unexpected.

Chapter Sixteen

John went back into the house to find Chrissy and Jared sitting watching TV. Chrissy's face had a trance look. John was sure her mind was on recent events rather than the TV cartoon. The way she was clutching Jared so tightly indicated that her mind was still in turmoil. He was surprised Jared wasn't complaining about her tight grip. She didn't even acknowledge John's presence. He wasn't sure if it was through choice or if she was too deep in thought.

It was time for some more phone calls, heading for the study. John called Mr. Delvietti. His call went through immediately when he mentioned Chrissy's name as his subject of interest.

"Well, Delvietti, you made a big mistake coming into my home territory. I protect what is mine. Final count one dead and one injured for you, and all mine are safe." He paused. There was no reply.

"This is a warning. You will desist from trying to kidnap Mrs. Lambert. The opportunity to snatch her will not happen as I will glue myself to her side. If any further attempts occur, there will be more deaths of your cohorts. I will deliver them personally to you, and a police escort for your arrest as a conspirator in this crime. Do I make myself clear?" John stopped talking. The threat made, he waited for a response.

"Mr. Taylor, do not make threats you cannot back up. There is no way you can get near me personally or otherwise. I resent your tone and message. Be careful. You are not invincible. Do I make myself clear?" The dial tone kicked in. John was left hanging.

He was satisfied with his call. He had never expected anything other than the threatening message in reply. But he knew the ground rules were set. That was his purpose for the call. The battle line was drawn.

His next call was to Joel.

"Joel, this is John. What shift are you on?"

"Days for the next two weeks. How is Chrissy?"

"Chrissy is fine."

"Where is she? I know she isn't at her place. I got the puppy for Jared."

"Chrissy and Jared are at my place. I needed her to be here so I could protect her 24 hours a day."

"What about the puppy?"

"You can bring it when you come over. I need you to stay in the house with them. I have a few errands to attend to. I can't take them along. Will you come?"

"Yes, of course. I want to see Chrissy and Jared. When and for how long?"

"Tomorrow night, and I will be out until the wee hours. But I will come home as soon as I can. I realize you will need to get some sleep before your day shift starts. Two officers are watching on the street, but I need someone inside with her. As you know, there was another failed attempt to kidnap Chrissy. So, someone must be with her at all times. Luckily, I stopped them from hurting her. One man is dead and the other one injured." John's voice was cold when he explained this.

"I was concerned when Max Kelsey told me about another kidnapping attempt on Chrissy. I am glad you were able to stop them." Joel was relieved it had failed.

"Yes, I am glad too."

"I am sorry to hear Chrissy is still in danger. I hoped that it was over for her sake. Why do you think they want her?" Joel's voice was puzzled.

"That is what I intend to find out, as soon as you get here to look after Chrissy, and bring your gun." Leaving the added message of 'shoot to kill' unsaid.

He continued on a lighter note. "Bringing the puppy will take some of the sting out of your being here for Chrissy's protection. Oh yeah, bring the rest of the puppy trappings. I will pay you for it. Is the puppy house trained?"

"Yes, it knows it has to go outside."

"Well, when you are outside, stay near the terrace so you can quickly get back inside. That won't make Jared happy, but there is no other choice right now. Keep as much as possible near the family room as that is on the house's protected side. The puppy can romp there more freely with Jared."

"I'll be there at about 7:30 after I pick up the puppy gear."

"Make it for dinner. I'll have things in place for a nice meal for you. That will give you more time for shopping." John gave him his address before hanging up.

The doorbell rang.

John was not expecting anyone, but it must be okay. Otherwise, the police at the curbside would have stopped them. He opened the door.

A police shield was exposed, announcing the plainclothes man. There stood the obnoxious Detective Delaney. Why would he be here?

"Yes, Detective?"

"Is Mrs. Lambert here?"

"Yes. What do you need her for?"

"I am still involved in tracking down information on the Frank Doherty murder. You, I believe, were there that day also. So, I will speak with you too. Can I come in?" Detective Delaney looked ready to give John a fight if he refused. He looked like he had his argument all ready.

"Yes, come in. Mrs. Lambert is here, but I will speak with you first." John took Delaney into the study at the back of the house.

They had no sooner entered the room when John got to the point. No invitation to sit down or anything. "I am not too happy about how you interrogated Mrs. Lambert. What in the world were you thinking? The officer with her told you she had just come from the hospital after a kidnapping. Your highhanded attitude set Mrs. Lambert's progress of recovery back considerably. I think you need a lesson in diplomacy." John's appearance was as threatening as his voice. "Now say what you are here to say. Then you are out of here for good. Do I make myself clear?"

Detective Delaney was not about to back down. The homicide was his investigation, and he was the one asking the questions here. "Mr. Taylor, what were you doing at Frank Doherty's place that day of the stabbing?"

"I was following someone for a client of mine. The subject entered the house I followed. I did see the body at that time. My subject must have gone through the house quickly and out the back door, so I followed. After climbing over several fences, I lost him. When I went back towards the house, I spotted Mrs. Lambert approaching, so I stopped her. She ran, and I followed. Mrs. Lambert fell hit her head and was knocked out. While I was leaning over her, someone hit me from behind. When I regained consciousness, Mrs. Lambert and I were tied together. I am sure you have learned all those details from her."

"I understand you were a Calgary cop at one time and are now a P I. Do you think that gives you the right to conduct my investigation?" Delaney's manner was quite arrogant.

"No, but I know you aren't supposed to browbeat innocent women who are in a precarious state."

"When you were at the Doherty house, why didn't you report the murder?"

"Well, frankly, I was kinda busy. After all, I wasn't there for the victim but for a job and the subject that was fleeing. Then I tried to intercept Mrs. Lambert. I fully intended to call the police when my subject got away."

"Your subject, who was he?"

"That is private information relevant to my client only."

"I think not," Delaney said huffily. "Who is your client?"

"Max Kelsey. Inspector Max Kelsey, to you."

Delaney had tangled with Kelsey a few times, so he backed off on that one.

"That took the wind out of your sails, didn't it? I will say this much. I was so close behind my subject that he didn't have time to stab the victim before he took off through the back door."

Delaney had had enough of this guy's smart talk, so he asked to see Mrs. Lambert.

"I think not. You have asked questions of Mrs. Lambert before. So, her story won't be any different. I will verify, Mrs. Lambert did not enter the house," John said firmly. "Mrs. Lambert is my client now. I feel it is unnecessary for her to talk to you further. You have heard my views on the events. So, I think it is time for you to leave." John was heading for the door. Delaney was still rooted to the spot and made no effort to move.

"The questioning is not over until I say it is. When you were inside the house, what did you see?"

"As I was chasing my subject, I was looking for him. I did not take in much in the way of details other than to note a man on the floor with several knife wounds but no evidence of a knife." John indicated that the door was for leaving.

Delaney gave up and preceded John to the door by keeping a few paces ahead of him in the hopes of encountering Mrs. Lambert. He could hear a TV coming from the front of the house but not near enough to be viewed from the hallway. John picked up the pace to escort him to the door and off the premises.

"Goodbye, Delaney. Don't bother to call here again."

"Taylor, you'll be hearing from me if I deem it necessary." Nodding, he went out the door. He was not pleased with the interview. Especially when he hadn't been in control, this did not sit well with him at all. Shaking his head, he strode to his car.

Chrissy looked up as John entered the room. She had the reassurance that everything was okay with the admiring look he sent her way. Jared wanted something to eat.

The TV program was interrupted by a paid announcement by the Charity Gala, which drew their attention. Hammond appeared. He was featured shaking hands with several teenagers. His smile broadened when a young girl tripped and fell against him. John's mind queried this man's credibility. What was Chrissy's connection with Hammond? He had to find out. Why would they have this type of paid programming during a cartoon?

The cartoon returned, depicting a rabbit leaping over a fence and landing on a dog. The playful dog proceeded to shake the rabbit off. Jared's voice came over the sound wanting something to eat.

Chrissy's usual response to Jared's hunger was to provide him a meal. They hadn't discussed how things were to operate. Would John delegate stuff to her?

She noticed that John had no personal mark on her tour of the place except for the study. Chrissy was sure that was the only room he spent time in, other than the bedroom.

She liked the decor of the place. She wouldn't change much if it were hers. Except, maybe a few fascinating pieces she could picture here and there. A few personal items exhibited around would complete the décor.

She didn't realize she had been staring at John while having these thoughts. His look had changed, from admiring to enquiring.

What was she thinking about? Is she still thinking of her four ridiculous rules?

When I see her sitting in my home, it feels homey. Not just an empty house as he usually felt when in residence.

Jared's voice cut into their thoughts. "Mommy, why are you and John staring at each other? You aren't saying anything."

She broke eye contact with John. In an embarrassed voice, she said, "Jared, was I staring at John? I must've been daydreaming while looking in his direction."

"Jared, would you like something to eat? I will phone out for a meal. What will it be Chinese, Italian or Pizza?" John was covering the lapse in conversation with a distraction.

"Pizza! Pizza!" Jared's face became animated, knowing that he had a choice.

"One giant pizza coming up. Maybe your mom could help me with the toppings. I'll order pizza for the guys out in the squad car too." He strode out of the room, saying over his shoulder. "Coming, Chrissy?"

Having no recourse, she got up to follow him. She was almost to the kitchen when he said, "your friend, Delaney, was here to see you. But I ran interference for you and answered his questions. I didn't think you wanted to see him again."

Chrissy breathed a sigh of relief. "Thank you, John. That man has the mannerisms of a bull."

"Yes, he does have an abrupt manner, which I don't like either. But I hear from Max that he does have a good record in solving homicides." John passed the kitchen and headed for the study. She broke out in a grin. Bingo John was going into the study to phone, his comfort zone. She brought up the rear with a lighter step. She knew that she was dead on with John and his mansion.

He was relaxed behind his desk when she entered. A pen in his hand poised to write down the toppings for the pizza. She noted the scratchpad had the pizza's logo and phone number. He must eat a lot of pizza or Italian pasta.

"Jared likes most toppings except olives and peppers."

"Is he big on meat?"

"Yes, he can eat the meat lovers' one but no anchovies."

"Good, I like the meaty ones. I was going to get it half and half, but now that I know Jared will enjoy meat, we'll just order that. Drinks?"

"Milk for Jared. I'll just have mineral water."

"You and I are having wine. I have a nice vintage I have been saving for such an occasion as this. It is a Beaujolais." He picked up the phone to order the pizza.

Chrissy wandered around the study. His mark was definitely here, with a well-used chair and lamp near the fireplace. There were several books on the table nearby.

The fireplace laid for use. She pictured the fire blazing, the wood crackling, and flashes of sparks. John with his feet on the huge hassock, reading in his chair. Chrissy was fingering the books. Mostly detective stories with a copy of Tennyson's poems handy, surprising her.

Finishing his call, he was watching her. "Tennyson was my mother's favorite. She gave it to me the day that they left for Europe. I do pick it up now and then. It brings them into the room with me."

Chrissy was touched by what he was saying. He was admitting he was lonely and missing his parents.

There goes his loner image. "What no comment?"

"No, I miss my parents too. They never saw Jared, and that makes me sad. Jared would have loved them." She had a melancholy expression on her face.

Chrissy thought she should get back to Jared. She felt vulnerable right now, and she was feeling too close to this man in his personal domain. John had saved her life twice. He had just helped her evade the despicable Detective Delaney. It was time to enforce her special rules upon herself rather than John.

Chrissy's expression became stern.

"Chrissy, is something wrong?"

"No, nothing is wrong. I had better get back to Jared. I don't like to leave him alone."

John held out his hand. "Let's go see what he is getting up to?" Chrissy stared at his hand.

"Chrissy, what are you thinking?" His hand still held out towards her.

She dropped her thoughts instinctively, reaching out and placed her hand gingerly in his. Then looked up at him with a soft look

John wrapped his fingers around her small hand, liking the feel of her hand in his. His eyes flew to her, capturing her soft look.

"Chrissy, Jared's waiting." John knew they were on dangerous ground, and he had to save them. They had to be in each other's company for a while yet. Was she acting this way because he saved her? Her defenses must be down.

"Yes, Jared is waiting." Chrissy started moving with John towards the door, their hands melded together. Their hands snapped apart as Jared's voice entered the area.

"Mommy, is the pizza coming?"

"Yes." Chrissy's eyes moved quickly from John to Jared guiltily. "Yes, Jared, the pizza is the meaty one."

"Oh boy, I love meaty pizzas. They are so tasty." Jared started leaping up and down.

"Yes, champ, I do too." John automatically catching Jared in mid bound and raised him above his head. He held him there while Jared giggled and giggled.

"Let's go get the plates for our feast." Plunking Jared on his shoulders, he headed down the hall to the kitchen.

"Duck your head." Jared scrunched down as the kitchen door came into their sight. John leaned forward, almost making Jared appear to be standing on his head. The two were laughing gleefully. Chrissy stood, watching, and listening to their spontaneous laughter, and chuckled too.

She felt their relationship had gone from duty to much more. Was it her being grateful for her recovery from her latest attacker? But there had been no one since Todd. Having a man in her life was a new experience, as it was for Jared. They were to be closely linked together until this is over.

Jared was not one for being backward for his age. He loved to ask questions.

"John, why are bad men after mommy?"

"Jared, I wish I knew. It really has me disturbed, not knowing. But I promise you. They won't get her no matter how they try. Whenever we are outside for any reason, I want you to keep your eyes peeled for anyone who seems to take an interest in your mom and let me know instantly. Can you do that?"

"Yes, I don't want them to get her either. John, will they ever stop so that we can go home?"

"Jared, I just don't know, but I'm working on it. I don't want them to have her either. Besides, don't you like being here in my home?" giving Jared a fake punch in the shoulder.

"Yes, but I would like it better if we can go outside and play, and I do miss my friends at Playschool," Jared added his big blue eyes, looking up at John.

"Yeah, friends are good to have, aren't they? I miss my friends too. But I do like being here with you and your mom. How about we go to the park tomorrow? We will take the police guard along for protection."

"Will we be all right?" Jared's eyes brightened.

"Of course, it should be fun."

"I still won't see my friends."

"I am your friend, Jared."

"Yes, but you are my new friend, and I miss my old friends."

"Soon, it will be over. I promise then you will be with your friends again. Now, let's get these plates and napkins back to your mom before she comes looking for us." John had the bottle of wine tucked in his hand and the napkins in the other. Jared was carrying the plates carefully. His feet were shuffling along so he could firmly control the dishes.

John could proudly introduce this boy as his own. He had never really thought about being a father. He was pleased about his home now that Chrissy and Jared were here to share it with him. John knew if they stayed here permanently, he could make this a real home. And not feel like he was just a guest, as he did now.

His eyes went instantly to Chrissy. She was sitting on the couch with her eyes turned towards a little patio outside the French doors. Maybe she wanted to be out there to enjoy the late afternoon sun. It was small compared to the enormous terrace off the family room and study. John wondered what she was thinking about. Whatever it was, she hadn't noticed that he and Jared had returned.

Some birds were flitting back and forth in the trees near the patio, chirping at each other like they were playing tag. The sky was clear, and the sun was starting to lower.

Chrissy was unaware of this activity. Her mind had drifted far away, wondering when her life would return to normal. Would she have any clients left, or would she have to start over? Selma and Dave must be worried about me. I must call them. Why didn't I enforce my four rules once I got here? Was it because of the latest kidnapping attempt, or was it because John helped Jared over his fears? It was so good to hear Jared laugh. She had been afraid that this afternoon would have turned him into a frightened boy again or make him resent the staying inside.

John was standing nearby, opening the bottle of wine. He was hesitant to disturb her.

Her eyes raised to John. His hands were twisting the wine opener, but his eyes seem to be devouring her. She felt self-conscious, dropping her eyes, color rose into her cheeks.

Chrissy finally became aware of Jared's twittering as he placed the plates on the low table with a napkin near each plate. He was talking about the pizza coming soon.

"Soon, Jared. The pizza will be here soon. Wonderful Jared, you are setting that so perfectly." Jared grinned at her then swung to John to see if he had been watching.

John must have suddenly been aware of Jared's eyes. Embarrassed, he dropped his eyes to the wine bottle, saying. "I'll have to go back and get the glasses."

Jared sped out of the room, yelling. "I'll get them."

The doorbell pealed, getting John's attention.

Chapter Seventeen

John walked to the door expecting the pizza, but instead, it was Joel.

"Joel, what are you doing here? I thought you were coming tomorrow night."

"I am, but I just had to see Chrissy for myself and give her these flowers. It seems so long since I have seen her." He stood there with a dozen pink roses in his hand. He was still in uniform, so he must have picked up flowers on the way from the station.

"Is it the pizza?" Jared asked as he arrived behind John. The glasses suspended in his tight grasp. "Hi, Joel, have you come to have pizza with us?"

"Hi, Jared. No, I just came to see your mom for a minute to give her these flowers." Joel was looking expectantly for an invite.

John finally spoke. "Yes, sure, come on in. Chrissy's in the parlor off the living room." Joel was bringing Chrissy flowers. That meant their relationship was more like a courtship. Why wasn't he happy about that? Joel was a nice guy.

Jared was talking a blue streak, telling him about the bad men after his mother. Joel was following him, listening intently, and adding a few comments.

The doorbell pealed again. This time it had to be the pizza. John was pulling money out of his pocket while opening the door. The box was huge, like a whopper size. He had said their largest pizza. The young man was smiling as he spoke the amount of the bill. John handed over some money, which included a healthy tip. The young man leaped off the veranda with glee.

As there was only one box and a paper bag, he assumed the patrol car officers were enjoying their pizza. Looking out, he saw them wave, acknowledging their bonus dinner.

John entered the parlor. Joel was standing with Chrissy, not touching, but very close, linked by the flowers. They were talking adamantly, and Jared was looking from one to the other as they spoke.

"Joel, you will stay for pizza? There is lots here. Will you serve, Chrissy, while I get Joel a plate and a glass?"

Joel dropped his hand and turned. "I guess I could stay," smiling at Chrissy.

"Yeah, this is a big pizza." Jared chimed in gleefully.

Chrissy held out the roses. "John, will you put these in a vase with water for me while you are in the kitchen?"

"Yes." John came over and took the flowers, while Chrissy took the pizza and the paper bag containing Jared's milk.

John left the room, staring down at the delicate pink roses. He placed the flowers on the counter. Where would Gretchen put a flower vase? He found one finally in the cupboard over the fridge. He arranged the roses. Grabbing a plate and a wine glass, he headed back to the parlor.

They were standing near the window, silhouetted by the sun. Joel was holding her hands while she was eagerly talking to him. He was hanging onto Chrissy's every word.

John said brightly. "Joel, here is your plate. Chrissy, I thought you would be serving the pizza?"

Jared leaped up. "I'd like some. Mommy and Joel are too busy talking." John sat down, setting the extra plate and wine glass across from him, serving Jared his food and milk. He then poured the wine. John served out three liberal pizza pieces.

"Hey, don't you two want pizza?" Chrissy kept talking, but her feet were moving very slowly towards the direction of John's voice, but her eyes were still on Joel.

"Are you enjoying yours, Jared?" questioned John.

"Yeah, John, it is good. It has double cheese, the way I like it."

Jared was taking another bite. A long string of cheese followed the pizza to his mouth. The string of cheese finally broke off, attaching itself to Jared's chin. He quickly cleaned it off with his other hand, eating the cheese looking guiltily at John. But thankfully, John was looking over at his mother and Joel.

As they came closer, he could hear that she had been telling Joel about the kidnapping. Joel was concerned and was asking questions. Chrissy answered in a whispery voice, glancing toward Jared to see if he was listening. Jared was too involved in the pizza's cheese strings.

They each took a plate from John and picked up wine. Then Chrissy directed Joel to a corner of the room where there were some seats and a coffee table.

John joined Jared in creating long cheese strings with his first piece, much to Jared's approval and enjoyment. His giggle heard around his mouthful.

* * *

The next day went without incident. John and Chrissy kept Jared amused, playing games, and Gretchen was doing the weekly cleaning. Periodically Chrissy would leave and speak to her. John wondered what they were talking about. But when Chrissy came back, she did not elaborate on what was said.

She had been asking if she could help Gretchen with some of the cleaning, while asking questions about John's parents and their life while they were in residence. Gretchen continued cleaning while she talked.

"Mr. and Mrs. Taylor were easy folks to work for. They had a busy lifestyle, with his real estate and her charity organizations. Two afternoons a week they would spend together in some activity or just sitting in the garden talking. They were very devoted to each other."

"When John stayed for a visit, they both rearranged their schedules to be with him. They eventually decided to move to England. John moved in, but he still seems to act as a visitor. To him, the house was still his parents."

Chrissy was not surprised at this last comment because she had already surmised that. She went back to John and Jared as she could see Gretchen wanted to do the vacuuming.

Later in the day, Gretchen was in the kitchen making dinner. John had told her that Joel would be a guest, so to make something special. Chrissy wandered in, asking, "Can I help you with the dinner?"

"Yes, if you'd like. You could peel some potatoes." Gretchen could see Chrissy wanted to talk some more. That always slowed her down, so she put Chrissy to work helping.

Chrissy was thankful to be doing something at last. Just sitting inactive was making her stir crazy. She had a busy life usually, trying to fit everything in during the day and evening while also allowing Jared a reasonable amount of her attention. Since she had arrived here, she had more or less sat around feeling useless. Besides, Gretchen was someone new to talk to. Gretchen knew that she was curious about the Taylors.

"Mr. Taylor was a generous man that was meticulous about his attire and his manner. He was a gentleman in every sense of the word. Mrs. Taylor was beautiful with a figure that models would envy. Her attire was stylish for a charity function or a casual day off with her husband."

"They were both tidy people, so it was never a problem getting my day's cleaning done. Mr. Taylor was always slipping me extra money for my children, saying, "take them out for a day of fun. But I always used the money to buy them some clothes. My family fun didn't require money. We spent a lot of time hiking in the woods and having picnics. My husband joined us when at home. He was a traveling salesman with quite an extensive district. I was happy that it ended when Mr. Taylor asked him to work for them."

Chrissy was enjoying her melodious voice, and the insight into John and his parents. She finally finished peeling the potatoes, rinsing them and putting them on the stove to cook. Gretchen had a roast in the oven that she had surrounded with carrots and whole small onions. Chrissy watched her make a parfait dessert.

"John is an easy person to work for too." Gretchen continued. "He would sit like you are and listen to me talk about my family. His parents probably made him mature before his time. I doubt they even realized what they had done. That is the trouble with only having one child and busy lives."

"John loved to hear about the frolicking and the arguments of my children, who were close in age. Now, they are older, but they still love that rivalry as three boys usually do. My sons are in high school. Now they compete on the playing field, not so much Danny, who is into computers. I think Danny's future will involve computers in some capacity." Gretchen looked to the doorway as John entered.

"What are you two talking about so intently?"

"I was just talking about the boys to Miss Chrissy here. She sits lapping it up as you used to John." Gretchen said with a big grin.

"I thought maybe Chrissy was quizzing you about my secrets. She has been in here for quite a while." His sparkling eyes softening his comment.

Chrissy gazed at him. She felt guilty and said, "why would I be interested in you? Gretchen has so many interesting stories about her sons." His expression changed. He felt disappointed at her words somehow, and Gretchen took pity on him. "Well, I have been spinning some yarns about your mama and poppa too."

"Mama and poppa? When has anyone ever address them like that? You know I only ever called them mother and father."

Gretchen chuckled. "Yes, you did, but they loved you a lot even if they made you an adult before your time."

"Now, Gretchen, no giving away secrets. I had better separate you two. Coming Chrissy?" John held out his hand with a wistful smile. Chrissy took his hand to be pulled from the chair.

"Jared is wondering why you were away for so long. Hadn't we better be getting back to him?"

They strolled towards the den. "Chrissy, I will be going out after dinner. Joel will be staying with you while I am gone."

"So, that is why Joel accepted my invitation so readily. You had previously arranged for him to be here. I wondered how he found out I was staying here. I should have known."

"Chrissy, I have to find out what is going on out there. I do not want to be caught unaware at the Charity Gala. I need to know what I'm up against. My concern for you and Jared is paramount." His expression showed his concern.

The ringing of the doorbell announced Joel's arrival with the new puppy.

Opening the door, Joel reached forward, giving John the dog carrier. Then left to get the puppy's necessities from the car. Chrissy had gone to get Jared.

Jared came running. "Puppy is here," jumping up and down.

"Yes, Jared." John lowered the cage to the floor to unlatch the door. Out sprang the sandy-colored puppy heading towards Jared, then jumping back, leaping to Chrissy, then frolicking around to John, greeting them all happily.

Jared finally cornered the squirming puppy in his arms. The puppy was excited and wiggling profusely, licking at Jared's face, his face full of happiness. Jared looked at Joel coming in the door. "Joel, you brought me a puppy."

"It was a lonely puppy that needed a companion and playmate. So, I instantly thought of you," jostling Jared's hair.

"I want to be the puppy's playmate. Can I keep him?" Jared's eyes zoomed first to John, to Chrissy, then Joel, all in his quest for yes.

"Yes, you can keep the puppy," Joel said chuckling. "But you have to promise that you will take care of it. Keep puppy with you at all times when you are not at Playschool."

"I promise, I do, I do. Oh, I love you, puppy!" Kissing the puppy between licks.

The three adults looked on with big grins. Their lives were changing with this bundle of wriggling, boisterous puppy.

Chrissy was thanking Joel and kissed him on the cheek. John thanked him too.

Joel bent over and picked up the puppy bed. "This was the most comfortable looking dog bed I could find. Not that I think it will get much use, knowing little boys want their puppy to sleep with them."

"Does puppy have a name?" Jared asked after another lick.

"Yes, the owner gave it the name Alfred, but I think you should name him Alfie. Although the puppy's papers read Alfred Alonso the III."

"Yes, yes, I'd like Alfie better than Alfred." Jared finally let go of the wriggling puppy. His arms were getting tired from trying to control the rambunctious dog. Alfie boisterously leaped to each of them then ran in circles.

Jared called. "Alfie, Alfie, come here." The puppy leaped towards him. "See, Mommy, he comes when I call him. He knows his name."

"Yes, I see." Chrissy was wondering what she had gotten herself into, letting Jared have such an energetic pup. John was pleased with Joel's choice. The dog would be medium-sized, not too big for Jared.

Joel and Chrissy stood close together, looking on with pleasure at the puppy's antics. They kept throwing smiles at each other. She was happy Joel was here. She could relax now. Joel was so easygoing and fun to talk to. She looked over at John, who was bent down, patting Alfie and talking to Jared.

John would be gone. I can be myself with Joel without feeling awkward.

The dinner went well. John liked Joel, and he kept up a running commentary with Joel's subjects that were eclectic and interesting.

When John served dessert with Jared's help, the conversation switched to amusing Jared. The two men gave antidotes from their childhood. Joel came from a family of four boys, so his stories of hilarity in-jokes played on each other had the dining room filled with booming laughter. John relaxed, enjoying the endless stories too.

Finally, John excused himself when Joel offered to help Jared settle the puppy for the night and offered to read a bedtimes story.

"Sorry to run out on the dishes, Chrissy. But I need to get downtown while the street people start their moves for the evening. The answers are out there somewhere. If only I can tap into the right person, I will have it made. Stick close to Joel, won't you?" John squeezed her hand. He then reached for his glass, picked it up, "Salute," finishing the wine in one swallow.

That was when Chrissy noticed John's attire was more casual than usual. The clothes to help him blend into the night, with the night prowlers who roamed the streets.

"John, be careful. I wish I knew what was going on too. But I am concerned about you. It was nice with the stories during dinner, not having that clouding my mind. You probably don't realize it. But it muddles the back of my mind constantly. These men are dangerous.

Your life isn't worth sacrificing if you can resolve this at the Gala."

"Chrissy, that is true, but if I find out something positive tonight, it will prepare me for what is coming down at the Gala. I will be careful. I have been doing this long enough to count my cards and leave when the cards fall against me. Lady luck is part of my armor against the odds."

John leaned into Chrissy. He brushed his lips to her lips so fast, removing them fleetingly. Her eyes widened. John left without another word.

She heard Jared's yell, "Mommy, are you coming to kiss me good night?"

She headed up the curved staircase, whispering, "John, be careful."

Chapter Eighteen

John was not making the contacts he wished to. The night was turning into a total loss. No nibbles, no bites, just rejection of his offers of money. Someone had to know something. He would have to get back soon so Joel could go home. He should have told him to bunk in one of the spare guest rooms. Chrissy could have seen that he was comfortable.

John was just pulling out his cell phone to call when a shadow entered his doorway space. He continued with the phone call but was evasive when he asked how things were going. Joel had agreed to stay, commenting that he was off the next day. Chrissy agreed to make him comfortable. John finished with a statement. "Not too comfortable. We don't need a permanent guest." Accentuating the idea with a chuckle.

Slipping the cell phone back into the case on his belt, he could hear the shadow breathing heavily off to his left. He got the whiff of alcohol. The breathing was male that he felt sure. He was playing a waiting game, wanting the shadow to make a move. John was bunching his muscles to strong-arm him if he had plans to frisk for his wallet.

The breathing changed, less ragged ready to speak. A voice said, "I hear the bucks are flowing for a river of information on the gala entertainment."

"Could be." John was still holding his stance.

"If you make the river flow, you might be able to catch the pot of gold at the bottom."

"Pot of gold that is a fairy tale." John wanted more before he shelled out anything.

"Oh, the pot of gold is real if you keep the flow from damming up."

"How much water are we talking about?"

The raspy voice said. "Two hundred gallons."

"Maybe half the water should do it." John still wasn't making any moves towards his wallet, not yet until he got some positive info.

Raspy said. "One hundred fifty gallons minimum."

John had a fifty in his left pocket, so he pulled it out. A little light glowed for an instant from a pencil flashlight. Fifty gallons isn't a trickle."

"The trickle will increase if water flows." John could play this game of water too.

"A gust of wind will roar blowing out the lights at eleven. The lights will appear when the prey is in place. The sacrificial lamb will be the bait of compliance. Except the sacrificial lamb is being elusive. The stalker is getting nervous and may have to retreat. Then blood will be spilled in his hurry."

"Cut the double talk. What lamb?"

"A pretty lady," Raspy said facetiously.

"Why that particular lady?"

"Because she has links with the prey."

"The beautiful lady I know has no links." John was trying to puzzle the connection between Chrissy and Alan Hammond.

"The link was made when the prey viewed her up close. That is when she became the sacrificial lamb for the prey."

"That was all a mistake. I know I was there with her."

"The stalker has heard otherwise. His informant is never wrong." Raspy muttered. "The trickle needs to increase."

John drew out another hundred from his left pocket, holding it out. The light flashed. A hand snatched it away.

"The lamb was viewed and accepted as dinner at a gala banquet."

"Do you mean he intends to get to know her at the gala?" John was amazed. She was unaware that she had that effect on men particularity, not Alan Hammond. Incredible, Chrissy was to be Dinner at the gala.

Now he understood the invitation from Hammond.

John felt Raspy pushing past him, fading into the night. Dumbfounded with the information that he had received,

John went looking for Max Kelsey.

How could Hammond even think of Chrissy as his? Chrissy was not a doll or bimbo. She was just Chrissy, pretty, kind, and friendly.

John was having trouble fitting Chrissy into this latest scenario. Mr. Hammond was harsh, conniving and a wheeler-dealer. Poor Chrissy was not going to be a meal for anyone, and definitely not a sacrificial lamb, not his Chrissy.

His foot went down more heavily on the gas pedal, finding Max Kelsey tonight was imperative. A couple of red lights cooled his fury. He was driving fast but not unrealistically.

He went to headquarters. The guy on duty said Max was home tucked in bed. It was a quiet night.

John knew Max's address. He knew full well Kelsey's quiet night was over. He intended to cause a stir with Max. Pulling up to Max's house, there was no sign of a light on downstairs. A faint light was showing upstairs, probably a night light. John parked and made for the door. Ringing the bell was useless because no one came. So, he started pounding on the door. Lights appeared in several windows. A harsh voice wanted to know who was there. The porch light flashed on, framing John in bright light.

"Open up, Kelsey," John yelled loudly.

The door was whipped open, and Kelsey stood there with a gun pointed to the floor. "Are you crazy, John?"

"No, just angry and worried."

"Come in. Don't you realize that some people like to sleep? Buddy, you are disturbing a beautiful dream. Just because you know my address doesn't mean you have to show up here, you know. I finally got a quiet night, and then you."

John pushed past Max.

"Well, I am not having a quiet night. So, why should you sleep when I'm not able to."

"Have you gone mad? Having to watch that lady is making you stir crazy. It was your idea, you know."

"Uncle Sam, I know why they want Chrissy so bad. Why they are trying to kidnap her."

"Why?"

"She is the sacrificial lamb in the game that Hammond and Delvietti are playing."

"What in the world are you talking about? Sacrificial lamb?"

"The Gala, Chrissy is to be the sacrificial lamb."

"You aren't making any sense. Come, I will make some coffee." Max headed towards the kitchen, snapping on the light. He moved to the counter where the coffee maker stood awaiting action. He put his gun on top of the fridge out of harm's way. John was watching Kelsey, trying to calm down his fear for Chrissy.

"I didn't know you wore pajamas to bed?"

"Well, you and I haven't been night buddies where sleep is concerned. Besides, it is a good thing I am, or I would have come to the door in the buff. You would have liked that, wouldn't you?"

John laughed halfheartedly. "Not really, you aren't my type."

"Quit the crap. What is this all about?" Max had set the coffee to perk. He walked to the table, sitting down, indicating the other chair with the movement of his head. "Talk, John, and it better be good. By the way, where is Chrissy? Who is minding the lamb?"

"Joel, a cop friend of Chrissy's, is watching out for her. I needed to get out on the street to get some answers. Boy, did I get a whopper of an answer? It seems that Delvietti intends to use Chrissy as a sacrificial lamb to get Hammond in line about something. I didn't find out 'the something' yet."

"But why, Chrissy? She doesn't know either of them."

"No, but when Chrissy was kidnapped the first time, she must've made an impression on Alan Hammond because the word is that he wants her for dinner."

"Dinner? Why are you talking like this? Are you on drugs or something?"

"Hammond has decided that Chrissy is either going to be Mrs. or Mistress to him in the very near future. Delvietti knows this and wants to make use of it by using her against him in some deal. Delvietti isn't happy about Alan's compliance or the elusive sacrificial lamb."

"This is too farfetched. Chrissy isn't the type to get mixed up with their kind. John, think about it."

"Yeah, I have thought about it. I know Chrissy isn't the type. But for some reason, that hasn't stopped Hammond from expressing his desire for her. Her name, apparently, is being bandied about by his enemies. Hence the attempted kidnappings of Chrissy. She is too sweet for either of them." John's heart sunk every time he thought about her being with Alan Hammond in any capacity.

Max was staring at John, trying to fathom this absurd idea. The coffee stopped perking. Max got up to get two coffees, his mind whirling around in thought. As he walked back to the table with two steaming cups of coffee, he looked intently at John. There was more to this, or why was John so upset?

John accepted the mug from Kelsey.

Kelsey looked at John inquiringly. "John, are you sure about this?"

"Well, I just paid a hundred and fifty for the information. This info is what Raspy came out with."

"Raspy? Who is Raspy?"

"Raspy was a shadow in the doorway that dropped the news. I never made him. I was too shocked by his news to notice him when he slithered away."

"You're slipping, John. You used to be more careful than that. Is there something about Chrissy you want to tell me?"

"No, other than she is too sweet to be involved in any of this. She is a lamb compared to the two low-lives." The shock was still chilling his insides.

"I thought you liked Alan Hammond."

"Yeah, the first time I met him, I did. He was quite the politician and played the part well. But being kidnapped sort of changed my attitude towards Hammond's political facade. Chrissy was appealing that night. She tore a strip off of Hammond, and her anger lit up her whole being. So much so that Hammond must have decided to renew their acquaintance.

"What do you propose I do, John? Especially at this time of night. Have you fallen for Chrissy too? She must be quite the lady." Max chuckled. John had never gone beyond a few dates with anyone. Even with the women he and Laura introduced to him.

"We have to protect her. They can't be allowed to use her."

"John, you are protecting her, and I have two perfectly good cops sitting outside your house 24 hours daily. What more do you want?"

"Can't you pull Delvietti in for questioning or something?" John was clutching at straws. "Raspy indicated the Gala was the location of the event. He said, a gust of wind will roar, blowing out the lights at eleven. The lights will appear when the prey is in place, meaning Alan Hammond. The sacrificial lamb will be the bait of compliance, meaning Chrissy. Except the sacrificial lamb bleating well is being elusive, meaning Chrissy was not cooperating with their efforts to kidnap her."

"Evidently, when Hammond kidnapped her, she captivated his interest. Apparently, Alan intends to seize Chrissy for himself at the Charity Gala. He sent me a personal invitation to be present. Somehow Delvietti found out that he wanted Chrissy. Delvietti will do whatever it takes to get Alan's cooperation, which means using Chrissy as the sacrificial lamb. I am worried that something will happen to her in the crossfire between the two."

"John, be realistic. There is nothing I can bring him in for that would provide you with answers. You were with the police for long enough to know that. Besides, you're the famed P I. How come you aren't doing your own investigation? Could it be that Chrissy is creeping into that stone you have for a heart?"

"You are funny, ha, ha. I am just worried about her, that is all. Chrissy is a nice lady and a mother of a cute little boy." John wasn't about to voice feelings for her to anyone.

"John, go home. Get Chrissy out of bed and have coffee with her if you can't sleep. I am going back to bed and sleep for the rest of the night. Now go home and protect Chrissy. Then you won't have her on your mind as a lamb because Delvietti won't get her."

John was sitting at the table, looking gloomy.

"John, go home. Get some sleep. The gala event is three days away. Are you still taking Chrissy?"

"Yes, if this is going to end, she needs to be there. So, you better have some of Calgary's Police Department's finest close at hand that night. You need to use some of your FBI techniques, Uncle Sam."

"John, the CPD will be there. You might not see them, but they will be there. Now, go home to your Chrissy."

John glowered at Max.

"She isn't, my Chrissy."

"Maybe not, but I bet you wish she was." Max started laughing. "Admit you have fallen, fallen big time. Oh, by the way, how good a friend is Joel to Chrissy? They have been alone together for a long time. Aren't you worried?" Max laughed heartedly.

John glared some more but didn't answer. It was time to go home. Joel was not a subject he wished to explore. Not right now anyway.

Max slapped him on the back as they headed to the door. He was anxious to get rid of John and back to bed.

Their goodbyes over, John was out of the door. Max was taking the stairs two at a time. "Sleep, heavenly sleep."

* * *

John made as little noise as possible when he arrived home. Heading for the kitchen, he wanted a stiff drink but settled for a beer. A sleepy Joel appeared. "Well, did you find out anything?"

"Oh, yes. Much more than I bargained for." John was looking at Joel, tipping his beer in Joel's direction, in question.

"No, not for me, thanks. What did you find out that has you in shock? You don't look too healthy around the gills. Was it that bad?"

"Oh, yes, that bad. Delvietti wants Chrissy for a sacrificial lamb, and Hammond wants Chrissy for Dinner."

"What in the world are you talking about?"

"Simple Hammond wants Chrissy as the next Mrs. and Delvietti wants to use Chrissy against Hammond, to make him comply with something he wants or something he needs to happen."

"Chrissy? That is utter nonsense. She won't have anything to do with Hammond."

"We know that, but evidently, Mr. Smooth Politician doesn't think that way. Hammond thinks Chrissy is perfect for the role, and he intends to let her know this at the Gala."

"What are we going to do to stop this insanity?" Joel was getting as worked up as John

Uttering the words had John fuming again. "I am going to keep her out of both their clutches."

"What about the Gala? Are you still taking Chrissy?"

"Yes, I think she needs to be there."

"For what reason? You are putting her in direct danger." The horror was in Joel's voice.

"Max Kelsey and some of CPD's finest will be nearby."

"How do you know that?"

"I just came from Kelsey's place."

"What did he think about Chrissy and these two low-lives?"

"He wasn't impressed with the ingrates and their intentions. He found it hard to believe at first. But he knew I wasn't kidding."

"You're right; anyone can see that this has amazed you," exclaimed Joel.

"Yeah, mind-boggling, isn't it? She is too good for the likes of them. I am going to . . . Chrissy, I didn't know you were up?" John had spotted her in the doorway and ended his comments quickly. He didn't know how much she had heard.

"Mind-boggling? Too good for who?" Chrissy eased in to stand beside Joel.

John and Joel exchanged glances. John hadn't wanted her to know anything, and reading Joel's expression, he didn't either.

"Chrissy, couldn't you sleep? Do you want me to get you some warm milk? Is Jared sleeping okay?"

She wasn't about to be put off that easily. "Too good for who?" Her hands flew to her robe covered hips.

"Chrissy, do you know how cute you look in that silky pink robe with tousled hair and sleepy eyes?" John was trying to think quickly for a way to cover up the situation.

"Yes, Chrissy, you do look adorable." This from Joel.

"I am waiting. Too good for whom?" Chrissy punctuated the whom! John should have realized Chrissy's stance wasn't for effect but anger.

"Joel was asking about the Gala. He wants to attend with us."

John uttered quickly. "I was telling him it might be feasible, and then I started describing Mr. Smoothie Politician to him. He was saying that you were too good for Alan or me for that matter." John glared at Joel, defying him to speak otherwise.

Chrissy eased her stance.

"I don't think that about you, John, but I would about Mr. Hammond. I can't say I particularly liked him, even though his public image was a smooth manner. I hope he loses the election. I certainly won't vote for him." She was trying to puzzle out the irritation on both their faces. She felt sure she was being snowballed.

"What did you find out tonight, John? I am sure you have already shared it with Joel." Chrissy noticed the quick look between the two men. Bingo, something was going on.

"I didn't find out much. Just that whatever is going to happen will happen at the Gala. But we already surmised that it would be there." John didn't tell a lie, only a half-truth.

She stood glancing from one to the other. Their expressions looked too innocent now to be the whole truth. John's jutting jaw was firm, so she doubted she would get more out of either of them tonight. She showed her ire by storming out of the kitchen without so much as a goodnight.

Joel shrugged, and John sighed with relief. He whispered, "that was too close." John stood up. "Time to head for bed," giving Joel a meaningful look in case Chrissy was listening outside the door.

Joel wanted to say more to John but accepted his lead.

Chrissy knew something wasn't kosher about John's explanation. There was nothing she could say that would convince him to come clean. She had waited outside the door to hear more. Chrissy made a hasty retreat upstairs when John elected immediately to retire for the night.

She had ducked into Jared's room so that John would think she was checking on Jared. She stood listening intently because his room was close to the stairway. But the two men only exchanged goodnights after arranging the time for breakfast.

She waited, hoping John would go to his room before she left Jared's room. So, he wouldn't see that she was waiting around to hear the men talking. But she was caught red-handed when John came in for his nightly check on Jared. Chrissy blushed to the roots of her hair when he found her standing there just inside the door.

"Aah, Jared is okay. I just checked on him."

John observed the blush but did not acknowledge it, just said, "Jared sleeps soundly, doesn't he?" Going over to the bed and touching Jared's cheek gently in a caress.

Chrissy made a hasty retreat into her bedroom.

John had to figure a way to tell her about Hammond wanting her. He intended not to let that happen. She belonged to Joel.

There was whining from the corner of the room. John walked over. The cover was moving, lifting the blanket on the puppy's bed, two brown eyes greeted him.

"Had enough sleep, have you? Let's you and I go for a nightly stroll." John lifted the puppy to head down to the terrace and the shrubs nearby.

"Well, Alfie, do you like your new home and your new master? Pretty special, isn't he?" John put Alfie down. He headed for the hedge instantly. After Alfie stiffed a few times, he traipsed up onto the terrace, barely making each step. Then he came to John's feet with a little yip. John picked him up and retraced his steps to Jared's bedroom.

"You know that you and I are going to become good buddies, because we're both going to protect those two forever. But in the meantime, you will have to grow a little." The puppy settled into his neck and was going off to sleep. John put him back in his doggie bed and covered him. John went over to Jared. "I would like you as my son." He leaned over and kissed him on the cheek. Jared squirmed, then smiled. Then settled back into sleep.

John went to his room. When he passed Chrissy's room, his mind flipped to how to tell her about Hammond's intentions. He moved on silently to his bedroom.

Settling into sleep wasn't easy. His mind churned. He figured the direct approach was best. He just knew he had to let her know before the Charity Gala. He couldn't have her walking in there blindly, not knowing.

Chrissy was not going to take this too well. She had expressed how she felt about Hammond when she saw him campaigning on TV. She called him slimy and conniving. So, she wouldn't take kindly to his plan for her.

Hammond had a lot of nerve with his intent to approach her at the Gala?

John agreed with Chrissy. Alan was a slimeball.

Chrissy entered his room. She floated towards the bed in a gossamer gown of white. Her long wavy tresses of red flowing around her shoulders. She was smiling. There was a gleam in her sparkling eyes. John just lay there waiting, not saying anything. He wanted her to set the mood.

She lifted the sheet and climbed into bed. "I couldn't sleep until I knew what happened tonight." She was lying facing him. Her hand came up to caress his cheek.

John didn't move. He didn't want to make her aware that he slept in the buff.

"John, what were you and Joel talking about?" Her hand was caressing his face in detail. Her fingers were very light over his cheeks, his jaw, his chin, and lips. John tried not to tense.

"Joel and I were discussing the puppy."

"John, there was more. I heard Hammond and Delvietti." Her fingers were trailing down his neck to his chest, looping playfully in the curly mass there.

"Hammond? Delvietti? Why would we be talking about them?" John wanted to cover her hand and control its wandering, but he just laid there not moving.

Chrissy's fingers were meandering around his chest and over his shoulders.

"John, you are keeping something from me. I know it." Chrissy's fingers had gone to his waist. John wanted to stop her, but then he didn't. How far would she go for the information she sought?

"Chrissy, I would never hide anything from you." John's muscles were tensing. He didn't know how much more he could take without responding. If she kept on, she would find out just how well he could act in response.

She hadn't stopped caressing his waist. How far would she go to persuade him to talk? His naked torso was alive with feelings.

Chrissy's fingers were easing lower to his knotted muscles in his flat stomach. John knew he should stop her, but his arms and hands were ignoring his body's demands.

"John, you are a liar." Her fingers were creeping lower.

"Liar? Stop right now." John sat up, reaching for the light. When he looked back at Chrissy, he was staring at an empty bed. His brow covered in sweat.

"My god, it was only a dream." John didn't know whether to be happy or sad. He just knew it was time for a cold shower

Chapter Nineteen

In the morning, John couldn't meet Chrissy's eyes when he arrived in the kitchen. His dream too recent in his mind seeing her in that glossy sheer white nightgown that didn't hide her luscious curves. His muscles tightened, just thinking of her wandering fingers.

He felt something on his foot, looking down, it was Alfie. Saved by a puppy. Jared wouldn't be far behind. John reached down to lift the puppy as he said, "Good morning."

Joel's good morning drew his eyes guiltily to him. Joel sat at the breakfast table with a coffee. Jared was soon standing beside John, looking up at the pup.

Alfie was trying to wriggle free, so John released him. Jared went charging after him. Chrissy's voice following. "Jared, come back. Breakfast is ready. Alfie needs to be fed too."

John sauntered over to the counter for some coffee. With a steaming coffee, he slid into the seat opposite Joel.

"Alfie is quite the pup. I hope he is house trained, or Gretchen will have my head."

"I told you last night he was except for the odd dribble if he gets too excited. That is normal for most puppies." John knew his comment had been ridiculous, but he knew his guilt was even more ridiculous.

Joel was off duty today, so there wasn't any need for haste. He still wanted to approach John for more details. The truth was that he wished to be assigned to protecting Chrissy at the Gala. How was he going to work that he didn't know? But he knew John had an in with

Max Kelsey.

They managed to get through breakfast without any reference to last night. Jared kept trying to feed the puppy under the table. Each of the adults took turns correcting him on this practice.

Chrissy knew she had to pin one of them down as to what John had found out last night. Chrissy felt she would have better success with Joel. John could be so stubborn. She found this out on past occasions. *How do I get Joel alone?*

Joel intended sticking around until he found out more details from John. He had to get him to intercede with Kelsey to have him at the Gala. Joel needed to be there for Chrissy. *How could he get John alone?*

John wanted a more decisive plan for the Gala now that he knew something was going down that night. He wanted her to be safe at home. But he also knew that she was the key to everything. Her absence just meant she would be a pawn sometime in the future. *How could he avoid Chrissy? The answer, keep Joel and Chrissy together.*

After breakfast, John excused himself from the table, saying he would have to go out. "Joel, is it possible for you to stay with Chrissy and Jared?"

Joel smiled at Chrissy. "Of course, I'll stay. We can help Jared start the puppy training. Can't we, Chrissy?"

She smiled back, responding to Joel's pleasant smile. Such a kind, caring guy, so open and straightforward, not like John. "Yes, of course. Alfie needs some guidance starting now. Jared needs to learn the do's and don'ts of puppy care."

John, run away. It is easier to avoid my questions. Oh well, I will have Joel alone.

"John, are you going somewhere in particular? Maybe I should go with you," Chrissy asked John sweetly.

"No, that won't be necessary. Joel will be here, and the police are outside. You should be safe as long as you stay inside or on the back terrace, and only if you feel the need for fresh air." John's answer was as sweet as Chrissy's.

Joel was happy to spend the day with them. "Jared, let's get Alfie outside for a romp in the bushes." He came to his feet with Jared following in his footsteps.

"Come on, Alfie. Let's go outside," Jared called.

"Jared, do not go away from the terrace area and stay with Joel." John admonished as he gave Jared's hair a ruffle to take the sting out of his command. "Alfie must be trained to stay close too." Looking meaningfully at Joel, wanting his instructions obeyed to the letter. Then John exited the room in the direction of the stairway.

Joel, Jared, and Alfie headed out the door. Jared was giggling happily at the puppy's antics.

Chrissy put her elbows on the table and let her head fall into her upraised hands. Why wouldn't he tell her anything? Doesn't he realize I need to know? Why do men act in this macho way? I am strong enough to take anything as long as I am prepared. Darn you, John.

Chrissy sat there feeling dejected. She despaired at being a prisoner. She couldn't break out of here without probable consequences for Jared and herself. What happened to her life? My business is falling apart daily. Oh, to be Jared's age and accept things as they are. But I am not his age. I hate being held a prisoner.

"Chrissy, are you all right?" John had come back into the kitchen.

"Oh, yes, why would anything be wrong? I am under house arrest while my business is deteriorating daily. My life is not my own to govern. You won't tell me what I need to know. No, I am not fine. I am furious." She had gone from tragic to anger as her comments progressed. She lifted her head and glared furiously at John

"Chrissy, I know things are bothering you. The Gala is in two days, and that should end it."

"John, will it be over? Will the Gala give us all the answers? What guarantee are you willing to give me?" She was glaring at John, not willing to be appeased.

"I hope so. Of course, I would love to say it will be over, but we don't know. As to guarantees, I can't, but I wish I could." John was meeting her angry eyes with understanding.

"John, if the Gala doesn't answer the threat against my life. I intend to leave here and distance myself from you. Maybe it is my association with you that is keeping this going." Some of her anger was subsiding.

"Chrissy, you can't do that. I won't let you. It is you that is being kidnapped, not me. Please, Chrissy, be reasonable? We can only hope that the Gala will end it all." John was worried that she might leave without his knowledge. He felt that he was responsible, chasing her into this mess. Suppose she had rung the bell. Not getting an answer, then she would have just walked away and no kidnapping.

"Another thing, John. How can I go to the Gala? I have nothing to wear? I need to go shopping. This Charity Gala sounds posh."

"I don't think that is wise right now. My mother still has some formal gowns in a walk-in closet upstairs."

"But, John, they won't fit me. They will be out of date fashion-wise. They are probably the wrong color." Chrissy was actively throwing out complications to his suggestions. She wanted to leave here and go shopping.

John came around the table and reached for her hand gently, pulling her out of the chair. "Come on, and we will go and look at the dresses. I think they will fit. My mother is about your size. Maybe you can get Gretchen to help you alter them. She is coming in today to clean. While he was talking, he was guiding her to the stairs leading to the second floor.

"But, John, the styles will be outdated and too old for me. The color for sure. I can't wear your mother's dress." John continued pulling her along as she was talking. They had reached his mother's bedroom closet. John dropped her hand, opening the cupboard's sliding louvered doors, displaying dresses and suits arrayed on racks.

"My parents didn't take everything with them. I haven't had the heart to get rid of them. They're not dead, only living in England." His hands were skimming over the dresses, lifting them out to see them with a close eye. He slung a couple over his arm.

"Try these, Chrissy. I do believe they are your style. My mother probably never wore them. She had a fetish for evening wear, buying them in case. I know they didn't go out that often formally."

"I want you to try these on. I will leave until the viewing." John slipped out of the room, brooking no arguments.

Chrissy looked at the lovely gowns he had placed on the bed. They were gorgeous. The color would suit her perfectly. She knew there was no point in arguing. Slipping a dress over her head, it slithered down her body like silk. It was a gossamer dress in green chiffon. The shoulders were bare except for the straps that were so narrow they were almost nonexistent. The material was clinging at her waist and hips. It felt luxurious. She was observing herself in the vanity mirror when John's reflection joined hers.

"Lovely, I thought you would look good in that green with your red hair. Now try on the other one if you aren't sure about this one." John's reflection disappeared. She removed the dress. She hadn't wanted it to fit, but it graced her figure like it was made for her.

She picked up the other dress. It was a white dress comprising of lace and seed pearls. It to slithered down her curves like a glove. This one showed off her creamy bare shoulders. The dip in the front showed off her cleavage.

When John appeared instantly in behind her, Chrissy whipped around. "Have you been watching me undress and dress?"

"Not at all. I just figured you were the type that didn't take long to change." A tongue in cheek comment. "That looks lovely on you, like a princess. You will have to have a coiffeur come to style your hair." Lifting her tresses lightly with his finger letting them fall away from his hand. She usually had it in a ponytail or clipped back. "I think the green, don't you?" John's eyes were almost devouring her. "That is lovely, but the color doesn't show your hair off the way the green does. It turns your hair into flames."

She was watching his image in the mirror. His reflection was so close to her, and she felt a funny fluttering in her heart.

"Chrissy, do you agree?"

Her eyes drew back to the dress. She was a fairy princess, but she agreed with John the green dress did more for her hair, making it come alive.

"Yes, I think the green dress. This dress is beautiful, though."

"I like the illusion of strapless with those tiny straps on the green dress," John said, his grin wickedly making him look like a naughty boy. "I don't think there is much need for alterations. But you could get Gretchen's opinion on that."

John walked to the closet and pulled out a velvet green evening coat. "I think this will be the perfect completion to the outfit, don't you?" Whipping it around her shoulders. Chrissy's hair glowed as it fell over the velvet when John lifted her hair, letting it flow through his fingers. John liked their portrait in the mirror.

* * *

When Joel and Jared, along with Alfie, returned, talking and yipping together. John was waiting. "I have decided not to go out, so it is all right if you leave now, Joel. I will handle things from here." Joel was surprised. Flustered, he made his goodbyes to Jared and headed towards the door, hoping to see Chrissy before leaving. Chrissy was coming down the stairs.

"Joel, are you leaving? John, aren't you going out?" she was confused.

"John has changed his mind, so I don't need to stay any longer. Goodbye, Chrissy, I'll give you a call. Maybe we will go out sometime."

"Goodbye, Joel. Yes, I would like that." Her voice held her puzzlement at John's sudden change in plans.

John had made this decision while watching her in the mirror.

"Goodbye, John, see you around sometime." Joel left with John's words of goodbye.

John headed towards his study, hoping Chrissy would not follow. He felt sure that Jared and Alfie would keep her busy. John knew he was avoiding her because he still didn't have the solution as to how to tell her, knowing she might refuse to go to the Gala.

When it came time for lunch, he went into the kitchen at Jared's request. He picked up his sandwich plate and drink, saying, "I am expecting a call. I want to be in my study to take it." With that, he left the room, not waiting for a reply.

Chrissy's sound of amazement was faintly following him down the hall.

After lunch, in the afternoon, Chrissy and Jared played games and frolicked with the puppy. Finally, settling Jared with his usual cartoons, Chrissy went back to the kitchen to clean up. Taking some cookbooks down, she looked up recipes for dinner. Chrissy spent a quiet afternoon by herself as John had made it clear that he wasn't to be disturbed. She decided to ask Joel for dinner tomorrow but wouldn't admit it was to get back at John for his rejection.

* * *

The next day things hadn't changed. John was very chummy with Jared. But didn't encourage much in conversation with Chrissy. She tried once, but he cut her off with an excuse that Alfie needed to go out. He and Jared took off with Alfie bounding after them.

The day progressed with John continuing to be evasive. Chrissy was seething inside. She was trying to get up enough nerve to intrude into his study, where he kept disappearing. She could try Joel when he came for dinner tonight.

She needed something easy so she could spend more time with Joel. Would John come to dinner if Joel was here instead of hiding in the study like he had last night? I need to know the facts? How can I find out? I am the one that is involved. Yet I am clueless as to what is going on.

Her mind kept circling these thoughts. What if she refused to go to the Gala? Would John change his mind then and tell her what was going on? I want to go, especially now that I have such a pretty dress. But I am afraid of the unknown. Maybe I should stay home, but no then I would still not get any answers. I need my life back to recover my business. I can't even go home to pick up messages. Clients must be calling because I certainly haven't been able to ring them.

I need something to keep me busy. I am tired of circling to no avail, and it is giving me a headache. I wish I had brought my files with me. But John did not want me to contact anyone from here. So, whoever was looking for me couldn't find me. Well, they found me anyway. I might as well look for the phone numbers for my clients. I should phone and apologize for missing my appointments. I must try to recover my Interior Decorator business.

I will try to get Jared to have a nap so I can take care of this. She felt excited at the prospect of recovering her business and a future. This gave her an incentive to busy herself as it was almost lunchtime.

She aroused Jared to take Alfie out before lunch.

"Mommy, we have such a good time out there. You should come

with us."

Jared was excited at being let free from the house. Alfie, sensing Jared's excitement, barked and circled around him.

"Where is John? Is he still in his study?" Chrissy questioned.

"No, he is outside. He said he needed fresh air to think." Jared wished to share his fun with John.

"Stay on the terrace." She went back to get lunch.

Jared ran off with Alfie trailing, both bursting with energy. He tried a new game of playing hide and seek with the puppy. But Alfie found him every time. Then he heard his mother calling him for lunch. He ran eagerly to the kitchen.

John was sitting at the table, eating. Chrissy asked John what he thought might be expected of them? With the personal invite to the Gala Charity Event by Mr. Hammond. She hoped that John might say something that would give her a clue as to what was going on.

Jared sat across from John, asking him questions about training a dog. He went into great detail while they were eating. Thankful to put the Gala Event aside.

Jared's eyes kept closing. Romping around with Alfie had made him sleepy.

"Eat up, Jared, you're falling asleep. I think this afternoon, you should have a nap."

"Oh, Mommy, you know I don't like going to sleep in the afternoon. I'm not a baby anymore. I don't need a nap." Jared was trying to hold his eyes wide because he was sleepy.

Chrissy was looking at Jared and his wide-eyed expression and tried not to chuckle.

"Jared, I think you should listen to your mother. You don't have to sleep, just rest. You can take Alfie with you." John felt it was time that he spoke to Chrissy. He almost had the words ready in his mind.

Chrissy inquired, "Jared, are you finished? It's time for your rest. No, don't give your sandwich to Alfie. You shouldn't feed him at the table."

"But, Mommy, he likes me to do that."

"I know, but it is not good manners to feed the dog at the table. He has his own dishes in the corner. That is his eating area."

"Listen to your mother. She is trying to help you train Alfie. Do you want me to take you upstairs to get you settled for your rest?"

"Okay, you can put me to bed. C'mon, Alfie, we are going upstairs." Jared followed John and Alfie. John figured Jared would settle into a nap if Alfie were allowed to cuddle up with him. He thought that Alfie was due for a rest, so it wouldn't be long before they would both be asleep.

Chrissy tidied up the kitchen and took out the cookbooks, needing a recipe for a casserole dish for dinner. She hadn't mentioned to John yet that Joel was coming.

Her attempted talk with John, so far, had been disappointing. Now her strategy was to get Joel to talk.

John came back downstairs to speak to Chrissy. It was only fair that she knew what was going to happen., He was leery of how she would feel about Hammond's idea of a relationship. When the phone rang, he hurried to the study to take the call, reprieve with a sigh.

The call took longer than expected because he had to make several other calls as a result. He looked at his watch and wondered where the time had gone. The afternoon had almost faded away.

* * *

Jared was napping when the puppy gave him a whack. He giggled, pushing him away, but the puppy wasn't giving up waking his master. He wanted to play. Jared finally sprang awake when Alfie nipped at his ear. He let out a laughing yelp.

"I am awake. Do you need to go out?" Jared headed for the room with the French doors to the terrace, with Alfie trying to grab his feet.

Unlocking the door, Alfie ran through the open door. Bursting out onto the terrace, he raced in circles. Alfie was inviting Jared to join him. As Jared approached the puppy, Alfie being in a playful mood ran around Jared in circles. Jared made a grab for him. Then Alfie raced off the terrace heading down the path towards the goldfish pond. Jared hesitated. He was told never to go off the patio, but Alfie started yipping invitingly. Jared glanced at the house then ran after him.

"Come back, Alfie. Come back." But the puppy was really into the game as he frolicked towards the pond. Breathlessly, Jared caught up to him. Alfie was taunting the fish, leaping forward, then when the goldfish swam towards him, jumping back out of their reach. Jared came up behind him. "Got you." He grabbed for the puppy.

But Alfie wasn't about to be caught. His wiggling body was prancing away from Jared. It was like a game. Alfie would let Jared catch up to him, then leap out of his reach. A continued cat and mouse game to the dense stand of trees at the bottom of the garden.

Alfie disappeared into the trees. Jared once again hesitated. What should he do? John had never taken him this far. But he had to get Alfie back.

So, he ran into the woods hot on puppy's tail. Alfie was circling the trees in and out, leaping over little shrubs, hesitating invitingly until the laughing Jared caught up, only to turn and jump away. The frolicking stopped when the puppy let mother nature take over, squatting on the spot. Jared stood poised, ready to leap on him when he finished. But Alfie had other ideas. He was back into the game, hopping over shrubs and circling trees. Jared was laughing.

When the thought suddenly popped into his head, he didn't know where he was. The trees were surrounding him on all sides. They were huge, and there were no paths. He stopped his face showing his fear.

Alfie came over and licked his hand, sensing something was wrong. Jared patted the puppy, but his concern now was, where are we? How do I find the house? Mommy will be worried. John will be angry with me because he said not to leave the terrace.

He had to find his way home before his mommy knew he was gone. He walked back, but there were houses, not open gardens when he came out of the trees.

A more subdued Alfie was following him, sensing his fear. Turning, Jared walked the other way to get out of the trees. But again, no garden or fish pond. They were lost. Tears started to flow. Alfie made little noises like he felt Jared's fear. Jared bent down to hug the puppy, and tears began to flow. Slowly at first, then the sobbing was more intense. Alfie licked his face comforting him.

"Come, Alfie, we need to find mommy." Giving another sob, he stood up. The puppy started his circling antics, but Jared cried harder now, putting a stop to the puppy's frolicking. Alfie followed Jared as he went in a different direction.

Jared was getting tired. But he had to get back before mommy missed him. They walked and walked, coming out of the trees, still no fishpond.

Then his tiny mind went to his mother's disappearance. Would the bad man come to get him? He sank down in defeat. He wiped his eyes to clear them so that he could see. He now had no idea which way to go. Would the bad man come? No, he had to hide. He ran back into the woods. The shrubs were too small to protect them. What do I do now?

My mommy will cry if she can't find me anymore. Sob. The puppy gave out a yelp. He was running away from him but looking back at him to follow. Jared ran after Alfie only to find the puppy had no real direction because it plunked down, waiting.

Jared spied a larger shrub, which would give him some protection from the bad man. He crawled under with the puppy behind him. He curled up in a ball with the puppy in his arms, letting the tears flow.

Would the bad man hear him? He put his finger to his lips, saying "shh," to Alfie, making himself smaller.

Back at the house, Chrissy, unaware that Jared was missing, was making a snack. Jared would be awake soon. He was hungry after a nap. Climbing the stairs, she heard no sound from Jared's room. He must still be asleep. She entered the room.

No Jared. No puppy.

Chapter Twenty

Where could they be? Jared must've gone to the bathroom. Chrissy went back down into the kitchen, picking up the plate and glass and went over to the breakfast nook to place the snack. Jared will want to watch more cartoons, but she didn't want him spending all his time in front of the TV.

Now, where was Jared? He should be down by now. He is always hungry after his nap. She went to the washroom off the den, but no Jared. He must be in with John, walking on down the hall to the study.

"John, have you seen Jared? He is awake but not in the washroom. He always comes to the kitchen for a snack."

John quickly vacated the chair where he was reading. "Let me go upstairs. Maybe he went to the washroom upstairs instead." He headed for the stairs. As he passed the room with the French doors to the terrace, he glanced in, noticing the door was ajar. I'm positive I locked the door. He must have let Alfie out.

Chrissy, who was hot on his heels, bumped into John. She was starting to panic. "John, where is he? The puppy is missing too." Her head was moving around seeking.

John headed to the door. It was indeed, ajar. Looking out, expecting them to be on the terrace, but no Jared, no Alfie.

Now he was getting a sick feeling. Had someone been lurking about waiting for the opportunity to snatch Chrissy again? Jared and Alfie must've played right into their hands. However, he wouldn't express this thought to Chrissy. He didn't want her freaking out.

"Maybe they went to the goldfish pond, but I doubt they would. Jared knows not to go that far. Chrissy, why don't you wait here while I look around the house. I told him not to go off the terrace. But Alfie may have gone around the house."

"I can't just stand here. I want to look too." Chrissy was trying not to panic. Too late, her insides gave off a sick feeling as it contracted into fear and dread. "John, they are gone." Her voice screeched.

"Don't panic. We haven't looked around the house. Alfie must have left the terrace and ran around the side of the house. You stay here. I will look for them."

"But, John, we would hear them surely."

"Not necessarily. Wait here. I will make better time on my own." He leaped off the terrace, rounding the house. He could see no one. He continued around, but there was only Chrissy with a worried look and tears in her eyes when he arrived back at the patio.

"Maybe he went to see the goldfish."

"No, John, I told him not to go there without me, and you did too."

"Yes, Chrissy, but boys will be boys, and goldfish are an enticement. You know that." He wanted to reassure her, but he also wanted to race to the goldfish pond. If only they would be there. Not the other alternative. "Chrissy, promise me you will stay in the house and wait for me."

"But, John, I have to come with you." He didn't want Chrissy available for anyone else to find. So, he said, "you have to stay here in case Jared comes back. He will be upset if there is no one here."

He couldn't wait any longer. He took off quickly in the direction of the pond. He came to an abrupt halt as he neared the pond. No one was in sight. Where were they?

Apparently, Delvietti had ignored his warnings. No, he wouldn't think that way. He ran past the pond towards the trees. Puppies get very playful and love to run.

He plunged into the woods. As he rushed through the trees, trying not to make too much noise, to hear sounds from Jared or Alfie. Playful puppies usually barked.

He cleared the trees to the other side. No Jared, only houses, turning, he went to his left. But again, when he escaped the woods, no Jared. Changing direction, he called Jared's name, still no one. He got a sinking feeling Delvietti had Jared. Where would he take him?

How could he tell Chrissy what happened? He had failed them again. He felt heartsick. Why hadn't they heard Jared when he came downstairs? Alfie and Jared usually were quite noisy.

Just then, he heard a whimper, or so we thought. Was it wishful thinking? He stood listening. He waited, but no more sound. Where did he look now as he looked around? The trees in this direction were reasonably open.

Yes, there it is again. A definite whimper was coming from the shrub. He ran over, pushing aside the branches. "Jared, are you here?"

Alfie gave a yip at the sound of his voice, pulling the limbs aside further, seeing Jared and puppy curled up in a ball together. Jared was trembling.

"Jared, you frightened me. Why did you leave the terrace?" He lifted Jared with puppy locked in his arms, so John had quite an armful. He didn't care, so relieved Delvietti didn't have them.

"I am so glad you found us. We were lost. I was afraid the bad man would find me and steal us away. I told Alfie to 'shhh," his voice wavered. He wanted to hug John, but Alfie would fall.

"Jared, why are you out here?"

"Alfie needed to pee. Alfie kept running away from me when I tried to catch him. He wanted to play after his sleep. He just kept going and going and going. Then I was lost." Sobs racked his body. The puppy whimpered in sympathy.

"Your mother is frantic. Let's go back to her." Hugging the boy and dog tightly in gratitude that he had found them. His stomach still had that sick feeling, knowing how close they had come to losing them.

He walked speedily back to the terrace, passing the goldfish pond.

Jared commented, "puppy was teasing the goldfish, but he wouldn't let me catch him. He just kept running until he went into the woods. Then I was lost." The sobs came in earnest now. John set them down to free the puppy as it had started to struggle with Jared's crying. Then he picked up Jared, who locked his arms around John's neck, still crying profusely.

Hiccupping, he managed to murmur, "I walked out of the trees, but there were only houses. Where did the garden go?" crying again, Jared burrowed deeper into John's neck.

"Now, now, Jared, you are safe. You went the wrong way," patting his back soothingly. "We have to get back to your mother. She is upset at losing you."

John sped towards the house at a fast gait with puppy trailing his crying master.

As they came into view of the terrace, Chrissy yelled in relief. "You found them." She ran down the stairs towards them. The puppy was barking loudly, running to Chrissy. But she wanted Jared. When she reached them, Alfie was jumping up on her.

"You found them. Where were they? Come to mommy." Jared turned, reaching his arms out to her. Transferring into her arms, she hugged him tightly.

"Mommy, I was so scared. I was lost. Alfie wouldn't stop running. I tried to catch him. I did, Mommy. I was so frightened. I wasn't bad. Alfie wouldn't stop." He had his face in her neck, sobbing abundantly.

John had his arms around both of them. The adrenaline was still high. He quickly glanced around, but he couldn't see anyone observing them. But he was still concerned they might be there. "Let's get back to the house. I don't think we should be out here any longer. There may be someone else here."

As they cleared the door into the house, Chrissy's fear made her speak out.

"John, why didn't you hear them?" She scolded him angrily. "You are supposed to be protecting us, not off reading." She knew she was unfair as Jared had been sleeping. But her fear and panic had to be taken out on someone, and John was the only one here.

"Chrissy, I am sorry. I feel awful. But I honestly never heard them, or I would have stopped them. I must've dozed off. But even though I slept, I usually hear sounds. Alfie is frisky after sleeping, and Jared is usually laughing." He had failed them again.

Chrissy realized they both were to blame. She should have checked on Jared. But instead, her mind was wondering about making dinner or how she could get Joel alone to question him. Her guilt was an added weight.

Jared was still clinging to Chrissy. There was no way he was separating from her. She held onto him tightly, knowing how easily he could have disappeared into the clutches of Delvietti. The man that John and Max talked about. *Would he have insisted on her coming to him in trade for Jared?*

Feeling John's arms tighten around them both, made her look at him, seeing his regret plainly on his face. She relaxed in his arms, knowing that he wasn't the only one to blame.

The doorbell rang.

They didn't want to be separated, but someone had to respond to the summons. The doorbell was resounding again. John dropped his arms and headed for the door.

It was Joel.

He couldn't deal with this right now. "Joel, what are you doing here?"

"Chrissy invited me for dinner," giving John an odd look. Had she not said anything to John.

"Come in. I will get Chrissy." How would Chrissy act? Was she over her fright?

"Joel, you couldn't have picked a worse time to put in an appearance." He gave Joel's back an angry look as Joel passed him.

Joel must have felt the hostility as he turned to say, "is there something wrong, John? I get the feeling that you don't want me here. Is that right?"

"No. No, it isn't you, Joel. It is just we had a bad experience just before you arrived. I wasn't over it yet. Chrissy and Jared are in the kitchen. Jared is having a snack." He wasn't about to enlarge his previous comment, or Joel would reprimand him, which he would rightly deserve.

Chrissy was sitting close to Jared, watching him eat. Her heart was settling down at last, but she couldn't take her eyes off him.

She was surprised when John walked in with Joel.

"Joel, I forgot you were coming." *Now, why did I say that? You'll make him feel uncomfortable.* She added quickly. "Forgive me for that silly comment. Of course, I remembered honest."

Joel looked at her questioningly. Something was wrong as both John and Chrissy were acting strangely.

Jared piped up. "Hi, Joel, I was lost. Puppy and I were together, and John found us," he said in all innocence.

Chrissy looked at Jared in horror. Joel will wonder where she and John were while Jared got lost.

"Hi, Jared. How did you get lost?" A look of shock on his face, then his eyes swung from Chrissy to John.

"Alfie ran away from me. I couldn't catch him. He went after the goldfish, so I tried to catch him. But he ran into the woods, and I had to follow. Then I couldn't find my way home." Tears in his voice at the memory.

John and Chrissy both said at the same time. "Jared was napping." Then they both clammed up.

Jared ran over to John. "I didn't mean to go off the terrace. Alfie wanted to play."

John picked him up.

"Jared, it is all right. But I must say you frightened your mother and me. Please, don't ever do that again. If Alfie runs away, come and get me, and I will find the puppy, okay?"

Jared was nodding yes. Then he hugged John tightly. "I love you, John."

Joel remarked. "Apparently, this is not a good time to be here. Should I leave?"

Chrissy quickly rescued the situation. "Joel, I invited you for dinner, so please stay. Perhaps you can sit and talk to me while I cook dinner. Sorry, it is going to be a bit late. Jared's disappearance upset me. It is taking me a while to get my thoughts together. I was going to have a casserole made ahead of time, so we could sit and talk while it was in the oven." She gave him a beseeching smile for his understanding.

John mumbled, "Jared, do you want to come to the study with me? We can play snakes and ladders. You like that game." Giving Chrissy a look, but she was focusing on Joel for forgiveness.

The evening progressed with lots of interesting conversation, everyone trying to put the incident behind them.

Joel was happy he stayed, taking in John's stories with interest. Tales of funny and lighthearted incidents of his Private Investigator experience.

When it was time for Joel to leave, John debated whether to include himself seeing Joel to the door. But instead said. "Jared, bedtime. Say goodnight to Joel."

"Goodnight, Joel." Running to John, indicating that he wanted on his shoulders. Chrissy was still not happy with their budding relationship, but she smiled at Joel instead.

"I will see you to the door, Joel." Rising to follow Joel as he stood in the doorway watching Jared and John make their way down the hall. John was tipping this way and that to the accompaniment of giggles.

Realizing Chrissy's body was close behind him made him turn and give her a big smile. "Chrissy, will it be all right if I come again, I do so enjoy your family?" Chrissy glanced down the hall at John and Jared. *Yeah, we do act like a family. I will have to bring out the rules again.*

* * *

The much-awaited Gala night arrived. John arranged a hairstylist for the late afternoon for Chrissy's hair and makeup treatment. When the pampering was complete, Jared expressed. "Wow, Mommy, you are beautiful." John was in total agreement.

They were leaving early because John wanted to familiarize himself with the place thoroughly. Needing to meet Max to get the lay of the land before sitting down for dinner.

Chrissy did not have jewelry with her for an evening dress occasion. It didn't occur to her that it would be necessary.

John appeared behind her in the mirror with a box in his hand. "My dad bought these for my mother when he made an exorbitant commission on a complicated deal. Mother left them in a vault in the house. I phoned her for permission to make use of them tonight.

Opening the box, he lifted out the necklace of green emeralds encased in pearls. The jewels were not overly large but sizeable. The pearls were enhancing them to a green glow.

He laid them against her throat and slid the locking clasp into place. Then he delicately removed the emerald earrings, holding them against her ears. Chrissy was so entranced with the green radiance against her pale skin. She didn't respond by taking the earrings from him. So, John caressed her ear with his finger, feeling for the pierced hole for the earring. His fingers, feathering against her lobe, slipping the earrings through to fasten. John repeated it on her other ear.

Her eyes watched the minuscule movements of his hands. Then flew to his, only to see them dark and devouring.

She dropped her eyes to the full picture in the mirror. Was this the same couple that had argued angrily, nose to nose? She didn't think so. This couple was two entirely different people. The mirror image, casting an illusion of a loving couple who wanted and needed each other.

Chrissy closed her eyes. This cannot be. Then she opened them again. John had stepped back. The illusion was gone.

John was standing back, admiring her beauty. He broke the spell by saying. "It is time to leave."

She turned to pick up the evening bag that belonged to John's mother. Even the high heels were hers. Chrissy took in the full picture, gazing at herself in the mirror. The grandeur was there, but the person looking back at her wasn't the Chrissy she knew, but the image of someone else, perhaps John's mother.

John's voice called her, bringing her out of her reverie. Chrissy did something so unusual for her. She winked at the image in the mirror, and the image winked back. Chrissy knew then that all would be well.

As Chrissy floated down the stairs, John, Jared, and Gretchen were staring up at her. Three different expressions, John's admiring, Jared's in wonder, and Gretchen's in approval.

Jared breathed. "Mommy, you are a real angel."

"Yes, Jared, a real angel," John whispered huskily. He held her evening cape. He laid it tenderly around her shoulders, lifting her hair and letting it flow down her back. Most of her curls were on top of her head. John's fingers lingered.

Jared was jumping around in excitement, and the puppy was yipping in harmony. She bent down to place a kiss on Jared's forehead.

"Be good for Gretchen, and go to bed when she tells you."

"Mommy, angels do not tell boys what to do. They grant wishes."

"Well, this angel does because she left her magic wand upstairs," Chrissy said with a grin.

"Goodnight, Gretchen. I hope Jared's good for you."

"Miss Chrissy, you are beautiful. Don't worry, Jared's always a good boy." Gretchen gave a little laugh. "You look after Miss Chrissy, John, or you will get what for from me." She gave off another little laugh.

John gave Jared a high five and Gretchen a wink, whisking Chrissy out of the door. He wished he had a Mercedes, but his car would have to do.

* * *

He pulled up in front of the convention center that had been reserved for this Charity Gala event. He slipped out, going quickly around to help Chrissy. John looked very handsome in his tuxedo, Chrissy noted. She took his hand, letting him pull her to a standing position. The high heels gave her some height against John's tall frame.

John tossed the keys to the boy jockeying the cars around. Then he put out his arm for Chrissy to take wanting and needing her close until he found out who was coming tonight, and what was going to transpire.

He knew they were early but was surprised to see that Alan Hammond had not put in an appearance. The center was full of people milling about. He spotted Max and his wife, Laura, talking to Mayor Reardon and his wife, Diane. John led Chrissy over to join them, introducing Chrissy to everyone. The mayor's attention was drawn away to meet someone else, and his wife went with him.

John and Max were busy looking around. Laura asked Chrissy about the prospects of seeing some of her ideas on Interior Decorating. The men were exchanging hand signals and head movements, communicating with undercover cops in several areas. They were hoping the outer doors would be locked. Unfortunately, the doors were propped open to let in the night air, making security more difficult. John was surprised to see the open doors as the Gala was by invitation only. These open doors were conducive to uninvited guests.

Laura and Chrissy were running out of topics of conversation. Chrissy noticed the interest that Max and John were giving to their surroundings. She felt nervous on remembering that someone wanted to kidnap her for nefarious reasons. The key to the mystery was at this evening's Gala Event.

Chrissy glanced around, admiring the exquisite formal evening dresses. Happily, she was every bit as nicely attired as anyone here, realizing the magnitude of this Gala. A small orchestra was playing off to the left of the stage on a raised platform. There were gaily decorated tables of eight filling the room. The head table was on the stage, which she felt was befitting to Mr. Hammond's popularity and importance.

Due to the circumstances she had met Mr. Hammond, she was surprised that she could associate these qualities with him. Chrissy wasn't into politics but had been paying more attention. Since seeing his campaign speeches on television.

John and Max were working the room, guiding the ladies about greeting many of the guests. John seemed to know everyone. This surprised Chrissy. Her picture of him was as a loner and not very sociable. Tonight, he had destroyed that image. He was very popular with the men as well as the women. The number of women greeting him made her aware that he was a very sought-after bachelor.

The looks Chrissy was receiving from the women weren't always friendly. The men's attention trained on her more than made up for the disagreeable looks of envy from the ladies.

There was a fanfare from the orchestra. Alan Hammond and his followers swept into the hall. All eyes were swinging in their direction. Alan Hammond was waving and shaking hands as he strode around the front of the room.

He reached his seat on stage, still waving. Instead of curtains, there was a backdrop entirely across the stage with pictures of Alan Hammond presenting cheques to several charities in the past. A microphone appeared at his elbow. He swept it into his hand, greeting the crowd with a flowery speech.

"Thank you, everyone, for your generosity in bidding on the auction items to be presented later after dinner. This Charity Gala is to raise money for three charities that are near and dear to my heart."

Max and John exchanged glances, leaving unsaid the crap that was spilling from Hammond's mouth.

Alan finished his speech by saying. "There will be fifteen more minutes to mingle. Then everyone should find a table to sit at. I would like to mention. There are two people in the crowd tonight that will be approached to join me at the head table on the stage. Terrence Lewis, my right-hand man, will be approaching them shortly."

It was at that point that Joel came in their direction. He was carrying a tray of drinks. Chrissy's eyes widened at seeing him.

Joel asked, "would the lovely lady like a drink? And I mean lovely lady."

"Thank you for the drink and the compliment." She took the glass and raised it to her lips in a special salute to Joel. Now she knew there would be more police here undercover because neither John nor Max acknowledged knowing Joel. They did take drinks from his tray. Joel moved on, disbursing the rest of the glasses to people nearby.

They were wending their way to tables on the far side of the room, away from the open doors.

Terrence Lewis, with an attractive blond, appeared in front of them.

"Miss Lambert and Mr. Taylor, you are invited to join Mr. Hammond at the head table." John's eyes flew to Max. They had not expected this.

Terrence Lewis had Chrissy by the arm, guiding her towards the stage before John could protest.

Chapter Twenty-One

The attractive blond took John's arm, guiding him to the stage. He wanted to protest, but Chrissy was too far away from him as the crowd filled the space between the tables.

John looked back at Max, indicating that he should follow Chrissy.

Everyone was craning their necks to see the flaming red-haired beauty that was requested to join Alan Hammond. Who was this mysterious lady? She looked so regal in her green gown with glittering emeralds, sparkling in the lights trained on the stage.

Terrence guided Chrissy across to the seat beside Alan Hammond. Alan came forward to greet her, and he held Chrissy's hand. He was retaining it in such a tight grip that she couldn't break the connection. "Miss Lambert, I am so pleased you were able to join me. I have wanted to meet you again. You made quite an impression on me the first time we met."

Chrissy was smiling for the benefit of the crowd, but her eyes were saying otherwise. "I am surprised you remembered me. Our last meeting was so brief. Not exactly pleasant, as I recall." Chrissy was trying to extract her hand without success. She didn't want to be too obvious, as she was in the spotlight.

The blond was guiding John towards the seat beside Chrissy.

John reached over, sticking his hand out to greet Hammond. "Hello, Alan, nice to see you again." Hammond had to release Chrissy's hand to acknowledge John's greeting.

"Taylor, how nice to see you again. We seem to meet at charity affairs, don't we?"

"What can I say? You are a true benefactor of the underprivileged and the handicapped." John's voice was a bit on the flippant side.

Alan Hammond captured Chrissy's hand again, guiding her to the seat beside him. John had no choice but to drop into the chair on her left.

Alan was ringing a spoon on his crystal goblet to get the people's attention. Terrence Lewis appeared with a microphone.

"Ladies and gentlemen, I hope everyone has found a seat in preparation for the tasty meal that will be served shortly. But first, I would like to introduce the guests at the table with me. Starting on the far-right, Mr. and Mrs. Ralph Conner. They have been very supportive of my campaign and my dear friends for many years. The next couple needs no introduction, Mayor Reardon and his lovely wife, Diane." Some of the crowd clapped.

"On my left is a very dear lady that I had the pleasure of meeting under unusual circumstances but has never been far from my thoughts since, Miss Chrissy Lambert." Holding his hand out, pausing in such a manner that the crowd clapped, thinking she had to be a celebrity. Chrissy blushed prettily but didn't raise her hand or move her body in acknowledgment.

She was shocked when Alan Hammond picked up her hand and brought it to his lips, bowing to her as he did so. Confirming to the crowd, she must be a celebrity or royalty. The gallant kiss was payment in homage.

Chrissy was giving a weak smile in response, wishing she was anywhere but here.

Alan retained her hand as he continued the introductions. On Miss Lambert's left is Miss Lambert's friend and mine, John Taylor. The couple on his left is Monica Gerhardt and her husband, Steve. Monica Gerhardt, as you probably know, spearheads these charitable gatherings. She is on the board of several of our needy charities." Monica stood, acknowledging the clapping.

"Now, ladies and gentlemen, dinner will be served following the grace.

A man all in black stood up at the nearest table below the stage.

The room went quiet, and the blessing began. After the Amens, Alan said laughingly, "now let's eat."

The room became inundated with waiters and waitresses bearing trays of salads.

Alan Hammond sat and turned to Chrissy. "Miss Lambert, I so wanted to contact you ever since our last meeting."

Chrissy was still trying to extract her hand gently. The people were looking directly at them and discussing who she might be.

Chrissy said, "it is Mrs. Lambert, not Miss, and I have not missed seeing you." Her voice was barely above a whisper.

"Well, my dear, we will have to change that, won't we?" Alan Hammond said meaningfully.

John leaned forward. "Alan, what have you been doing since we last saw you?" Hoping to calm Chrissy down because they were entirely in the spotlight.

"John, you are a lucky man to know this sweet lady. You will have to bring her for dinner to my house in Mount Royal. We must make a date before the evening is over. I will speak to Terrence. He is my press secretary and knows my schedule."

"I don't know about that, Alan. Chrissy and I are quite busy. Our social calendar is quite full, isn't it, darling?" Taking Chrissy's other hand and bringing it to his lips in a repeat of Alan's introduction.

Chrissy's head swiveled to John, a shocked expression on her face. John hoped Alan didn't see it, squeezing Chrissy's hand companionably.

Alan had to release Chrissy when her salad appeared before her, but his expression was that he was not pleased with John's show of affection for Chrissy.

"Well, John, you'll just have to break a social date. I must have this lovely lady to grace my table. I want her to be hostess at a dinner that I am giving for some compatriots of mine. Would you do that for me, Mrs. Lambert? Chrissy? That is such a nice name. We don't want to be formal here amongst friends. Call me Alan."

Chrissy was out of her element, so she let John answer for her as his leg movement indicated.

"I don't know, Alan. Chrissy is quite a busy lady. Aren't you, darling? Are you aware, Alan, Chrissy has a four-year-old son? A real charmer, that lad." John was laying it on thickly, trying to save Chrissy.

She was eating the avocado salad to keep her hand occupied and out of Alan's reach. She was having difficulties swallowing. Even though the salad was delicious, one of her favorites.

"John, yes, I was aware Chrissy had a son. Jared, isn't it?"

So, Hammond had been looking into Chrissy's life for information. He should've known. John hoped his 'darlings' showed that they lived together as a couple, rather than just for protection. Hammond must know that Chrissy was living in his house.

"Yes, Jared. So, you do know Chrissy better than I thought." John said meaningfully.

"Oh, yes, I made it my business to know all about young ladies that catch my eye. Chrissy, you are displeased that I have made some inquiries?"

Chrissy said politely, "no, Alan, not at all." But the voice she used told the opposite.

Alan ignored or didn't understand because he said, "you will rearrange your social calendar to be hostess for me." Apparently, 'no' wasn't an option.

Chrissy didn't know what to say now.

"I will consider it, but I doubt it is possible." Turning to John, she said sweetly, "do you, dear?"

"We will have to let you know, Alan. Give me your number. I will call you." John replied, trying to bring things to a stalemate.

Terrence appeared at Alan's side at a hand signal from Alan. Alan dipped his head to Terrence. Terrance whipped out a card presenting it to John as though prearranged. John pocketed the card, thanking Alan for his promptness in producing the number, not dreaming it would happen.

John and Chrissy hadn't eaten much of their salad. Alan hadn't even lifted his fork before the waiter appeared, asking if they were finished. The time had passed in innuendos while others ate.

John scanned the room while waiting for the salad plates removal. Max was scanning the room too. Their eyes finally came into contact.

Max gave him the finger to the nose, a secret message that John understood, 'this is not good, keep your eyes peeled.'

John lifted his spoon and tapped his cup accidentally as he set it in the saucer. John's way of saying, 'I will.' John's eyes scanned the room again. He was glad that Max and Laura were sitting at a table close to the stage. They had discussed their strategy ahead of time. But never dreamt that he and Chrissy would end up at the head table. He should have known.

Max didn't figure anything would happen before the auction, but he wasn't sure.

Chrissy was answering Alan's questions about Jared. A safe subject, she hoped. John turned to make some effort to talk to Monica and her husband. He did know Monica from other social gatherings.

John was still scanning the room ever so casually as he talked. He wanted to join Chrissy and Alan in their conversation. He got his opportunity to speak to Chrissy when the mayor engaged Alan's attention.

"Darling," John lifted Chrissy's hand, kissing her palm caressingly. "Are you enjoying the evening?"

Chrissy felt the kiss kindle a heat throughout her body. Chrissy was undeniably out of her element with both John and Alan. She didn't want to play these types of games.

"Yes, darling. I can't think of anywhere I would rather be." She almost choked on that last statement.

A waiter put a hot plate in front of her containing lobster tails, rice pilaf and various vegetables arranged in an enticing decorative array. She noted the sizzling butter, sitting over an orange flame, was placed beside her plate to complement the lobster.

If Chrissy's stomach wasn't so jumpy, she would have devoured the lobster, her favorite cuisine. She dipped a bit of lobster in the butter. Her fork disappeared from her hand. "Be careful. You don't want to burn yourself." Alan dipped the lobster, then held it to Chrissy's lips. She was too stunned by the new ploy of Alan's to object. She opened her lips to receive the morsel. Her hand reached for the fork.

"I think I can manage to be careful," she said sweetly. Alan released the fork, knowing full-well people would be looking at their byplay.

John was furious as he turned back from a conversation with Monica to see Alan feeding Chrissy, intimately.

What was Alan doing? Was he trying to show the crowd that there was a relationship between them?

John was furious. He missed Chrissy's remark, but he did see that she had recaptured her fork. John decided it was time to lay a bomb ready for fusing.

"Alan, I am surprised that Mr. Delvietti isn't present this evening. I understand he is a very good friend of yours." John had a pleasant smile on his face. Alan's countenance changed to a stern look.

"Mr. Delvietti? I don't recall knowing a Mr. Delvietti. Although I have heard the name before." He tried to look vague.

"That is odd. When I was speaking to Mr. Delvietti, he said he knew you quite well. In fact, he planned a surprise for this evening with you in mind." John was enjoying himself. Chrissy was even grinning slightly.

Hammond glanced around quickly, scanning the room, noting the wide-open doors. He should've insisted they be secured. It was too late now, but he would insist on it before the auction commenced.

John winked at Chrissy then pulled his ear. A signal to Max that he had planted the bomb, they had discussed. Max pulled at his ear in acknowledgment, switching his eyes to Hammond, noting his agitation. The fuse was lit. Fear was there in his expression. Even though he had a benevolent smile on his lips. *Way to go, John.*

Laura knew Max wasn't happy about something, but she didn't know what. Too bad Chrissy and John were at the head table. She would have enjoyed the dinner more if they had sat together.

John was talking to Chrissy, letting Alan get his equilibrium back. Alan was talking to the Mayor and Diane.

Now, Chrissy knew for sure that something was going to happen. Something was going on between Mr. Delvietti and Alan Hammond, or why would he be so upset? She noted that although John was attentive to her, he was scanning the room periodically. In her nervousness, Chrissy started eating intently, eyes on her plate. John was eating like he didn't have a care in the world, which was infuriating to Chrissy. He held their conversation on the topic of a tasty dinner. And not giving her a chance to query him.

She jabbed him under the table, indicating her unhappiness at John. She had a right to know what was happening. After all, she was in the limelight here. But how could anything happen in full view of all these people? How could it?

Alan was calling for her attention back to him.

"Chrissy, how was your dinner? Did you enjoy the lobster? You look like a lobster person to me. I was going to have Filet Mignon, but I do enjoy a good lobster, now and then. I felt it was appropriate as I wanted to butter up these good patrons. So, they would liberally part with their money. No pun intended." He gave off a chuckle as the waiter started clearing the plates.

As soon as the plates were removed, a voice behind her said.

"I hope you like your dessert, madam. It is deep-fried ice cream with a peach brandy sauce." Chrissy's head whipped around at the sound of his voice. It was Joel. Chrissy hoped Alan thought she was startled by someone behind her rather than her knowing the voice.

"Yes, that does sound yummy." Giving Joel a wink, then leaning into his arm ever so slightly, as he placed her dessert on the table in front of her. Joel never acknowledged the touch, placing a dessert in front of Alan with the same flourish. Joel gave him a winning smile, as though he thought Alan was Mr. Wonderful.

John rationalized. *Don't overdo it, Joel.* He placed a dessert in front of John. Barely acknowledging John while slipping a paper out a bit on the far side of the dessert plate and sliding it back in, pulling his hand away. Joel served Monica and her husband. Then left the stage with his empty tray.

Chrissy and Alan were discussing the dessert. Alan looked like he wanted to feed Chrissy again, his eyes following her dessert spoon's contact with her mouth.

John figured that Alan was too busy to notice his sleight of hand. He palmed the slip of paper.

Monica was too intent in talking to her husband, exclaiming over the dessert, to notice John read the note.

I HAVE SEEN TWO FIXTURES THAT DON'T BE-
LONG HERE.
TWELVE O'CLOCK AND TEN O'CLOCK.

John dropped his napkin to slip the note inside his pocket, so he didn't misplace it. Then he surveyed the room, spotting the fixtures that Max had fingered.

Although they were in tuxedos, their bulkiness made them look out of place. A couple of Delvietti's more promising hoods, sticking out like sore thumbs.

The two men were not what John wanted to see. He hoped the hoods came in the open doors and were not part of the guest lists. John reached for his ear, looking toward Max. Then continuing past as he turned his head towards Chrissy.

"Darling, I see you are enjoying your dessert. I have only tasted a bit. But I know it is something that would appeal to you." Chrissy smiled at him, jabbing his leg with her hand that had been in her lap under the table. John knew Chrissy was letting him know that she was aware that he was up to something. He suggestively licked his lips. Chrissy shuddered then gave him another poke. *What had got into John? Wasn't he overdoing his role?*

He grinned as he put a spoonful of dessert into his mouth, letting his tongue follow the spoons removal.

Chrissy's stomach knotted. *Why was she reacting this way? This was just John, remember.* Thankfully Alan called her attention back to him.

"Chrissy, will you sit next to me when we leave the stage when the auction starts?"

She was at a loss of what to say. Rather than have a scene develop if she refused, she nodded her head yes. She knew her voice wouldn't be able to express the yes required of her. She fervently hoped that there would be a seat for John too.

Joel had given Max a dessert, slipping him a piece of paper too by dropping it into his lap while he joked with Laura. She was enjoying the familiarity of this young waiter, hoping that Max was otherwise occupied as he had been during most of the dinner. Joel was now openly joking with the whole table delaying, his leaving.

Max opened the note.

> THERE ARE DELVIETTI MEN AMONGST THE
> WAITERS.
> I COUNTED AT LEAST THREE.

Max said, "waiter, are you busy on the 12th. I would like you to serve at a party? I will be giving?

"The 12ᵗʰ, I think so."

Slipping the note back to Joel. "I will give you my address and the particulars later.

Joel appeared at the head table. "Coffee or tea, sir?"

"Coffee will be fine. Have you been doing this long?" John inquired conversationally.

"No, not too long. I got the job because of the three Ds in our midst. They made it easy to get the hang of things, helping out with my training."

John nodded his consent to the message, taking a closer look at each of the waiters, wending their way amongst the tables.

Joel had moved, serving the rest of the table. He wanted to yank Chrissy away and disappear into the night. It was making him ill to see Chrissy fondled over by Alan Hammond. Joel knew that she was in so much danger from Delvietti and knew that he had to be around here somewhere. Joel felt sure. He hadn't spotted Delvietti yet. Joel was glad when he could leave the stage. So, he didn't have to watch any more of Chrissy's dinner partner that had monopolized her attention from John.

John had made two of the D's easily. They were not very polished in their duties. Not knowing the finer arts of serving to the right, removing to the left. Their actions were mechanical rather than smooth. One was even slopping coffee over into the saucer. Now, where was the third?

Studying the room carefully, the third was blending in better. It wasn't until a waiter walked companionably with one of the D's. It had to be the third one. Otherwise, why would they be talking so companionably?

John lifted his spoon and made a decisive ping against his cup before he stirred in some cream. Max repeated the action. John knew Max had spotted the three Ds.

The players were coming out of the woodwork. John wanted to excuse himself, but he didn't dare leave Chrissy. He had to get her out of harm's way, as quickly as possible, when the deal went down.

He kept glancing at his watch in a rather obvious way. As though he was bored and wanted to get to the auction. Max and he had arranged that if they thought they knew when it would happen, they would look at their watch several times then ease their hand up their arm. Eight was the wrist, nine was about five inches above, ten was the elbow, and eleven was the shoulder.

The way Delvietti's clan was moving amongst them, John figured it had to be when the waiters could still access the tables for positioning. So, John slipped his hand up to his arm until he reached his elbow. His watch read 8:45. The three D's actions didn't seem pronounced enough yet.

Max looked at his watch, angling it as if it was difficult to see in the bright light. A message to John, he agreed. Max excused himself and headed out into the hall. He had to locate his man that was communicating with his crew. He wanted them expecting something between now and ten o'clock.

John wasn't available now that he was on stage with Hammond. John would stick to Chrissy's side like glue. She can still be a sacrificial lamb if they weren't careful.

Max was able to radio in for additional black and whites to be in the general vicinity. He handed the radio back to Eric, telling him to make the men aware to expect activity in the next hour.

Instead of going directly back into the hall, he toured the place and glanced outside. But couldn't see anything out of the norm.

As he made his way back to his table, he issued a sigh of relief. The doors on the far side had been closed. Hammond must have arranged that. He must've been feeling vulnerable with the doors open too. He indicated to Laura not to ask questions with the shake of his head. She normally queried his movements.

"What will be, will be." he breathed out.

* * *

Hammond breathed a sigh of relief. Terrence had obeyed his instruction to seal the doors on the far side of the hall. John had made him nervous, mentioning Delvietti. Why would John refer to Delvietti if he didn't know something was going on between them? This was not good. Delvietti had been quiet for a month now. Hammond's fears had eased, which had returned instantly, since John's casual statement. It would be just like Delvietti to break up his party. Delvietti likes sensationalism.

Chapter Twenty-Two

Alan speculated about John's comment about Delvietti and tonight? John must've arranged for Max to be here because Hammond had not seen his name on the guest list that he had perused updated to yesterday. There were a few names that he didn't recognize, but that happens at such big affairs. But Max must have had an invitation to get in the door at the front entrance.

"Chrissy, are you enjoying the evening so far?" Alan inquired, coming out of his distraction.

"Oh, yes, but a bit overwhelmed being up here in view of everyone. I am not used to the limelight. I doubt I could handle it on a regular basis. I don't know how you manage it." Secretly, she was pleading. *Forget me.*

"I seem to thrive on the exposure. It is only a matter of time before you accept the spotlight as normal. Politics and popularity go hand in hand. You will get used to it if you are around me. Chrissy, I want you to be part of my life. I need a hostess to help with my parties and my campaigning. Can I count on you?"

John's pressure on her leg let Chrissy know that he had heard Alan.

"I am sorry, Alan. I don't think I can perform that kind of a role. John and I are very busy socially since we are an item now."

Then John said right on cue. "Darling, I wish your ring had been ready for this evening. I wanted Max and Laura to see the ring on your finger. They are finding it hard to believe that I am actually engaged to you. They both thought I was a permanent bachelor."

"I didn't know you and Chrissy were that serious, John. I thought you were just friends. Otherwise, I am sure I would have heard through the grapevine." His voice was stiff. He had lost some of his smooth veneer.

"You knew we were living together, didn't you?" Lifting Chrissy's hand, kissing her palm gently.

Alan's face was annoyed now. John reckoned by his comment about the grapevine, meant that Hammond was keeping tabs on Chrissy.

Chrissy leaned into John. "Yes, darling, it is a shame my ring wasn't ready. I would love to show it off to Laura and Max. Darling, are you sure you aren't going to miss bachelorhood?" Chrissy asked slyly.

"Of course not, darling, because I have you." Again, he kissed her palm.

Don't overdo it, John or you will make it unbelievable.

Chrissy turned to Alan. "I guess I won't be able to be a hostess for you, after all. Sorry."

Alan was slowly recovering from this latest setback. His plan of winning Chrissy to his side tonight was disappearing. He had been so sure he could charm Chrissy into being part of his life.

His lips spread into a charming fake smile. "Chrissy, perhaps I can persuade John to release you for a couple of occasions I have in mind. Did I tell you how charming you are tonight? You outshine every lady in the room. I particularly like the emeralds you are wearing."

John cut in. "That was my engagement present to Chrissy. They are an heirloom passed down through my family. My mother wanted me to give them to my bride-to-be. I guess that is because she wants to be sure that I go through with it this time. You know mothers. I guess she has decided she wants grandchildren while she is still young enough to enjoy them."

Alan's smile slipped a little, but he cheerfully said, "Congratulations, John, I guess you could sort of say that I was your benefactor." He paused.

John looked at him inquiringly.

"Yes, John, I was instrumental in getting you and Chrissy tied up together. If tied separately, this union might not be. Then maybe I could have persuaded Chrissy to join me and my campaign." Alan said with a subtle emphasis on the 'me.'

Alan looked at his watch. It was nearly ten. He could hear that there was quite a bit of activity backstage. The auction was set for ten, looking around at the tables. The waiters were clearing the rest of the dessert plates, cups and saucers.

Some chairs had appeared just below the stage for the head table patrons. Terrence appeared at his elbow with a microphone.

"Ladies and gentlemen, I can tell by the activity backstage that the auction is about to begin. I hope everyone has enjoyed the meal that was provided for you. Thank you, Monica. As usual, you have outdone yourself with an excellent cuisine for the occasion. Remember, folks. This dinner was organized to make you feel very benevolent. To make you dig deep and empty your pockets into our three charities. Let the auction begin."

The head table cleared first, and the white tablecloths whipped off, replaced with rich, bright red ones to best show the auction items.

Alan took Chrissy's arm before John could, leading her to the side of the stage in preparation to take her to the chairs set out for them in front. There was movement on stage, removing chairs and positioning tables. The noise escalated.

John was having trouble keeping up with Chrissy and Alan. Chrissy let out a shriek. Her screech barely heard above the noise.

A man had closed in behind her putting his arm around her neck. Another man grabbed Alan. They were both dragged through the backstage door.

John couldn't get through the doorway. It was solidly blocked, much to his amazement. John went across the stage, dropping down near Max.

"They have Chrissy and Hammond. Let's go."

"Yes, I heard Chrissy scream," Max said on the run. "Where are we going?"

"His goons stopped me from following, so we need to get to the back entrance before they leave the building."

Three waiters were trying to dissuade anyone from leaving. They were reassuring the people that the lady had screeched because she tripped. "Please, go back to your seats because the auction is about to begin."

John looked around. The two Delvietti men from the table nearby had disappeared.

Max held up his shield. John and Max pushed past the waiters. The three waiters had their hands full of frantic ladies and men trying to leave to stop John and Max from exiting.

Max yelled, "now," as he saw Eric. "Backstage area at the back of the building." Eric redirected the men to close in.

Max and John raced towards the backstage doors. This time, not only were they kidnapping Chrissy but Hammond too.

With all the confusion on stage, most of the guests were unsure what exactly had happened, if anything. The auction set up on stage was complete. The guests had settled down to usual conversations. The Mayor and his wife, Diane, were in the front row seating with Monica and her husband along with the Conner couple. The Mayor was conversing in a low voice with his wife. "That was rather odd when Alan and Chrissy disappeared backstage. I wasn't exactly looking that way with all the upheaval of moving the chairs and tables. I swear that something happened that was irregular. Did you see anything?"

Diane looks at her husband's calm exterior, knowing the concern he concealed to keep everyone thinking that nothing unusual was happening. She was proud of his ability to display a mask of calm.

"Yes, it looked like a man had Chrissy with his arm around her neck, but I couldn't be sure because of my blocked view by the men moving the chairs."

"Why would they take Chrissy, I wonder? Did it look like Alan was taking her?" Wonder in his voice.

"I have no idea. I was trying to get out of the way of the chair removal."

"I hope they are all right. Let's hope they appear before the auction starts. It looks like the auction is about ready."

A shot sounded from outside the building. Diane's eyes went quickly to her husband. He patted her hand that she had placed on his arm. "It is probably a car backfiring. Keep calm. We don't want these people panicking."

The auctioneer was calling for the first item to be spotlighted. The auction had begun.

Max and John were running towards the back of the building. Eric hot on their heels. They reached the backstage door. The corridor was empty. Then they heard a shot. They turned only to be stopped by the goons that had immobilized John on stage. Before Max could lift his gun, the thug knocked it from his hand. John palmed his knife and stopped the attacker after Max. Max and Eric were grappling with another assailant.

John jumped over the body slumped down on the pavement. He ran across the parking lot as three police cars were heading quickly onto the roadway. John heard someone run up behind him.

"There they go." The voice belonged to Joel. "The Delvietti-men took Chrissy and Hammond, didn't they?"

"Yes." John was still running full tilt to his car, which was close to the front entrance. You could hear sirens in the night air.

The car valet saw what was happening and threw John his keys.

John reached his car wishing he had an automatic opener using his key. He leaped inside, leaning over to open the door for Joel. Then he shoved the key into the ignition and took off. Wishing he had a radio band to hook up with police calls. Where were they? What direction did they go after leaving the parking lot street?

The sirens sounded like they were heading for the industrial area. Possibly Delvietti's warehouse, where they took Chrissy before. John focused the car in that direction.

"Joel, did you overhear anything pertinent when the three D's were together?"

"No."

"How did you ID them?"

"It was the way they handled themselves. Their method of handling the trays and the dishes. They took one tray to my three. Undercover duty at least gives us some insight into the job, so we blend in. These three never blended in."

"Good work, Joel."

"Yeah, but they still have Chrissy. Where were you? I thought you were supposed to stick to her like glue?"

"Yeah, but the cleanup crew were blundering idiots. They got in my way. Delvietti's goons had the doorway blocked. I could risk my life at that point, but I thought Max and I together could save her."

"Where is Max?"

"Last time I saw Max and Eric, they were fighting off one of Delvietti's goons."

"Two against one that should come out in their favor, surely?"

"I hope so, or I have a lot of explaining to do to Laura, Max's wife. She is one tough lady where Max is concerned. She would not forgive me for running off without helping."

John drove around the block, casing the warehouse. No sign of anyone. But that didn't mean they weren't here. He remembered from when he last saved Chrissy that he couldn't see any signs of life then either.

"Joel, I know of a way in if they haven't sealed it up since I broke Chrissy out last time." Joel looked at John.

"You mean this is where they took Chrissy last time?"

"Yes, and I found a way in that wasn't guarded. However, we may not be so lucky this time." John looked at Joel. He was taking it hard the abduction of Chrissy. They had to save her.

They parked a block away. Joel and John had just gotten out of the car when Max and Eric pulled in behind them. John walked back to speak to them.

"So, you finally got away from that goon. Took you long enough."

"What do you mean? We were here before you got out of the car."

"Where are your black and whites? Where were they and your men at the Convention Center? Why weren't the kidnappers stopped?"

"My men fumbled the ball only because Chrissy had a gun against her head, and so did Hammond. They got off one shot trying to take out a tire, but they missed. The blacks and whites lost them."

"Max, I want to go in alone, but I will probably need backup, so I want Joel with me. We both have a vested interest in this." Right now, Chrissy was the prime concern.

"And?" Max inquired.

"You and your black and whites be in place when we make a hurried exit from the building. Have you figured out why Delvietti wants Hammond?"

"Not really. Just like we haven't been able to tie Frank Doherty to this either."

"Maybe we are about to find out. Let's go, Joel. Max, if we don't make it out in fifteen minutes, storm the ramparts." Max gave John a thumb's up.

They synchronized their watches, and John took off. Joel was right behind him. They quickly walked the block leading to the warehouse, working out hand signals to communicate once they entered the building. They approached the warehouse, at a slow pace from shadow to shadow. They made their way to the window, which was still accessible to John's amazement. Someone wasn't on their toes. Joel dropped down behind him quietly.

They crept along, skirting the three men, supposedly keeping the place secure. They were busy trading conversation while enjoying a cigarette. Their confidence was evident by the fact that they weren't even bothering to look around.

John and Joel quickly slipped past them without detection. John made for the place where they held Chrissy the last time, but she wasn't there. Evidently, it was going to be more challenging to find her this time.

John's signal to Joel, this was where Chrissy was before. Joel was disappointed that she wasn't there. It meant they were using her to keep Hammond in line. John had warned him. But he had hoped that would be the last resort only if Hammond didn't cooperate.

Joel had his gun with him. He had drawn it from his shoulder holster after he entered the building. John palmed his knife to take out all obstacles, less noise that way.

They proceeded forward. John and Joel ducked out of the light when they heard voices coming from behind them. The three men went into the lit area. The three waiters from the center. John had hoped that they wouldn't get here so soon. No such luck, now it meant three more against them. Joel and John had arranged to save Chrissy at all costs, and Hammond only if they had no opportunity to get away without him. John had convinced Joel that Hammond and Delvietti deserved each other. Joel agreed with John's plan, wanting Chrissy safe.

A voice came out of an open door.

"You know, Alan, you were very foolish to get into the gambling racket, that is infringing on my territory. I know your place in the country has a gambling casino. I want it shut down. I want a signed agreement to that effect. If I hear you are running any more games in my area or otherwise, I will take you out. You'd better sign that you are out of action as of tonight."

"But I need the funds. My campaign costs are mounting. I need the money to keep my hopes alive. I must keep the currency flowing." Hammond was sweating and almost pleading.

"No deals. You sign. You stop now. Do I make myself clear? You ignored my first warning to your partner, hence Frank Doherty's demise."

"I won't sign it. I need the funds. You will still have your games. Mine aren't big enough to even put a dent in your profits."

"Wrong answer. This pretty lady here is not going to be so pretty if you don't sign." Joel tried to rush in. John grabbed him and shook him into facing reality. Now wasn't the right time. The door closed, and the voices sounded muffled.

"They're going to hurt Chrissy," Joel whispered. "We can't let that happen."

John hissed. "Fine, get yourself caught. Who will save Chrissy then?" John was looking around. They needed a diversion away from the room Chrissy was in.

John spotted a fuse box. He could pull the fuses. But that would only put everyone in the dark, and Chrissy might get hurt. Not a feasible idea.

John knew that it had to be something pretty powerful to bring Delvietti and his thugs out of there. He was still looking around when he spied a bunch of stacked boxes with danger signs on them and the word EXPLOSIVES.

Now, that could cause a powerful diversion to persuade Delvietti and his thugs out of the office. But the explosion would have to be far away from the offices.

The door opened again.

"You know you are being foolish. Begging won't save this pretty lady for you." Delvietti must have been running his hands over Chrissy. Hammond yelled out. "Keep your filthy hands off her. Chrissy, I am so sorry I got you into this."

"Never mind the chatter. I want that agreement signed now." again, Delvietti must have run his hands over Chrissy. She yelled out this time. "Keep your filthy hands off me, you idiot." Hammond didn't sound like he was ready to give in. John felt sure his apology to Chrissy was meaningless. He would sacrifice Chrissy without a qualm. John knew that Hammond would lose anyway, and hurting Chrissy wasn't necessary. Delvietti would kill Hammond before letting him leave without signing the agreement.

John and Joel's insides were knotting at the pictures Hammond and Chrissy were painting. The door closed again as one of the goons walked out. John stepped out behind him and used the blade. The thug gave out a gurgling sound and collapsed slowly to the floor. Joel was there to help drag him behind the boxes of explosives. The diversion had to be now. They couldn't wait for Max.

Grabbing a couple of boxes of explosives each, John was hoping there were detonator caps inside one of the boxes. They didn't have time to search for a particular one they needed. Not if they were going to save Chrissy.

Not wanting to block their window of escape. John went in the opposite direction. John and Joel were stealthily working their way to the back of the warehouse. Now the three goons were trading words, enjoying another cigarette.

John opened the boxes with his knife. He winced at abusing the blade that way, but Chrissy was more important than the knife. He just realized she was everything to him. Joel would have a battle on his hands when this was over.

John had experience in explosives from a summer job with a demolition crew. One of the boxes held detonator caps. The Lord was with them. John attached the wire to the boxes with Joel's help. Then they strung out a long line which John intended to light. He gave himself extra line to make it back to the front of the warehouse, hoping it would go off before Max stormed the ramparts. He glanced at his watch. Five more minutes that should be enough time.

John touched Joel's hand, then pointed. Joel took off, and John lit the fuse. Thankfully, he had never given up the habit of carrying matches. They could hardly have asked the smokers for a match.

John was close on Joel's heels as they raced to get back behind the boxes outside the office, where Chrissy and Hammond were being held. They dived behind the cartons as the first box detonated. The office door flew open two goons ran out. The second detonation brought Delvietti to the door. The two goons were on the run, and the three smokers were yelling. The third box detonated, and Delvietti left at a run also.

Joel and John leaped into the room. Chrissy sat tied to a chair. Delvietti must have knocked her around while they positioned the explosives. Her head was forward as though one of the blows had knocked her out. "Hammond, you are a slimeball. I will see you never get into office," John stipulated.

Joel was untying her. John knelt before Chrissy. "Chrissy, wake up. We have to get out of here." He ran his hand gently down her face. When her bonds fell away, Chrissy started falling sideways. John whipped her up into his arms. "Let's get out of here. We can use the front door."

Joel asked, "what about the slimeball here?"

"Never mind him. Let Delvietti take care of him. I want to stop Max. Let these two men fight it out."

Hammond was pleading, offering them large sums of money. Calling them names as John with Chrissy and Joel headed out the front entrance.

"Joel, you head off Max and the black and whites. I'll head for the car. I want to get Chrissy to the hospital."

Joel yelled, "The hospital is on Kensington Drive, Stanhope General."

Chapter Twenty-Three

J oel took off at a run, racing to the back of the warehouse. Max and Eric had their guns drawn. There were various black and whites positioned around the warehouse, with men hiding behind them. Max was rallying them to enter the warehouse when Joel raced into view.

"Stop, John has Chrissy. He is heading for the hospital."

"What were the explosions?"

"John set off some boxes of explosives as a diversion."

"Where is Hammond?"

"We left him inside for Delvietti. That slimeball was letting Delvietti knock Chrissy around rather than give in."

"Give into what?"

"Hammond apparently is running a gambling casino at his country home. Delvietti objected to that. Frank Doherty was his partner. His death was a warning to Hammond that he didn't heed."

"I agree to let them fight it out between them. So, we won't storm the warehouse. All right, fellas, let's pack it up." Max thanked the officers and sent them back to their duties.

"Joel, do you need a ride? I take it, John has gone without you?" Max saw himself in this eager young man when he was his age.

"John needed to get Chrissy to the hospital. Yes, I'd like a ride to the hospital, thanks."

Max said. "Fine, I'll take you. Stanhope General, I presume?"

"Yes."

They piled into the car. Kelsey put his emergency light on the roof. He took off for the hospital, hurrying but didn't run red lights. It wasn't that much of a hurry. The flashing light just cleared some of the slower traffic to the side of the road along the way.

They met up with John. He was pacing back and forth outside the full waiting room.

John looked like death warmed over with his face expressing his concern for Chrissy. "She was still unconscious, although I called to her constantly on the drive to the hospital."

Joel took up the pacing with him, and the two men talked of their worry for Chrissy. Max sat, watching the two of them. Which of these men would actually end up with Chrissy? Max knew John was aware that Joel wanted Chrissy, but Joel seems to be oblivious to John's feelings for her.

Max was greatly amused. Although John was aware of Joel's feelings for Chrissy, he wasn't jealous of him. John must like Joel too much for that. It would be a case of winning Chrissy's heart. Max knew John well enough to know he intended to win, and Joel could continue as a friend.

Footsteps resounded down the hall towards them. It was Dr. Gord Abbott. He looked after Chrissy the first time she came in. He had remembered her because she had been a kidnap victim.

John and Joel collided in their turning towards the doctor. They wanted the information the doctor would impart as he stopped near them.

"Mrs. Lambert has a concussion and multiple bruises administered by a jagged object. A large ring is my guess. Are either of you next of kin?"

"No." The two men said in unison. "We are just looking after her right now."

Dr. Abbott was looking at them intently, thinking, what an odd remark.

"Can we see her? We have to see her. She means a lot to both of us." John spoke instantly.

"Yes, she has regained consciousness, but we want to keep her overnight for observation." If they are looking after this woman, how come she is in this condition?

It was at this point that Max came forward. "How is Mrs. Lambert?" Three men inquiring after Mrs. Lambert, was he the one that beat her? Max pulled out his shield at Dr. Abbott's look of wonderment.

"I am Inspector Max Kelsey. Mrs. Lambert was injured tonight after being taken as a hostage."

"Hostage?" What was going on in this woman's life? First, a kidnapping now a hostage?

"I am sorry I cannot reveal the details, but they took Mrs. Lambert against her will. That is all I am at liberty to tell you at the moment."

"Well, Mrs. Lambert has multiple bruises about the head and a concussion. She has recovered consciousness, but I want to keep her in for observation overnight."

John and Joel had a stricken look on their faces hearing the details again. Should they have rushed the office instead of using the diversion? Would that have saved Chrissy from her injuries?

Dr. Abbott took a package out of his pocket. "Mrs. Lambert had these on her. They looked very valuable, so I thought I had better remove them and give them to her next of kin." He held them out to Max.

Max stared at the sparkling stones. Max visualized Chrissy as Laura, and he had greeted them at the Gala. The velvet evening cloak, the gown and the emeralds lay against her neck and dangled from her ears. A vision of loveliness with her flaming red hair.

Max looked at John and Joel. John piped up. "Max, those were my mother's. I loaned them to Chrissy."

Dr. Abbott was still looking at Max for instruction. Max said. "I will vouch for this man. He is telling the truth. They probably did come from his mother knowing him as well as I do."

Dr. Abbott passed the emeralds to John. John pocketed them quickly, not even glancing at them.

"Can I see Chrissy now?" John tried not to be too demanding for fear of putting the doctor off. He was so anxious to see her, and so were Joel and Max.

"Sure, she is in ICU, which is the room down the hall with the red light over the door." John and Joel smiled at the doctor.

Max inquired. "Do you mind if all three of us go in?"

"No, but I suggest one at a time, and I must caution you we have heart attack patients in there too."

These three men are really concerned about this woman. First, a kidnapping, then she is a hostage. How could that be? The first two men looked smitten over her. If they were looking after her, why was she still taken hostage and brutalized? There must be quite the story here, he thought, as the three men walked down the corridor, not talking just walking towards ICU. Dr. Abbott shook his head then headed back into the emergency and his next patient.

The men figured if they were quiet, it would be okay, so all three went in, wanting to see and hear Chrissy. She was lying looking so pale, her hair partly fallen from her cap of curls anchored to the top of her head. The pale face marred by the bruises darkening there. John wanted to lift her into his arms.

She must've heard their footsteps because she opened her eyes.

Joel was the closes. She smiled weakly at him, seeing his concern, and Joel grasped her hand. "Chrissy, I am so sorry that we couldn't stop this from happening to you."

Chrissy's eyes lifted to John, and Max then again to Joel. Not knowing her rescue details, but she felt sure they all had a part in it. "Well, it would have been better if you had gotten there sooner, but at least you saved me." Joel and John felt guilty they hadn't saved her before it became physical.

"They were not concerned for me at all. Mr. Delvietti was talking about maiming me. I shudder to think what they would've done if you hadn't saved me." She closed her eyes, hoping to shut out the horror of the images.

"Chrissy, I tried to get there before they did this to you. I even left Hammond to be dealt with by Delvietti. If he survives, I will personally see that he is brought down and never gets elected for office ever again." John had picked up her other hand wanting contact with her like Joel. Chrissy felt a tingle in her hand as soon as John touched her. Her eyes flew to his instantly. Had he felt it? He wasn't serious when he was playacting at the dinner table for Alan's benefit.

Her eyes shifted to Max. "Hi, I guess I didn't fare too well. They want to keep me in overnight."

"Sorry, Chrissy, that we weren't able to stop them from taking you at the Convention Center. I never wanted this to happen to you. If I had known, you would never have been on that stage. I mistakenly thought you were safer up there with John beside you. We expected the activity to come from the floor. We spotted five men from Delvietti's clan there, and we were keeping a strict eye on them. Three waiters and two were guests." Max continued.

"We never dreamed that the attack would come from backstage. It is my fault not pre-thinking this and having men back there too. I don't know how Delvietti pulled this off and got his men placed inside, but he did. He must be far more powerful than we gave him credit for. I won't make that mistake in the future."

Chrissy laid there listening to all three men taking personal blame for her bruises. But the fault was hers.

Chrissy looked at all three men. "It was my fault. I didn't play the part that John gave me as his fiancée. I could have refused Alan and waited for John, but I didn't. So, don't blame yourself any of you."

"Chrissy, we should have saved you before you got out of the Convention Center," John remarked with deep feeling in his voice.

"Chrissy, I wish you were not hurt. Just looking at your beat-up face makes me cringe inside. The thought of Delvietti touching you makes me furious." Joel said with deep feeling, lifting her hand and kissing it. He wanted so badly to comfort her. She looked at Joel. *Why didn't she feel a tingle from him?* She liked him a lot.

"Neither of you are to blame. I will get better. The bruises will disappear in a few days." She looked intently at John. She continued.

"I want Mr. Hammond's election hopes dashed permanently. I will help you to discredit him. He doesn't deserve the people's trust."

Looking at Max, she said. "Isn't there anything the police can do to stop him?"

"Not unless we can prove he is breaking the law. Perhaps raiding his country home when it is used as a gambling den. Then again, maybe Delvietti has taken care of him by now." Looking meaningful at John.

Chrissy closed her eyes again because the thundering drums

had taken over her head. John could see the exhaustion and pain there amongst the bruises. She probably has a headache from her concussion.

"Let's go now. We will be back for you tomorrow when they release you."

Chrissy's eyes flew open. "John, I ruined your mother's dress, and the emeralds disappeared." Tears started escaping. "The cape is still back at the Convention Center."

"Sssh! Chrissy, the dress isn't important. Dr. Abbott gave me back the emeralds. He retrieved them when you first came in for treatment. I will recover the cape, so don't even think about that."

"But they were so beautiful."

"No, Chrissy, you were the beautiful one, not the clothes," John said reverently. It was at that moment that Joel realized John was in love with Chrissy too.

Chrissy was too exhausted to keep on. A nurse approached to tell them that she needed rest.

Chrissy closed her eyes. She heard the nurse shooing them out until tomorrow. She remembered Jared, and her eyes flew open, but all she saw were their backs as they passed through the door.

Each man was feeling their guilt because they hadn't stopped Chrissy from being brutalized. They all hated Alan Hammond for allowing it to happen.

* * *

The next day when John arrived in the kitchen. Jared was in his pajamas playing with the puppy.

"John, I let Alfie out to pee. But I didn't go off the terrace."

"That's good." John picked up Alfie, who had scampered to his moving feet. "Well, boy, are you keeping this young man inline or is he keeping you in line?" Putting his nose close to the nose of the puppy. Alfie's tongue appeared for a lick, but John quickly backed away. Jared was laughing.

"I am keeping Alfie in line the way Joel showed me. Where is mommy? I went into the bedroom, but she wasn't there. So, she must be down here somewhere." Jared ended with concern, retrieving Alfie from John.

John picked up Jared and the puppy. He walked over to the chair and sat down before replying. Alfie was now trying to lick Jared's face as puppies naturally do. Jared giggled, but his face soon lost its laughter when John said, "Jared, your mom is in the hospital. She got hurt last night."

"But you said you would protect her. You said you would." Now Jared looked angry.

"I know I did. I tried to protect your mom. I really did. Joel and Max tried too, but the bad men took her away. We were too late to stop them from hurting her." Holding the boy and dog so tightly that the puppy was squirming.

John felt the pain from the memory of her pale skin blemished by bruises from the beating she had taken. The hurt was deep within him because he failed to stop it.

"Sometimes Jared, people promise things that they can't keep. I love your mommy. I love you, and it hurts me when you or your mom get hurt. All I can say is that I tried to protect her. But I just wasn't able to." The pictures of Chrissy's face and her unconscious body tied to a chair were all too visible.

He dropped his chin to the boy's head and held Jared and Alfie protectively. Chrissy, I am so sorry. Hammond is finished as a politician, and I intend to see to that.

"Will my mommy be home soon?"

"Yes, Jared, you and I will go to the hospital to get her. I am sure she misses you. When you see your mom, you will see bruises on her face, where the bad man hurt her. She needs you to be a big boy and help her get through this. She needs our love and support. Now, let's get some breakfast, then get dressed. Did you sleep well?"

"Yes, but I knew Alfie was waiting for me to wake up because I could hear him making noises."

John had been awake for most of the night with the memories.

"Coffee for me, orange juice for you. Cereal and toast for both of us. Does that sound good?"

"Yes, and I will feed Alfie."

"Sounds good," setting the puppy and Jared down.

Jared ran to the cupboard for the dog food. The puppy at his heels. John watched with pleasure the care Jared was taking, scooping out the measured amount Joel had shown him. His tongue was sticking out as he tried not to spill any as he crossed to Alfie's dish with the measuring cup. John wished this was a permanent home for Jared and Chrissy. But then there was Joel. He sighed and went back to his duty of making breakfast.

After breakfast, they headed upstairs to get dressed. John showered and shaved. He glanced at his tuxedo thrown over the chair, noting it would have to go in for a cleaning. It wasn't the proper attire for rescues in warehouses, but he had no choice. He felt terrible all over again for Chrissy. He was keeping her with him as long as he possibly could to protect her.

Jared kept coming to John. "Is it time to go get mommy yet?" A couple of hours passed, and his question answered. "Yes, it is time to go."

They put Alfie in his kennel, so he didn't tear up the place while they were gone. Alfie loved his lair, curling up and going to sleep.

Jared was in the car like a shot. They stopped at the gift shop to buy flowers for Chrissy. Jared was to give the flowers to her on their return home. They were lying on the back seat when Jared climbed back in after wheeling Chrissy out of the hospital. John ushered Chrissy into the front seat. He was treating her like she was a breakable doll.

Jared was plying Chrissy with questions. John was trying to steer the conversation in another direction.

When they arrived home, Jared was first out of the car with the flowers in his hands. John came around to open Chrissy's door. He reached in, taking her hand to aid her from the vehicle.

Jared smiled. "Mommy, these are for you from John and me," thrusting the flowers into her hands.

"Thank you, Jared. They are lovely," kissing Jared.

"Thank you, John." She looked at him shyly. Jared piped up. "Mommy, you didn't kiss John."

Chrissy and John eyed each other. "You're right." She leaned toward John and gave him a peck on the cheek, blushing prettily, and John grinned.

"Let's get your Mommy into the house. We have to look after her. I think she is still shaky." Chrissy put her free arm around Jared.

Chrissy was placed on the couch in the family room. John was making a fire while Jared put a blanket that John had given him over her legs.

Gretchen came in from the kitchen.

"Chrissy, oh dear, you don't look so good. I will get you a hot cup of tea. That will help fix you up." Chrissy wasn't used to all this attention. Gretchen picked up the flowers to put them in a vase.

When she brought the vase back, Chrissy saw the full beauty of the bouquet. It was tropical flowers of various colors with some rosebuds tucked in amongst the display.

She thanked John and Jared again. Jared insisted on another kiss. "Now, John, Mommy."

John was near the fireplace. "That's all right. Your mom already thanked me."

Chrissy was thankful and disappointed at the same time. When would she be leaving here? She hoped it was soon.

John said as though reading her thoughts, "Chrissy, until I find out that things are safe for you to leave. You will have to stay a while longer. I hope you understand that."

"John, I thought it was over. Why do I need to stay?"

"Until I am positive this business between Delvietti and Hammond has ended, you are not leaving here." He came over to her, leaning over and taking her face tenderly in his hands, grazing the bruises ever so lightly with his fingertips.

"Chrissy, I am so sorry." His eyes were devouring her. Chrissy felt warm all over. She knew she loved this man. But she also knew he was a confirmed bachelor. Besides, there was Joel.

The doorbell rang. Answering the door, Gretchen came back with Max Kelsey. Then she excused herself to get the tea tray.

"Chrissy, how are you?" Max came closer to the couch.

"Max, I am getting better. I am coming to grips with my ordeal." Chrissy smiled weakly at Max.

"Chrissy, I am so sorry we couldn't stop this from happening. Twice now, I have failed you. Laura is furious with me for letting it happen again." Max's expression was sorrowful.

"Stop, please, it was nobody's fault. It happened, and there is no going back. I need to forget. Everyone apologizing is only bringing it all back too clearly." Chrissy placed her hand on Max's hand, squeezing it in forgiveness.

"But the bruises are reminders of our failure."

"I will have to ask Gretchen for makeup to hide them."

"Who was talking about me? I heard my name," said Gretchen, rolling in the tea wagon.

"Gretchen, I was saying that I would have to ask you for makeup to cover my bruises if they didn't stop apologizing."

"Well, this tea will fix you up. Now everyone sit, relax and enjoy my tea cakes. I made them especially for Chrissy." Gretchen was busily pouring tea and handing it out to the men after serving Chrissy, urging the men into chairs near the couch.

John kept looking askingly at Max. Was it to be good news he had to impart? There was a little small talk before Max led the conversation back to Alan Hammond and Delvietti.

"The word is that Hammond was released sporting a broken arm. So, I guess he must have signed the agreement to give up the gambling casino business. Now, I hear talk that Delvietti pressured Hammond into announcing he is dropping out of the race as a pollical candidate. Apparently, Mr. Delvietti is a more powerful man than we gave him credit for."

John looked at Chrissy to see her reaction. She was stunned with what Mr. Delvietti had been able to accomplish with Mr. Hammond. Would John be taking her home now?

Max continued. "Chrissy, I will feel better that you stay here for a while longer. Until Mr. Hammond formally makes his announcement. Don't you agree, John?"

"Yes, I am not letting Chrissy out of my sight until I am positive that it is all over. Rumors are not good enough for me."

John switched the subject before Chrissy could reply and put up some kind of an argument.

"Jared, go get Alfie. I am sure Max would like to meet him."

Jared was off like a shot. Alfie was still in his kennel. He started yipping as he heard Jared's running feet coming his way. Jared bent down and opened the door. Alfie jumped up, trying to reach Jared's face, his tongue making licking motions. Joel had told Jared that he must take Alfie out as soon as he released him from the kennel, so they headed to the terrace. Alfie ran to do his duty, then came back when Jared called. He picked the squiggling puppy up. He raced inside, going directly to Max.

"Well, what do we have here? It looks like a Great Dane."

"No, it is a Cocker Spaniel. He won't be as big as a Great Dane." Joel had shown him many pictures of dogs. Great Dane's looked like small ponies. Cocker spaniels looked like Alfie.

"Are you sure? It looks like it has big paws to me." Taking the puppy from Jared and examining the puppy's paws. "Yup, a Great Dane for sure. Does this puppy have a name?"

"His name is too long, but I call him Alfie. He is a Cocker Spaniel. Joel said he was."

"Well, if Joel says he is a Cocker Spaniel, he must be. Joel must know his mother."

Jared looked at Max for a long minute, then he said, "how would Joel know Alfie's mother?"

"Well, Joel went to pick up the puppy from where it was born, so he must have met the mother."

Again, Jared looked at Max intently for a minute. "But Joel bought the puppy."

"Yes, but the puppy was part of a litter of puppies and was born to a mother dog." The fact appeared to be news to Jared. He would have to ask Joel. Joel only said he had bought a puppy for him.

Max passed the puppy back to Jared. Jared was looking at Alfie differently now. He couldn't fathom leaving his mommy. He would miss her too much. He wished Joel was here so he could ask him.

Max said goodbye to Chrissy and John. "We will not be pressing charges on Delvietti for Hammond's broken arm nor charges on Chrissy's behalf, which is a shame. We can't make it stick with Delvietti's powerful lawyers. But Delvietti has done us a service retiring Hammond from politics. Everything should be finished now." He gave Chrissy a slight bow as he and John left the room.

Chapter Twenty-Four

Joel arrived after dinner. Jared confronted Joel as soon as he arrived. "Why did you take Alfie away from his mother? You said you bought him."

Joel quickly explained how he bought the puppy after the mother had many pups, and children like Jared could take care of them as a puppy friend. Jared was thinking hard about that.

Joel walked over to Chrissy, apologizing again for her injuries. She accepted his kisses on her bruises. Joel explained to Jared that he was kissing her bruises away. Jared easily recognized the bruises were still there and said so.

"Yeah, but now they don't hurt as much, do they, Chrissy?" Her murmur no, they didn't hurt as much was observed by John. Joel loved Chrissy. She must reciprocate his feelings the way she so naturally accepted his kisses.

When Joel kissed her, she deemed it more like a brotherly kiss. Indeed, not the response she had with John.

John suggested watching cartoons to Jared. They all went into the family room. Jared was still trying to digest what Joel had said about dog mothers. They had so many puppies at one time that she was willing to give one to a boy like Jared to look after. Jared looked at Alfie, who was sleeping in his lap. He raised his eyes to his mother. He could never leave his mommy. Not even if there was someone else to look after him. He would have to love Alfie more so Alfie wouldn't miss his mother.

Chrissy and Joel were sitting on the couch. John was sitting in a nearby chair. He was getting ready to excuse himself to give Joel and Chrissy time together. A news bulletin interrupted the program they were watching.

The face was that of Alan Hammond, who had his right arm in a sling supporting a cast. Alan was saying. "Due to extenuating circumstances, I have to say that I am dropping out of the election with deep sadness. I will no longer be a running candidate representing this area, and I have resigned from my Senate seat. I want to thank all the people who have supported me over the years." He waved to the crowd as the picture faded out.

The adults sat digesting the news bulletin.

Chrissy said, "I guess it is officially over," stealing a look at John.

Joel replied, "Hammond deserves to be out of the race. Chrissy, you will be free now."

John appeared not to notice, instead apologizing for leaving them, indicating that he had some business to attend.

After the program was over, Joel helped Chrissy put Jared to bed, reading him a bedtime story. She sat on the other side of Jared, watching him.

She was so lucky to have Jared. She would never tell John, Joel or Jared that Mr. Delvietti had promised Hammond if he didn't cooperate, that he would kill Chrissy. She didn't know if that was just a threat or not. But she was just glad to be rescued before she found out. Fear set in for a moment, shattering her a bit until she closed off her mind.

When the story finished, she kissed Jared, giving him a squeezing hug. Jared accepted it joyfully.

Chrissy and Joel left after shutting off the light. Neither were aware of how Alfie separated from his mommy was affecting Jared. He felt sad. Poor Alfie would never have his mother's kiss. Jared sneaked out of bed to cover Alfie, adding a pat and a kiss.

Instead of TV, Joel and Chrissy sat talking. Joel remarked, "you will be free to go home now, I guess." Will that work in his favor?

"Yes, I am surprised John didn't remark on the news," commended Chrissy.

"Yes, I thought that too."

Chrissy inquired about Joel's life. Something that they had not discussed before now. She told Joel about her business and how she felt she had lost most of her clients due to her absence. Her home life and Jared's would be so different now. Both avoided talking about the previous night's ordeal. Neither broached the subject of their relationship, for which Chrissy was thankful.

Joel made an early departure after John returned to join them.

Chrissy saw Joel to the door. He kissed her on the lips lightly then on her forehead. Chrissy didn't seem to respond. Joel had been trying all evening to get a clue of Chrissy's feelings for him. But he was unable to detect anything positive. All he knew was that John was in love with Chrissy. But she was almost distant towards John, almost hostile, at times.

Maybe Chrissy wasn't ready to show her emotions since her traumatic experience. As Joel got to his car, he was trying to puzzle it through. But he didn't have a conclusion by the time he drove away.

John spoke to Chrissy. "Do you think you would like an early night? You have had quite a time lately."

"Yes, perhaps you're right. I think I will make my way to bed." She stared at John. He was avoiding looking at her. John's guilt was still evident. Perhaps it would help remove his guilt if she went home. Chrissy and Jared could leave tomorrow. She would try salvaging her Interior Decorator business. What was left of it? She would have to build it up again. Her livelihood depended on it.

How long had it taken for her to earn her reputation? Two years she thought. Hopefully, this time it would only take a year because she was no longer an unknown. Businesses could grow fast by word of mouth endorsements.

John was watching Chrissy. What was she thinking? Does she hate me for the beating she took for Hammond? Why couldn't I stop it from happening? She looks more delicate than usual. How can I ever make this up to her? He remembered going into that room and seeing her tied up in the chair, unconscious. His stomach clenched again. The memory was still too vivid.

"Chrissy, do you need help to get upstairs?" John inquired quietly, wanting to assist her.

"John, I am capable of managing the stairs. It is my head that hurts. I will be all right if I hold onto the railing."

He wanted to pull her into his arms, but he knew that she would probably reject him. He turned and walked back to his sanctuary.

Since Jared and Chrissy had come, he had finally felt more at home in this place. But he knew they would be leaving now.

When John finally walked up the stairs to bed, the sadness encompassed him. It was two o'clock, and he didn't think he would get much sleep. The end would be soon. He had seen it in Chrissy's eyes. The way she looked at him.

He did his nightly check on Jared. Jared's curled up body enclosed the puppy. John went over to pick Alfie up, carrying him to his bed and covered him. Alfie let out a couple of whimpers then curled more tightly in a ball.

John's stomach tightened. How could he live here missing Jared and Alfie and this nightly ritual? He settled the cover around Jared carefully. Then leaned over and kissed his cheek. He would miss this nightly routine once Jared left.

He walked further down the hall, glancing at the closed door. Once Chrissy left, would he hear from her? His steps continued on their way to his bedroom.

Maybe it was time to go and see his parents in England. How long had it been? At least two years or more. Was he that busy in his life that he couldn't take time to see them? They offered to come here, but he had put them off each time they mentioned that. Well, he would put it off no longer. He would phone his parents tomorrow just to hear their voices, to help alleviate his soon loneliness.

His lagging steps finally reached his bedroom door when he heard a noise from Chrissy's room. He turned back. Was she all right? Should he go see? He stood there, listening. Again, he turned around to enter his room.

There was another sound Chrissy must be having a dream. Did he go to her, or would she come out of the nightmare on her own? Maybe he could just peek in on her. Before he could finish his argument with himself, Chrissy gave a terrible scream. John was down the hall like a shot.

Racing through the door, he saw she was wrestling with the covers as though she was trying to cower away from someone. Her head was going back and forth on the pillow. Another scream emitted from her.

In seconds, John was on the bed with Chrissy in his arms.

"Chrissy, wake up. I have you. You are safe. No one will ever hurt you again. Chrissy, wake up." John was rocking her and holding her close against his chest. John was raining kisses on her forehead and temple. The nightmare still had Chrissy in its clutches.

"Chrissy, wake up. You are in my arms. You are safe. They will never get you again. Please, Chrissy, wake up." She could hear his voice pleading with her to wake up. Her eyes opened and closed, then opened. She could see the outline of John's head in the pale light from the moon. She felt safe as John held her. She sunk into him, riveting herself into his closeness. Her body was shaking from the trauma of the nightmare of Mr. Delvietti's threat of death if Hammond didn't sign. He had lifted a gun and was going to shoot her. Her thoughts were not for herself but Jared. He would be alone for the rest of his life. She had to avoid the bullet.

John's voice penetrated her horror.

"Chrissy, you are safe. You are here in my arms. No one will harm you ever again." How could he stop her shivering?

John lifted the covers and got in beside her, pulling her against his hard body. Chrissy's mind was still paralyzed, but her body reacted to the warmth. She burrowed against him until he felt every curve of her body. John crooned to her. Slowly ever so slowly, the shaking stopped. She was lying with her head on his shoulder, enclosed in his arms.

He kissed her temple, putting his hand up to caress her cheek. His fingers came away wet with tears.

He slowly felt the tension go out of her body. She whimpered once. Then her breathing settled into a slow rhythm of sleep. She was out of the nightmare. He would just hold her a while longer to make sure it didn't come back.

"Mommy and John, why are you in bed together? Is mommy okay, or is she hurting again?"

John opened his eyes instantly, hearing Jared's voice. Chrissy reacted more slowly, seeing the room sprayed in sunlight. Jared's face with Alfie held against his cheek came into view. She sat up only to find her legs entwined with John's legs.

"John?" Both were fumbling around to extract each other's limbs.

"Good morning, Jared," Chrissy said quietly.

"Jared has Alfie been out yet?" queried John, hoping to distract him.

"Yes. What are you doing in mommy's bed?" John was so grateful he hadn't made it into his bedroom and undressed before Chrissy had her nightmare. Except he must've kicked off his shoes at some point.

"Your mother had a bad dream. You know how your mommy holds you when you have a bad dream. Well, I was holding your mom for the same reason."

"But, mommy doesn't climb into bed with me once I wake up."

Chrissy was sitting on the far side of the bed with the covers up to her neck. John was perched on the edge of the bed, trying to locate his shoes with his feet and explaining things to Jared.

"Jared, your mother has been through some horrible times. She just needs someone to hold on to her and make her feel safe."

"But only a daddy gets in bed with a mommy."

John couldn't look at Chrissy. He had slipped into his shoes and was standing beside the bed. He put a hand on Jared's shoulder, frantically thinking of what to say next.

"Jared, I know I am not your daddy. But your mom needed someone and because she has no daddy. I had to step in to keep her safe."

"Does that mean you are going to be my daddy now?"

Chrissy finally came out of her shock of finding John tangled with her in bed.

"Jared, John is not your daddy. No one can replace your father unless I marry again."

"But John was in your bed like a daddy." Jared was persistent.

"Only because I had a bad dream, so it doesn't count," Chrissy said firmly, sending a glare John's way. What was he doing in my bed? Then the nightmare came back vividly, and she closed off her anger.

John was trying to defuse the situation and invited Jared and Alfie to join him for breakfast. Jared was distracted, he put Alfie down, and he left the room at a run, yelling. "C'mon, Alfie." He liked it when John made breakfast. He made it fun. Alfie was yipping and following after Jared's running feet.

John looked at Chrissy sheepishly.

"Sorry, I didn't mean to fall asleep. I certainly intended to be out of here before morning. I mean, I was going to leave as soon as you fell back to sleep." Chrissy was still glaring at him, wishing he would leave. She didn't want to discuss it until she had her clothes on. She felt so vulnerable in her frothy nightie.

He lamely said, "I'll go get Jared's breakfast." He headed out of the room. They would have to discuss this later.

Jared was still too taken up with finding John in his mother's bed. Jared innocently asked, "John, are you going to be my new daddy?"

The question hit John as soon as he entered the kitchen. He realized then that Jared was becoming obsessed with the idea.

"Pancakes or scrambled eggs for breakfast?"

"Pancakes, please. When can I call you daddy?"

John went to the cupboard and fridge to get the ingredients for pancakes. While he frantically wondered how he was going to handle this latest dilemma. How to explain about being found in his mother's bed when it was without her permission? Let alone as a daddy to be.

"Did you feed Alfie?" That may distract him.

"Yes, I fed Alfie. Can't you see he is eating?" Jared pointed over at Alfie. "When can I call you daddy?"

So much for distractions. I better do this head-on. "Jared, you can't call me daddy until your mommy and I marry. And . . ."

Chrissy entered the room before John could finish.

"Mommy, when are you and John getting married?" Chrissy's eyes flew from her son to John.

"What is going on here?"

"Mommy, John said I couldn't call him daddy until you and he married. So, I want to know when you are getting married?"

"Married?" Chrissy's eyes pinned on John with an intense stare. "Why would you tell Jared we are getting married?"

"I tried to explain that I would have to be married to you before he could call me daddy. Not that we were actually getting married." His voice had a request for understanding.

"See, mommy, John said you were getting married. When? I want John for my daddy."

"Jared, John didn't explain himself well. We are not getting married."

"Why was he in your bed then?"

"I believe we have already had this conversation. However, I will explain it again." Chrissy was throwing daggers at John. "Mommy was having a bad dream, and John helped me out of the bad dream by comforting me. Like I comfort you out of a bad dream."

"But you don't sleep with me." Jared wasn't about to be put off. He wanted John as his daddy. John was making pancakes as though that was his only goal in life. He was avoiding the looks Chrissy must be shooting his way.

"John wasn't sleeping with me. He was comforting me."

"But I stood watching you. You were both sound asleep for a while before I talked to you."

Chrissy was secretly saying to herself, why was Jared at the age when 'WHY' was so important?

"John had his clothes on, so he must have just sat on the bed."

"But he had the covers over him, and your arms and legs were tangled when you lifted the covers."

"Jared, I know it looked like John was sleeping with me, but that wasn't really what was happening. Now, you must accept my words on that." Chrissy was helping to get breakfast on the table. Food was the only way to distract Jared.

"Would you like maple syrup or blueberry syrup, Jared?"

"Maple syrup. Why can't you marry John so he can be my daddy?"

"Jared, this has gone on long enough. John and I are not getting married. You cannot call him daddy. Do you understand?"

"No." Jared was holding onto his hopes.

Chrissy looked at John in exasperation.

"Why were you in my bed?" John was caught, but he didn't want to talk about it in front of Jared. During all the talking or rather misunderstanding, John had accumulated a sizable number of pancakes ready for consumption.

"Let's drop the subject and eat," John said brightly, carrying the precariously high pile of pancakes to the table. "Jared, how many can you eat? Six?"

"Start him off with two." Chrissy interposed before Jared could reply. John plopped two pancakes on Jared's plate. Four on Chrissy's and four on his own before Chrissy could say more on the taboo subject.

Jared was industriously piling butter and syrup on his pancakes. Chrissy was still glaring at John.

"Not now, darling. Just eat up. We have lots of pancakes to get through." John said blithely.

"Don't, darling me. My name is Chrissy to you." Her no-nonsense manner brooked no argument, not in front of Jared. How was he going to worm his way out of this one?

Chapter Twenty-Five

Alan Hammond was no longer running for Member of Parliament or allowed to remain a Senator, so he had to bury his anger by hiding in his country home. But he was still contemplating having Chrissy Lambert in his life.

If he couldn't have his political career, he would still have his law practice. He wanted Chrissy as his wife and hostess.

The problem was how to go about that. John Taylor was protecting her. She was even living in his home for added protection since Delvietti had kidnapped her.

Delvietti would have to be dealt with too. Mr. Delvietti was a powerful man, but Alan was not one to let others ruin his life. He would use the law, of which he was a master, to shut Mr. Delvietti down. Alan had a lot of influential friends in high places. He intended to make use of those who owed him favors.

Now back to Chrissy Lambert. It is irrelevant that she was supposedly marrying John Taylor. Alan figured that was only a ruse because she resided in his home.

"Geoffrey, where does John Taylor live? He must have been on the guestlist for the Gala, find out from Rita. Then I want you to get Rita to send three dozen roses to Mrs. Lambert at John Taylor's place. Then I want you to deliver an invitation to Mrs. Lambert and John at his home."

Geoffrey took off to make the telephone call to Mr. Hammond's secretary, Rita. He passed on the information regarding the three dozen roses, and obtained John Taylor's address.

He returned to the living room where Mr. Hammond was enjoying a cigar in front of the fireplace. Geoffrey informed him that Rita dispensed the flowers, and he had John Taylor's address.

"Geoffrey, there are some pre-printed invitations to my city home. Bring one of them here with an envelope. I will fill in the information for their dinner to be on the 14th. Then arrange for a special dinner that night from that restaurant we used three months ago. Tell Antonio that it is an intimate dinner for three. He will know what best to serve and the wine." Alan dismissed Geoffrey. He sat back, enjoying his cigar and the fire. He visualized Chrissy reclining on the chair across from him. Her beauty reflected in the firelight, causing glowing highlights of flame in her flowing red tresses. He had to make her his wife.

Alan had a new goal in life, and his latest goal would not be thwart.

* * *

John had been avoiding Chrissy and their talk regarding him in Chrissy's bed. He had mainly spent the day in Jared's company or installed in his study with the door closed as a deterrent. Every time Chrissy knocked on the door, he talked out loud as though on an overseas call.

John didn't mean to fall asleep in her bed. But John knew that Chrissy wanted answers. The answer John would give wasn't what Chrissy wanted to hear. When he had the opportunity to hold her, he just couldn't let go. He fell asleep tired from lack of sleep lately. How could he tell her that?

Chrissy was getting angrier by the minute. She would just give him another twenty minutes. Then she was going to invade his private call. She would make him hang up to talk to her. She wanted an answer. Why was he in her bed when Jared woke them up?

Then Chrissy remembered the tangle of arms and legs. She had felt so rested and relaxed entwined with him. How could that be?

The front doorbell sounded. Chrissy walked to the door, not wanting Jared to answer it.

Without thinking of the consequences, she yanked the door open. It was Mr. Boots. She quickly slammed the door, but Geoffrey had stuck out his big booted foot, and the door twanged against it.

"Miss Lambert, I mean you no harm. I have something for you." Geoffrey eased the door open, sticking his hand out with the envelope in it. He smiled at her. She ignored his extended hand.

"Miss Lambert, I have an invitation for you, that is all. Please take it." Again, he extended his arm, indicating that she should take the envelope. Chrissy was holding back when John appeared.

"Geoffrey, what are you doing here?"

"Mr. Hammond asked me to deliver this invitation to Miss Lambert." John reached for the envelope.

"I'll take it, but don't count on a reply." He stepped back, keeping Chrissy behind him. "Please remove your foot. You have delivered your message."

John noticed a florist truck in front of the house. There was a messenger with an armful of boxes walking up the steps. Why would anyone be sending flowers?

Geoffrey stepped aside as the florist delivery man arrived on the veranda.

"Delivery for Miss Lambert."

John relieved the boxes off him, saying, "thank you." Promptly shutting the door.

"Chrissy, who would be sending you flowers?"

"I don't know. I appreciate the flowers. But I can't think of anyone that would send them to me." Taking one of the boxes from John and opening it.

"Yellow roses, and there is a card." Chrissy opened the card. She almost dropped it in her repugnance. "It is from Alan Hammond."

John held up the envelope from Geoffrey. "Here, open this one."

Chrissy obeyed. "It is an invitation for the two of us to attend a dinner at Mr. Hammond's city home. John, what is going on here? How dare he approach me after being tortured because he wouldn't cooperate." The horror came back to her. She dropped the invitation and the box of roses, stepping away with disgust. John dropped the boxes to put his arms around Chrissy.

"It is all right. I won't let you be hurt ever again."

Chrissy put her head on John's chest. He clamped his arms tightly around her. "Chrissy, he can't get to you. You are staying here for that reason. I thought it was over, but apparently, it isn't."

"How dare he invite us to dinner." Chrissy's voice reflected her distaste. John agreed, but then he thought that maybe they needed to accept the invitation to end this once and for all. He said as much to Chrissy

"But, John, I couldn't go there. You know how I feel about him. He gives me the creeps."

"Chrissy, we have to end this once and for all. We have to show him you are not available. Otherwise, he will keep trying."

"How can I show him I am unavailable?"

"We already started the charade the night of the Gala, remember. We pretended that we were engaged. Well, we will carry it one step further and show up with an engagement ring on your finger. We will invite him to our wedding."

"But, John, there is no ring. We aren't getting married."

"Well, he doesn't need to know that. I doubt he will feel the need to show up at our wedding."

"John, what if he does? Then he will know we were lying."

"Well then we will have to have a mock wedding, won't we? We can easily arrange that. Would you consider it if it meant getting rid of Alan Hammond completely? It would be worth the effort, I think."

"Fine for you to say, John, but it is me that creep is after." Chrissy gathered up the boxes and headed to the back of the house to throw them out. She tried stuffing them in the garbage can, but they didn't fit. She kept trying. John wanted to laugh, but he didn't dare.

"Chrissy, leave those. Gretchen will take care of them. She loves flowers, let her take them. It isn't the fault of the roses that we don't like the donor."

John drew her back into the house. "Gretchen comes tomorrow. They should be all right until then, as the air is crisp."

"Let's read the invitation. What did it say?" John went back into the hall to get the invitation Chrissy dropped on the floor.

MRS. CHRISSY LAMBERT
AND
MR. JOHN TAYLOR

ARE
INVITED TO DINNER
SATURDAY, AUGUST 14, 1999 AT 7:00 PM
555 ROYALTON AVE S.W.
MOUNT ROYAL
CALGARY AB
RSVP 555-9292

"Well, I think we should reply with a yes. I will pick up the ring tomorrow. We can buy you a new dress, or you can use the other dress of my mother's you tried on, which would you prefer?"

"John, I ruined your mother's beautiful dress. How can you offer me another?"

"Okay, we will go out and buy you one when we go for your ring. We must plan our wedding date. When would you like to get married? The wedding shouldn't be too far in the future if we want to deter Mr. Hammond? Do you?"

"Planning a wedding day is that necessary?"

"Yes, if we want to convince Hammond that we are serious. Otherwise, we will always be wondering if he will kidnap you again." She shuddered. It was far from a fun experience.

John declared, "okay if I make it for a month? How does a September wedding sound?"

"September will be fine. It is only a mock wedding. I can handle that." Chrissy nodded her head. "How much of a mock wedding will we be having?"

John thought quickly. "We will hold it in the garden. We will need guests. We won't be able to tell them ahead of time that it is only a mock wedding. Someone might let the cat out of the bag, agreed?"

"I don't know, John, that is hardly fair to my family and friends."

"It can't be helped. We will have to set everybody straight later. The minister won't be real. We can hire an actor to play the part. We will have a catered dinner in the garden if the weather holds."

"John, isn't that going to be a bit much?"

"Not if we want to convince Alan Hammond totally. Wait until Max hears this." John laughed. "Max will be in his glory, making remarks about the confirmed bachelor taking a fall."

"Max may be in his glory, but I am not, so don't laugh. I don't want to do this. I feel it is a lot to do just to prove a point. How can you expect me to sit at his table and look at him without remembering that night? John, you are asking too much of me."

"I know, but I will be with you. We will make excuses about why we have to leave early. I would do anything if I could spare you this. But we can't have Alan waiting until you are alone and capturing you again. We have to prove you are mine."

John understood her refusal, but he felt Hammond wouldn't give up. "Please, Chrissy. You know I wouldn't ask this of you if we could handle this any other way. Do you want this fear hanging over your head forever?"

"You make it sound easy, but I still have to sit through dinner with him. I won't be able to eat a thing."

"Fine, don't eat, just go through the motions. I don't expect you to be able to handle a conversation, so leave that to me. But the odd darling or sweetheart wouldn't go amiss." John grinned at her. Chrissy seared him with a withering look. Walking away from John, she entered the kitchen. She had to make dinner for Jared.

John went to the study to call Hammond. He didn't elaborate. He just said that they would be there.

Jared's bedtime ritual became John's because Chrissy disappeared to her room as soon as she finished the dinner dishes.

* * *

The next day they all piled into John's car. First stop, a jewelry store recommended during their surveillance duties in John's cop days by Max. He mentioned this particular reliable jeweler would take back any jewelry if a woman refused.

It was a small store but stocked in glitter. John dragged Chrissy in with Jared's help, along with her protests. She wanted John to pick out just any old ring as it was returnable anyway. A young lady was serving a young couple. They were all atwitter over several rings that she was showing them.

A man in a grey suit with a wine tie came from the back of the store. He had a charming air about him. "Yes, may I help you, sir?"

"Yes, my young lady and I are looking for a certain ring to express my love for her." John still had a firm grip on her like he expected her to run if he let go.

Jared was looking at some jewels in a case. "These look nice, John."

"No, I think we need something extra special," looking directly at the jeweler.

"Yes, won't you come to my office? I have just the ring you probably have in mind." John thought this was the best way to handle Chrissy so she wouldn't balk. "I am sure you have as I don't see anything here similar to what I have in mind."

The jeweler opened the gate and directed them through to an office on the right. There was an elaborate lighting system centered on the narrow desk, intricately designed in rich mahogany. The chairs in front were of the same design. It oozed authentic heritage.

Chrissy fell in love with the desk and chairs. She would have loved to get her hands on a set like that. She perked up, devouring it with her eyes. John saw her face animated with interest. He felt it was safe to let go now.

"John, this is beautiful. I think it would be perfect in your study." Chrissy ran her hand over the desk, marred only by a black velvet pad in the center.

"Chrissy, this desk isn't big enough. I quite like the desk I already have. There is room to spread out."

"But, John, look at the design of this. The maker made this with talented hands. You can see it." Chrissy was running her hand over the wood with a wistful look.

The jeweler entered the room with a covered tray.

"Please, have a seat. I believe this tray may hold what you desire." Suddenly noticing Chrissy's interest in his desk and chairs.

"The desk and chairs were a real find, when I was at an estate auction with my aunt. She was looking for a curio cabinet that would match her furnishings. My aunt got her Curio cabinet, and I picked up the desk and chairs. Now, shall we pick a ring for the lovely lady?" John lifted Jared on his knee.

The jeweler flipped back the cover over the tray with a flourish.

The rings sparkled in rainbow hues. Jared gave off a big 'OH!' Chrissy just stared. John looked pleased.

One ring stood out amongst the dozen rings displayed there, and it was part of a pair. The wedding band was encircling the diamonds in the other ring. One large and three smaller diamonds in a triangle shape on the engagement ring.

The other rings were fascinating and of various sizes and designs. But John could only see the first pair as binding love. The way they were united together.

The jeweler watched John and knew his choice instantly, so his gaze turned to the young lady. "Is there one, in particular, I can show you?"

Chrissy was studying the rings. Some were gawdy large diamonds and three smaller rings more in a taste Chrissy could appreciate, but the pair in the center was fascinating. It was the only pair joined like that.

Her eyes strayed to that ring. Then away as though she wasn't interested in any of the rings displayed there, running her eyes over them rather quickly. The jeweler was pointing to some of the settings, explaining their size and the quality of diamonds. But Chrissy noticed he skipped all around but never touched the pair in the center. John was watching Chrissy. He knew that the jeweler had picked up on his interest in the 'au pair.'

The jeweler stopped talking.

"You didn't mention the rings in the center. Are they not for sale?"

John's heart lurched. Smart man, he had her interest now.

"The gentleman expressed an engagement ring. These rings are a set that cannot be separated. This set has a quality diamond of 2.5 carats. The diamonds in the triangle are one carat each. The center diamond is not as large as others, but the entwined rings' intricate design makes up for the size. Let me try it on your finger."

John interrupted.

"No, let me try them on her finger," putting out his hand quickly. The jeweler placed the ring set in John's hand.

The salesman said, "some people are superstitious and don't like to try on the wedding band ahead of time. Can I separate them for you?"

John had picked up Chrissy's left hand. "No, I think these rings should not be separated at this point. Don't you, Chrissy?" John eased the ring on her ring finger. Chrissy watched the ring slip comfortably in place as though it belonged there. She was watching the diamonds winking at her, such a beautiful setting. John lifted her hand as if to get a closer look. But continued the motion and kissed her finger just by the ring.

"With this ring, I give you my love, and when we marry our lives will fit perfectly together as these rings." John's voice was solemn. Chrissy's eyes had followed John's action and speech as though in a trance. Why was he acting like a serious lover? These rings were only a temporary situation. Chrissy finally lifted her eyes to John's. There was love shining in his eyes. She had no idea that he could be such a great actor.

John never took his eyes off Chrissy. "We will take the au pair." Not even inquiring into the price. John just knew he wanted the rings and her. There would be nothing mock about the ceremony. He had a month to convince her.

He pulled out his gold card and handed it to the jeweler. Then he removed the rings to separate them, to place the diamond on Chrissy's finger. With a smile he was passing the wedding ring to the jeweler for a box.

Chrissy was speechless. This had to be an illusion. Jared's comment drew her back.

"Does that mean I can call you daddy now?" John was still watching Chrissy.

As this was to be a fake marriage, Chrissy held her comment for when they were alone. Her eyes dropped to the ring on her finger. It looked lonely without its mate like she felt without John in her life. Where did that thought come from? This is a mock wedding for Mr. Hammond's benefit only.

Chrissy's thumb was playing with the ring on her finger to make the ring feel real to her. She was engaged to be married.

The jeweler came back into the room, giving John the credit card receipt to sign. John barely looked at it, just signed. Then he accepted the ring box of black velvet, enclosing it into his palm with a thank you.

The next stop was for a dress. John and Jared sat on a loveseat of brocade, and Jared gazed around with interest. When Chrissy appeared with a dress on, John would shake his head 'no.' The couturier came with another dress for her perusal. John finally got up and started looking through the merchandise himself. The couturier followed him around, watching his eyes alight on a fabulous luminous dress in a reflective grey. It was a cascade of shooting rays under the lighting.

"This one, and it has to be her size because this dress was made for her." John's positive comment brooked no argument.

"But the price . . ."

"This one." John turned and walked to the couch.

The woman rushed the creation into the dressing room. Chrissy was ready to leave the room with yet another dress, but the couturier waved her back. "Monsieur wishes this one for you."

Chrissy went to pick up the price tag, but the woman snipped it off expertly. Chrissy knew it was beyond her pocketbook. Two ladies were undressing her while Madam was preparing the dress to slide over her head, melding it to her body. Another lady had swept her hair back and pinned it up until it fell invitingly around her face in wisps of curls. Chrissy wanted to see herself in the mirror. But Madam swept her out the door and into John's view.

Jared's whisper. "Mommy, you are glowing." Chrissy looked down. A cascading array of colors lit the dress.

She missed John's look of pure love. *This dress would be for her wedding*. The dress was too perfect for wasting on Hammond. One of his mother's dresses would have to do for the dinner. This was the dress he wanted when Chrissy became his wife in September.

"John, this is too much for just a dinner." She was wanting to keep the dress but knew it wasn't practical. Nor in her price range, the way madam snipped the price tag.

John ignored Chrissy after he gave her a caring look then turned to Madam. "The dress is perfect."

Chrissy was ushered out of the room. John handed Madam his

gold card.

Chrissy came back dressed in her own clothes. "John, I am not buying that ridiculous creation. Now, let's go somewhere else for something more practical." She grabbed Jared's hand and headed for the door.

"But, Mommy, John already bought it."

Chrissy whipped around. "Well, John, un-buy it. I will not wear that dress."

"Fine, then don't," John said breezily. He signed his signature. Then lifted the dress box and passed Chrissy on the way out of the store. Jared stepped out the door, right on his heels. Jared wanted the dress for his mommy too.

Chrissy realized it was senseless to stand there. John was not about to come back. She stamped her foot and took off after him. All the salesladies were sweetly saying goodbye and good luck. That dress was a significant bonus in sales for them all.

Chrissy caught up to John and Jared.

"I won't wear that dress, John. Do you hear me? I won't wear that dress to the dinner party." Everyone within hearing was watching Chrissy and John. He was walking along casually, as though there was nothing untoward going on. Jared was holding John's hand. John gave him a conspirator's squeeze and a wink as Jared looked up at him.

"Fine, Chrissy, don't wear it. Wear one of the dresses in the cupboard." He didn't use the word mother as too many people were listening to Chrissy's raised voice.

"I will," Chrissy replied with her nose in the air. She whipped past him in her fury to get to the car and away from the attention of her audience.

She went to open the car door yanking at it in her anger. The door was locked. Chrissy stumbled back, and the momentum made her slip, only to recover herself by holding firmly onto the door handle. She straightened. After John unlocked the door, she calmly got in the car as though nothing had happened. Her manner was so dramatic that her audience clapped at her performance. John grinned, saluted the crowd, and got into the car.

Chrissy ignored him, instructing Jared to buckle up. She refused to acknowledge the cheering crowd as they drove into traffic.

Chapter Twenty-Six

John cast a few glances her way. Chrissy was staring out the car window. She was out of the car and into the house before John could turn off the engine.

Gretchen was vacuuming the hall. She quickly stopped. "Something wrong, Miss Chrissy?"

"I am personally going to kill John after I get my anger under control."

"That bad, eh?"

"Yes, do you happen to have a gun?"

"No, but I have it on good authority that some of John's friends do." Gretchen was trying not to laugh. This girl was sure beautiful and was a real spitfire when worked up.

John and Jared appeared.

"Well, John, what did you do this time? She is looking for a gun." Chrissy headed out of the hall as soon as Gretchen spoke to John.

"Sorry, but I only carry a knife." John's voice was full of laughter. Chrissy's anger did not perturb him.

Gretchen sighed in relief. John, evidently, had things under control.

"She sure is something when she is angry, isn't she?" Gretchen said in delight, hoping John had noticed, giving him a hint if he hadn't.

"Oh, yes. Chrissy collected quite an audience. She had them totally engrossed with her performance. Isn't she a beauty?" John was openly admiring in his speech.

"Jared, go find your mama and try to calm her down before she finds a gun."

"A gun! She wouldn't shoot you, would she?" Jared said in awe.

"No, Jared, but she is pretty angry at my highhanded attitude."

"What is highi ... itoo?" Struggling over the words.

"The fact that I insisted on buying the dress against her wishes."

"But, John, she was so beautiful in the dress."

"I know, Jared. She will wear that dress, but not for Alan's dinner. I have other plans for that particular dress, believe me." John was grinning broader than ever.

Chrissy came storming back.

"Furthermore, I am leaving this house after dinner." She stood with her hands on her hips, defying him to argue. When John continued to smile broadly, she said, "come, Jared, we will go outside and play away from this . . . this . . ." She grabbed Jared's hand and dragged him away.

John couldn't help it. He laughed out loud. Turning to Gretchen, he said, "Boy, that is one rampaging lady." He knew Chrissy recognized it wasn't safe to leave.

"Do you know this house hasn't been this alive in a very long time?" Gretchen was chuckling too, as she went back to her vacuuming.

* * *

All Saturday, Chrissy was jumpy and unsettled. She did not want to go to dinner. The very thought of Mr. Hammond being anywhere near her gave her the creeps, and certainly not in that creation John had bought.

They had a distant truce ever since the afternoon of the dress purchase. John came into the room, Chrissy left. Meal conversation passed through Jared. Jared wasn't quite old enough to pick up on how to avoid the situation. John kept reassuring him in private that everything would be okay between them.

Time to get ready for the dreaded dinner. Chrissy was sitting watching a blank television screen, glaring and muttering.

Jared appeared at her side, patting her hand. "Mommy, it will be all right. John said it would. He said it is time to get dressed. He made me a cheese omelet for supper. He let me put my dishes in the dishwasher by myself."

Chrissy was taking her own sweet time about complying. She intended to make a trendy statement on being really late.

After another half hour, John showed up at the door to the family room. "Chrissy, tonight is important if we want to end this. You want to go home, don't you? Then we need to make an appearance tonight. Please, get dressed. I promise we will leave as soon as dinner is over."

Chrissy turned her glare on John.

"John, you know it upsets me being anywhere near that man. I wish we didn't have to go."

"I know, Chrissy, I don't like him touching you either. But we have to get him out of our lives. If there were any other way, I would go that route."

"John, I will not wear that dress."

"Fine, I am sure you will find something suitable in the closet in my parent's room," John said quietly and walked out of the door.

Chrissy arrived an hour later in a simple greeny-blue dress. It was a statement of luxury without sexiness. Her persona for the evening. She had pearl earrings, but her neckline was bare except for the natural draping of the fabric of the dress.

When she passed John, there was no wafting of perfume that Chrissy had worn on the Gala night. Her hair was pulled back in a severe, off the face hairdo. Yet to John, she still radiated sex appeal in her stance of haughtiness.

"I am ready. Let's get this over with." Eyeing John's appearance of elegance in his navy-blue suit. His broad shoulders were showing his masculinity.

John noted her perusal. "Do I pass inspection?"

Chrissy shrugged her shoulders as though he wasn't important.

Chrissy, you are something else. A beauty even dressed down as you think you are. That color on you makes your red hair glow.

"Shall we?" John held out her wrap. "Jared, go to bed when Gretchen tells you. I know she has made a special treat for your bedtime snack."

"John, I always go to bed when Gretchen tells me. Have fun,

Mommy. You look nice but not as nice as you did in that special dress," putting his face up for a kiss.

Chrissy kissed him and hugged him, releasing some of the tightness in stature. But she regained it as soon as she arrived at the front door.

Gretchen had watched the exchange from a distance, knowing that all was not well between them.

John went out of the front door, leaving Chrissy to follow. At least, he hoped she was following. He was dreading this dinner too. He still had to convince Chrissy before they arrived at Hammond's that she will have to put on a performance of being a happily engaged couple.

The car zoomed soundlessly through the black night, mirroring the atmosphere in the car interior's quietness.

John cleared his throat. Then he preceded to say. "If we are going to carry this off, we have to portray a loving, engaged couple. Please, Chrissy, let's make the best of the evening and get the dinner behind us. You and Jared will be going home tomorrow. That knowledge should make you happy, at least."

"All right, John. I will put on the performance of a lifetime, and tomorrow does make me very happy." Chrissy turned a forced smile on him.

"That is all I ask of you." John's smile was pleasant. He felt sure his charm was due to be tested.

* * *

Geoffrey pulled open the door at John's ring. He was relieved to hear other voices coming from the room off to their left. Alan, no doubt, always did things up big. His ego wouldn't allow anything less.

"Good evening, Miss Lambert, Mr. Taylor."

"Good evening, Geoffrey." John slipped Chrissy's wrap off her shoulders, handing it to Geoffrey.

John held out his arm. "Shall we join the others, darling?" When Chrissy slipped her arm through John's, he grasped her hand and brought it to his lips.

She smiled, and the tension eased. She was going to play her part. John was relieved.

Alan came forward as soon as they entered the room, grasping Chrissy's free hand. "It is lovely to see you, my dear. Come join me, and I will introduce you to my other guests."

John did not release Chrissy like Alan was hoping. They advanced to the center of the room. Alan dropped Chrissy's hand, separating from the charming pair.

Alan's introductions to the guest were over. John knew several of the men in attendance. Chrissy smiled gracefully and pressed herself closer to John's side, giving off the aura of a loving couple.

Ralph Bannerman made some remark to John about his female friend in a joking way. John replied in a clear voice. "Ralph, Alan omitted to tell you that Chrissy is my fiancée, and we are being married in a month."

Alan was not wearing a pleasant facial expression at that statement. This was not how his plan for the evening was to progress. Everyone had appeared to stop their conversation as the news flowed throughout the room. "Well, the bachelor has finally consented to join the rest of us in matrimony." Ralph pounded John on the back. "You sure picked a lovely creation, or did she pick you?" Ralph jested.

Alan was getting angrier at this exchange.

"Chrissy was receptive to my charms, weren't you, darling?"

"John certainly has charm. He swept me off my feet," giving John a soft smile and kissed him lightly on his lips. Then she laughed, defusing the situation.

"I see you made the right choice, John." Ralph was consumed by Chrissy's charm.

Conversation resumed as though nothing startling had been announced. John was proud that the gauntlet was thrown down at Alan's feet. Alan was not happy, in the least. It took him a minute to restore his composure. As a seasoned politician, he could transform his face at a moment's notice.

Geoffrey came in to announce that dinner was ready to be served. Alan announced. "It is time to enter the dining room. John, I took the liberty of placing name cards on the table. Would you follow me?" He had maneuvered to stand beside Chrissy during his announcement, putting out his arm in an engaging way, "shall we, my dear?"

Chrissy held back, looking at John.

John put out his arm. "After you, right darling." keeping Chrissy pinned to his side. Alan had no choice but to lead the way. His face was red, but not from embarrassment.

John saw his name on a card at the end of the table. He quickly pocketed it and continued after Alan dropping the name on the table beside the seat Alan was holding for Chrissy. John slipped into the chair as he flicked the other name card to the center of the table in a disguised movement of reaching for the napkin draped in his wine goblet.

Alan bent over Chrissy, whispering, "you are charming tonight, my dear." He glanced over at the chair beside her, seeing that John had installed himself there. His countenance slipped for a second. Then he glanced around all were seated. He turned on his charming smile.

"Thank you, everyone, for coming to share my repast. Gentlemen, for tonight, no business talk, just pleasure." He gave a laugh which didn't quite ring true. He seated himself. The caterers arrived, ready to serve the soup.

John enlisted Chrissy in a conversation about the trip that they were planning the next day. Alan interrupted.

"Mrs. Lambert, may I call you Chrissy? Chrissy, would you like to see my home after dinner? I think you will enjoy the tour. It is considered quite the showplace. It has been chosen for a documentary on stately homes in this area."

"Yes, I am sure John and I would enjoy seeing your lovely home," Chrissy said sweetly.

"I don't think John would care for the tour."

"By all means, I would like to view your grand home. Of course, I will join you both." John picked up Chrissy's hand. "Chrissy and I are interested in all old stately homes, aren't we, darling?"

"Yes, John has a beautiful home too. I have been fortunate to be his guest for the past month." She gave John a wicked smile as though it had an intimate connotation of their relationship.

Alan's stomach tightened in anger. Things were not going as planned, throwing off his appetite. Vera Caplan, who sat on his other side, drew him into a discussion which he could not politely ignore.

Chrissy and John ate the soup with the appreciation of an expert chef. They kept a light conversation going.

When the main course arrived, Alan poured more wine for Chrissy.

He picked up his wine glass and held it out towards Chrissy and said softly, "you are a picture of beauty that never fails to make me want more of your companionship. You, my dear, are beautiful, and I find you very charming."

He sipped his wine after he said, "to you."

Chrissy was smiling a false smile. What now?

John smoothly leaned past her, saying. "Alan, you can see more of Chrissy's charms when you attend our wedding on the 18th of September. You will come, I hope. It is to be a small wedding with intimate friends and family, isn't that right, Chrissy? We would like you to be there, wouldn't we, darling?"

"Of course, Alan. You must attend my nuptial ceremony. John and I would love to see you as part of our close friends." She gave both men a winning smile. "You will come, won't you, Alan?" she finished.

"Yes, I would like that very much," Alan said through clenched teeth. "I didn't know your relationship had advanced to that stage. You should thank me for bringing you two together."

"Did you introduce John to Chrissy? I didn't know that? They make such a sweet couple," interrupted Vera. "Congratulations to you both. I assumed that John was a confirmed bachelor from Ralph's conversation until meeting you, Chrissy."

"Well, with this lovely lady's charm, it was hard not to fall head over heels in love with her." John grinned at Vera. "Eligible bachelors are out of fashion now, I hear."

Alan observed the banter with a grim countenance. He could cheerfully have driven his fist into John's smiling face.

"Chrissy, I accept your invitation to the wedding, but secretly I had hoped it would have been me." Blatantly ogling Chrissy to annoy John. Alan picked up Chrissy's hand and placed a loving kiss in her palm.

Chrissy smiled, but inside she cringed. She wanted to rub her hand on a napkin. She managed to disengage her hand. *Would this dinner ever end?*

John drew Chrissy into a conversation to relieve the tension. "Darling, I have ordered the flowers and cake for the wedding, as we discussed."

Somehow, he had to get out of the private tour of the house. He knew Ralph well enough to rope him and his wife into tagging along when he got the brilliant idea of inviting Vera too.

"Would you and Jack like to join us? We will make it a group tour of this house after dinner? Alan is showing Chrissy and me around." Then John turned to Pamela Wright beside him. "Would you and your husband like to join us too?"

Pamela leaned forward to express her joy to Alan. "Alan, that would be wonderful. I have always wanted to see it. I do admire your home."

Alan was biting his lip. This was getting out of hand.

"Why, of course, Pamela, why don't I invite everyone." Safety in numbers, maybe he could get Chrissy away from John in the milieu. His countenance brightened. This might work out after all.

The servers removed the dishes. Alan clinked his spoon against his wine glass.

"I am going to interrupt dinner with a tour of my home. Dessert and coffee are to be served after the viewing." Everyone was rising in anticipation.

John let Chrissy pass him, but Alan pushed past him before he could follow.

Chrissy looked beseechingly over her shoulder for John. He would have to catch up with her in the hall where it broadened out. Alan had his arm around Chrissy's back, guiding her along, trying to put distance between them and John. But John was very ardent and kept up with them. Stepping in beside Chrissy, when Alan turned to the group to talk about the room they were viewing. Alan eased his arm away from Chrissy, pointing out a chandelier that graced the room. That was all John needed. He efficiently pulled Chrissy back into the group, slipping between the couples towards the back. Alan was still talking, so he couldn't physically stop John.

The rest of the tour went without incident. Being a true diplomat, Alan regaled them with stories of his trophies and valuable artifacts. He took so long that it wasn't unreasonable for John to thank Alan and give him their regrets. They wouldn't be able to stay for dessert due to another commitment. "We previously arranged for Chrissy to see her sister and her husband regarding the dresses for the wedding." He turned to Chrissy and smiled before adding as he turned back to Alan.

"Your invitation will arrive shortly. I hope you plan to attend?" John said with a smile.

"Of course, Cupid has to show up for the nuptials," Alan said ferociously.

Ralph interrupted, "do we get an invitation too?"

"Sorry, Ralph, I didn't know we were intimate friends, or I would have sent you one." John's voice filled with laughter, making it easier for them to slip away.

Geoffrey must have been listening because he held Chrissy's wrap when they neared the front door.

"Thank you, Geoffrey. A splendid evening," said John graciously.

Geoffrey's glaring countenance showed his ire, on his employer's behalf, aware of the evening's fiasco.

John quickly headed Chrissy to the car and escape. The very idea that Alan had touched Chrissy angered him most. What must it have done to Chrissy? She had been tortured because of this man. Thank goodness it was over. He was sorry it had been necessary, but he couldn't take the chance of another kidnapping. Obviously, Alan had not been ready to give up Chrissy, which was all too obvious at the dinner.

"Darling, you were wonderful," John said after they had been driving for a while.

"Drop the darling. There is no audience now." Chrissy was back to being herself. "John, I do want to thank you for saving me back there. He is such a formidable man. I find it difficult to outmaneuver him. I still can't figure out why he wants me the way he does."

John looked at her. She was utterly unaware of her charms.

"Chrissy, it isn't easy to handle a snake like him. We will have to go through with the wedding to make his separation final from you. But you can go home tomorrow if you so desire."

"I do desire. Is it essential to go that far as to have the wedding? I don't like the idea of misleading our guests into believing the wedding is real."

"Yes, with a man like Alan Hammond, it is absolutely necessary. You saw how he was tonight, trying to get you away from me. Alan Hammond can't believe someone wouldn't want him. His ego is such that he thinks he's Mr. Wonderful, and that you, Chrissy, should want him in the same way."

Chrissy fell silent. There was no more conversation between them. Except for a Goodnight as Chrissy headed up the stairs immediately upon their arrival at home. Chrissy and Jared were leaving tomorrow. John was unhappy with that thought.

Chrissy went immediately to shower. She stood in hot water, burning away the recoiling feeling that slimy man had made her feel all evening. How dare Alan touch her that way? Especially after letting her be tortured for his illegal conduct. How dare he even think she would enjoy dinner with him? Let alone get to know him more intimately. She scrubbed her skin until she was bright pink. Then she was able to put the evening behind her.

As Chrissy was getting ready for bed, she wondered why she wasn't happier about going home tomorrow. It was over. She no longer needed protection.

She looked around the room. She had felt so comfortable here. John had never made her feel anything but welcome in his home. He was such a caring man, taking Jared and her in, disrupting his life, and putting his personal life on hold for them. Why was she so angry with him? John deserved her gratitude. But Chrissy knew in her heart that she would miss John for himself.

She got into bed, pulling up the covers. She thought of the night that John had spent in her bed. Jared had been so surprised and felt that it meant John would be his daddy. Jared had really liked the idea. She had to be honest now. Her first reaction at waking tangled in John's limbs was how wonderful it felt.

Her body must've known how right it was too or why had they

both slept so soundly, especially John, who was still entirely dressed except for his shoes

What about Joel? He was a nice man. Except Chrissy knew John meant more to her, and she was leaving tomorrow.

She rolled over, sinking into her pillow. She had no claim on John.

It was a long while before she drifted off to sleep. She heard John come upstairs and check on Jared as he did every night. He seemed to be taking longer tonight. Was he saying his silent goodbye to this nightly duty? Did he wish Jared was part of his life? Straining to listen, had she missed his steps passing her door?

Finally, she heard him. His steps paused outside her door. What was he thinking? Could he care for her as a person rather than just part of a job of protection? Finally, his steps disappeared to his room. He probably left his door open so he could listen in case either of them needed him. She knew that tomorrow would come all too soon, and she truthfully was going to miss this man and being with him in his home.

Chapter Twenty-Seven

John contacted Max at the station. Max said it was a relatively quiet night, so he had time to talk. "What is on your mind, John?" He told Max about the dinner and Hammond's attempt to separate Chrissy from him. "I wish it hadn't been necessary for us to go there. Poor Chrissy must have been cringing inside all evening. To think that slimeball let Chrissy be tortured. Then he has the audacity to think she would ever like him as a man. It just makes my skin crawl every time I think of him touching her." Max could hear the emotion in John's voice.

"John, my man, you have got it bad. So, you fell in love with Chrissy, did you?" Max laughed with a triumphant sound. "You mean to say the mighty bachelor is due to fall?"

"Yes, but Chrissy doesn't know that." John was not the least bit upset with Max's ecstatic laughter.

"What do you mean by that statement? It sounds ominous."

"Well, to make sure Hammond stays out of Chrissy's life. We are engaged and are having a mock wedding in a month on the 18th of September."

"A mock wedding? Engaged? Why a mock wedding?" Max was enjoying this tidbit of information. Wait until Laura hears this.

"Well, that is why I am phoning. I need Laura and your help to pull this off."

Max jumped in, "Is the mock wedding for your benefit or Hammond's? Of course, we will help."

"The truth of the matter is although I set this up to get rid of Hammond, I didn't want to lose Chrissy out of my life. The wedding will be the real thing. Only Chrissy thinks it is a mock wedding."

"What happens when she finds out?"

"Well, I just have to convince her it is the right thing to do or get an annulment. I hope she doesn't insist on that," John said emphatically

"I don't know, John. That might not be such a good idea. You have to tell her. If the wedding is real, then it is complying without consent on her part. You have to tell her." Max, always the law officer. "Now, don't get me wrong. I hope you can pull it off, but isn't that kind of iffy? It just might make her furious."

Max knew his buddy had fallen in love if he would go to such desperate measures.

"That is the chance I am willing to take. I set this in motion tonight by inviting Hammond to the wedding."

"Hammond? Are you crazy?"

"No, but I do love Chrissy. I want to marry her."

"Well, just tell her and forget Hammond."

"I am hoping Hammond doesn't show. I am hoping that when we say our vows that we will both take them seriously. I know I will. Perhaps if I can be convincing enough, she will stay married to me. I intend to tell her that I love her as soon as she makes it to the altar. You should see her dress. She looks like an angel."

"What dress? You bought her a dress?"

"As soon as I saw her in the dress, I knew that was the dress for the wedding. So, I bought the dress for her." He paused, remembering that moment Chrissy floated towards him. The shifting color as she moved, drawing him to her beauty.

"And?"

"She thought I was buying the dress for the dinner when all I could see was her walking towards me at our wedding. Now, I need your help to pull this off. Laura can help with the arrangements, can't she?"

"Oh, yes, she will take great joy in getting this wedding in place. How the mighty have fallen." Max was enjoying this conversation immensely. His friend was soon to be a married man with a family.

"How about Jared?"

"Jared will be okay with the idea. He has wanted to call me Daddy ever since he found me in bed with Chrissy." John knew Max would love this next part, pausing to let that sink in.

"Bed? You and Chrissy?" Max yelled, getting everyone's attention in the police station within hearing distance.

John laughed. "It is not what you think. I was going into my bedroom when I heard a noise. I heard Chrissy scream. It was after her last rescue and her torture for that slimeball Hammond. She had a bad dream, and I ran into her bedroom. I tried to wake her, but she was deep into the nightmare. She was crying and shaking, so I lifted the covers and crawled in to hug her. She never woke up, but she must have come out of the bad dream at the sound of my voice. The next thing I knew, Jared was waking us up wanting to know if he could call me Daddy now because I slept with his mother."

Again, Max was laughing with glee.

"Of course, you must do the honorable thing and marry this lady."

"Max, I was fully clothed. We were both asleep."

But Maiden Chrissy was not aware you were in her bed. Therefore, you compromised her." Max said gloatingly.

"Come off it, this isn't the middle ages. But I am willing to marry the maiden. I just hope she will feel the same when the time comes."

"Aren't you afraid that if you leave it without telling her, in her anger, she will want the annulment? You are taking a chance, aren't you?"

"Not if the wedding vows go the way I intend them to. I fully intend to tell her I love her as soon as she reaches me at the altar. The wedding is to be on my back terrace. There is plenty of room on the lawn for everyone. Hopefully, the day will cooperate weather-wise. I just need Laura to arrange the caterer, the flowers and the guest lists. I will take care of the rest."

"I don't know, John. Won't Chrissy want some say in her wedding? I know Laura would."

John pondered that for a minute. "No, Max. It has to be this way, or I might not win her to my way of thinking. Max, they are going home tomorrow. There is no reason for her to stay any longer." John's voice reflected his sadness at the thought.

"Maybe you're right. Best of luck. I think you are doing the right thing. Of course, I am the best man. How about the maid of honor?"

"I never thought of that. Maybe I will have to enlist her sister in this too. Maybe she could help Laura make the decisions. Perhaps, Laura could be the maid of honor. I will have to give this more thought. Goodnight, Max." John's mind was pondering the latest glitch.

"Goodnight, John. Your nights are numbered. Bachelorhood goodbye." His laughter was still sounding when the connection broke.

John stopped in at Jared's room as usual. Alfie whimpered and wagged his tail. John knew Alfie wanted to be on the bed, curled up with his master. He went over and covered the puppy and gave him a loving pat.

"Tomorrow, you will be going to your new home," John whispered. He went over to the bed and looked down at Jared.

"You will soon be able to call me Daddy. I intend to adopt you so that you will have my name. I love your mommy. I want us to be a family, and I love you too."

John whispered the thought out loud to Jared. He pulled the covers up around him.

He walked to Chrissy's room and paused there listening. Would her nightmare come back? I hope not. Chrissy, I wish you did not want to go home tomorrow. I will be left alone in this mausoleum again. It was bad enough before, but it will be far worse now.

He continued to his bedroom, leaving the door open in case Chrissy had another bad dream.

Chrissy, you will soon be my wife. I just wish we could both be in agreement on a real wedding, not a mock one. Do I broach the subject ahead of the wedding?

* * *

When Chrissy got home, it felt so strange to be there. Jared, she knew, felt the same. He had expressed his disappointment at leaving John's with a sad look.

John had dropped them off but politely refused to come in. Chrissy figured he didn't like goodbyes. He had helped her bring their things to the veranda and then made a hasty escape.

She had been pleased with the life that she had created here and her Interior Decorator business. She had always loved this house with Jared. Now, as she looked around, something was missing. She knew it was John.

Chrissy went upstairs, and she wandered over to the spare bedroom where John had slept. She was standing, looking around when Chrissy noticed a sweater thrown over the back of a chair. She would have to return it to John. She picked it up, smelling his manly scent clinging to the garment, and rubbed it against her cheek.

She shook her head, remembering his hasty retreat with hardly a goodbye.

Jared distracted her, calling her to come and see. "Alfie is running around the backyard as though he has been released from a cage." Jared was laughing. His sadness forgotten at the sight of Alfie's playfulness.

Chrissy went outside to watch Jared and Alfie frolicking there.

* * *

It was two weeks later Chrissy was gathering up clothes for the laundry. She looked at John's sweater with a wistful look. She hadn't heard from him.

Should she call him? Why hasn't he called? Hasn't he missed his sweater? Why didn't she just return it?

Her thoughts were interrupted by the pealing of the phone.

"Hello."

"Chrissy, it is John. How are you?"

"Fine." Just hearing his voice made her heart flutter.

"How are Jared and Alfie?"

"They are having a wonderful time playing in the backyard. Jared doesn't like leaving him to go to school. Nancy comes over to check on Alfie when I need to go out."

"How is your business coming along? Are you getting your clients back?"

"Some, but the fact that I didn't show nor call to cancel appointments made them not receptive to my calling now. I will have to work hard to rebuild my business."

"I am truly sorry, but it was necessary. I am not sorry you had to stay here in my home. Gretchen misses you and Jared. She said to say hi the next time I called. Chrissy, I miss you both and Alfie too."

"I miss you too." Chrissy's heart skipped a beat.

"Chrissy, I walk into a room, and I feel your presence, but you're not there." John's voice had such feeling. *Could he seriously miss me?*

"Chrissy, can I take you out to dinner? Are you still wearing my ring?" Her eyes flew to the ring. She had never even considered taking the ring off.

"Yes, and yes." There was breathlessness in her voice.

"Good." John tried not to sound triumphant. "Will tonight be all right or tomorrow night or both?" He laughed, feeling elated. She was still wearing his ring.

"Tonight? I will have to make arrangements for Nancy to come. If not, could I bring Jared?"

She wanted to see him, not wanting to wait another day.

"I did hope for just you and me, but I know Jared will probably want to come too."

"Jared will only come if I can't find someone to look after him." She assured him.

"Great, will 7:30 be all right with you?"

"Yes, that will be fine," trying to curtail her happiness.

"Tonight at 7:30. I will pick you up then." John rang off a happy man.

Chrissy dialed Nancy right away. "Nancy, please say you will look after Jared tonight?"

"I can if you bring him here. Then he can sleepover, and you won't have to hurry home."

"Bless you, Nancy. I'll bring him over about six. Then I can come back and get ready."

"Chrissy, you sound excited. Who is the hot date?"

"John, the man I was staying with for protection."

"Sounds like he was more than protecting you."

"No, he was a perfect gentleman, but this is our first date."

"Well, congratulations. Six is fine." Nancy rang off.

Chrissy arrived at Nancy's before six. When she slipped Jared's coat off, her engagement ring glittered in the light.

"Chrissy, is that an engagement ring? You said this is your first date."

"It is a long story, but I am engaged, but I'm not."

"Sounds interesting. Let me guess to John, the perfect gentleman, right?"

"Yes, but it isn't what you think. You know I have been having problems and needed protection. Well, John gave me an engagement ring to deter a certain party who has been bothering me."

"Let me understand this. You are going out on your first date with the man that you are engaged to marry?"

"Yes, I told you it was a long story. But I haven't time to explain." Chrissy kissed Jared and ran out the door.

"You better tell me the details tomorrow, or I'll hold on to Jared until you do," Nancy yelled as Chrissy ran down the walkway.

After she closed the door, Jared said. "I found John in bed with mommy and now John has to marry her. Mommy said it wasn't necessary because John had his clothes on."

Nancy knew that there had to be more of an explanation than that. She wanted to grill Jared for more details. But decided to wait for Chrissy's long story.

* * *

Chrissy was walking down the stairs as John rang the bell. Opening the door, she greeted him.

John handed her flowers. They weren't roses. He didn't want her associating his flowers with Hammond's and put a blight on their evening together.

"Thank you, John. They are lovely. I will put them in water. Would you like something to drink?"

"No, thanks. I have reservations at Luigi's. He is expecting us shortly."

"So, I get to see the infamous Luigi that supplies meals for you."

"I was going to take you somewhere really posh, but I like the atmosphere at Luigi's. Besides, he has been bugging me to meet you.

Is that okay?"

"How does hc know about me?"

"Chrissy, I was ordering food for three. How could I do that without an explanation? If you would rather, we can go somewhere else?"

"No, Luigi's is okay."

John held out her coat for her to slip on, guiding her out the door. "Where is Jared? I half expected him to be here."

"Jared is over at Nancy's for the night."

"That's interesting." John gave her an exaggerated smirk. Naturally, Chrissy blushed.

When they arrived at the restaurant, Luigi gave them the royal treatment, hugging Chrissy and making remarks. "You sweet lady, you snared the bachelor at last. Yes, I can see why John will lose his bachelorhood so willingly."

Chrissy smiled sweetly but refused to comment. Luigi seated them with a flourish asking John if he could order dinner for them?

John replied, "that is fine with me. How about you, Chrissy, are you willing to trust this guy?"

"Yes, who should know better than the owner what the specialty of the house is."

Rather than a wine menu, Luigi arrived back with a bottle of wine.

"This is the best wine to compliment the dinner. I hope you approve." He gave John a sample in his glass. John stiffed its bouquet, then tasted it.

"Excellent, I couldn't do better."

Luigi spied Chrissy's engagement ring as he poured her wine. Putting down the bottle, he lifted her hand.

"Are you engaged to John? You are a sly one, my friend." He grinned at both of them. Chrissy blushed. John decided rather than an explanation, he would just say yes.

"Fast worker, aren't you? I thought you two just met recently?"

"We did. We are only sort of engaged," Chrissy put in.

"Is that a new type of engagement I haven't heard about?" Luigi was beaming at John.

Chrissy was blushing more. John decided to forget the explanation.

"Yes, we are definitely engaged." Extracting Chrissy's hand out of Luigi's possessively.

"Congratulations, dinner is on me, my friend," slapping John on the back. "It is about time you got roped and tied. When's the wedding?"

Chrissy intervened. "We aren't getting married, really."

At the same time, John said. "September 18th."

"There has to be a story here. You are sort of engaged, you tell me. You are getting married on September 18th, and the young lady says, not really. Are you getting married or not?"

"No," was Chrissy's adamant reply.

"Yes," John's positive. reply

Luigi's eyes looked back and forth between them. He scratched his head, then said. "When you finally decide, I want an invite."

"This is getting complicated," Chrissy said after Luigi left them alone.

"I know, but these are unusual circumstances to explain."

John was feeling devilish as he picked up his glass.

"Shall we drink to our engagement and our upcoming wedding?" He held his glass out to touch hers, which forced Chrissy to raise her glass.

After taking a sip, Chrissy said, "you are enjoying this, aren't you?"

"Chrissy, I have never been engaged before. Let me enjoy the feeling."

"Okay, but no telling anyone else, agreed?"

"Agreed."

She didn't know how she would explain things to Selma or Nancy. She had phoned Selma and had a lengthy conversation with her omitting the engagement.

"John, about the wedding, what is going to happen? Are we really going to hold a mock wedding?"

John did not want to lie, so he said, "Chrissy, we will pretend it is the real thing. We'll make up an invitation list after dinner and make plans as though it was the real thing, like going through the motions, even if I feel Hammond won't come. How's that?"

"Just go through the motions like it is the real thing?"

"Yes"

"Sounds like fun. Do you think Alan could still be interested in me? I don't know why. I have never considered myself special in any way."

"See, we probably will never need the information. But I would like to have the once in a lifetime experience of planning a wedding." John was hoping Chrissy would agree.

The dinner Luigi served was superb. The conversation was light. Both were giving each other insights into their lives.

After dinner, John tried to pay for dinner to satisfy Chrissy's feelings of deception. Luigi still insisted that the dinner was his gift. They headed home to Chrissy's.

John asked for some paper to make a list of details for the wedding. "Humor me, okay?"

"Okay."

The rest of the evening was spent with a lot of laughter as Chrissy teased John about the perfect wedding. He was playacting the woes of the bachelor that would soon be married. He even got down on one knee and proposed to her, and Chrissy accepted his proposal.

"Now, we are officially engaged," he said, and Chrissy laughed.

If you weren't such a chicken, John, you would tell her this was to be the real thing.

John gathered up the sheets of paper and stuffed them in his pocket, after which he said, "just think in two weeks, we will be married. Are you nervous?"

"Me? I can fake it with my eyes closed. What shall I wear?" Chrissy asked grinning.

"You can wear the dress I bought you since you refused to wear it to the dinner."

"That would be perfect for the wedding, wouldn't it? You know I just might wear it." *The wedding would be perfect with all the plans we have made tonight. I do love this man. Why don't I let him know?*

When John was leaving, he enclosed her in his arms. "Now that we are officially engaged. I think we should kiss."

"I think that would be in order."

John needed no other invitation. His lips met Chrissy's with a kiss that went on and on, sealing their two hearts together. When they finally came up for air, John rested his forehead against Chrissy's.

"You know if we kiss like that, we should be married. Goodnight, Chrissy." His lips engaged hers in a second passionate kiss. Then he sailed out the door before Chrissy could comment.

Wow, could that man kiss. She was floating on a cloud of bliss.

John drove straight to Max and Laura's house.

When Max answered the door, he took one look at John's face. "What canary did you steal?"

"I have just come from Chrissy's and look at what treasures I have brought," handing Laura the information for a perfect wedding, including the guest's list.

"How did you get this?" Laura asked in wonder.

"Simple, I played a game of pretend, only I wasn't pretending. I even proposed, and she accepted. I told her the engagement was official."

"How did she accept that?" Max inserted.

"Fine, except I feel she still thinks I am kidding. During our playacting, I think it became a real engagement, but I'm not sure."

"John, isn't that risky?"

"I plan to see a lot of her between now and then. It will be a real engagement, as far as I am concerned. So, I may just entice her into realizing it is real for her too." John looked victorious.

"Laura, these lists should help us. The one obvious change is the flowers, she wants orchids, but that shouldn't be a problem. Have the invitations been printed yet?"

"Yes, I got them back today. How did you get all the addresses without her catching on?"

"Did I ever tell you I have good acting abilities? I just asked, and she gave them to me."

"What does acting ability have to do with that, if you just asked?" Max wanted to know.

"I don't know I just threw that in," John said laughingly.

Max said in jest to Laura. "What should we do with this guy? He is far too happy, wouldn't you say?"

Laughing, Laura said, "there is always a cold shower."

"No, he deserves his happiness." Max grinned.

Laura was looking over the food list.

"That's funny. This list is almost a duplication of what I ordered from the caterers."

"I know, but I sort of steered her a bit and she agreed with me."

"I see that I'm the matron of honor. Did you steer her there too?" asked Laura.

"She did mention her sister. Then she changed to you after some thought. I didn't press her. The minister was all her doing so you can contact him, or shall I?"

"I think you should introduce yourself to him. That is on your duty list," Laura said, handing the sheet back to John.

"Do you want a drink, or are you too high on love?" Max inquired boisterously.

"High on love, so I'll forgo the drink, thanks. Chrissy is wearing the dress I bought for her. Wait until you see it. She is a dream, walking in it." John said admiringly. "Will getting a dress be a problem, Laura?"

"No, Max can spring for it, can't you love?"

"Yes, my good buddy is finally getting married. We have to do it in high style." Max was enjoying himself.

John took out his wallet and pulled out some bills, and handed them to Laura. "This is for the cake and whatever else you don't charge. Let me know if you need more. The cake description is pretty explicit. Do you think there will be any problem?"

Laura read over the description. "Not that I can see. I don't believe you got all this information without her knowing you would be using it." Laura shook her head in wonder.

"I told you I was a good actor," grinning profusely. "Look, I had better get going. It is getting rather late."

John kissed Laura, thanking her for her help.

Max grabbed his hand. "Only two weeks to go. You only get married once at your age."

"I hope so," John said, smiling as he left for home.

* * *

John was with Chrissy every opportunity he could find. They acted like an engaged couple with Jared joining in the experience. She was swept along with his good humor about his fading bachelorhood.

The kisses they exchanged daily were not platonic by any stretch of the imagination. John needed plenty of cold showers as a result.

Chrissy started hearing from friends who had received their invitation to the wedding. She kept the details to a minimum when asked about the ceremony.

Selma was hard to put off, so she explained that it was because of her situation with Mr. Hammond, but never clarified the exact circumstances.

Nancy's questions were more direct, having extracted details from Jared. Chrissy tried to play that down, saying she had a dream, and John was waking her when Jared came in and found them. "John is a gentleman from the old school," letting Nancy's mind take it from there.

Laura called to ask who was walking her down the aisle. Chrissy's instant reply was. "Jared, of course." They talked a while longer. After she hung up, she got the niggling feeling that this was to be a real wedding from the way John was acting. No, it can't be. She had to clear that thought away.

Chrissy went back to her drawings of a layout plan for a job she was working on.

* * *

John brought the dress over the day before the wedding.

"What is in the other box?"

"Laura said Jared is walking you down the aisle, so here is an outfit for him."

"John, why do I get the feeling that this has gone from pretending to a real wedding?"

"Has it?" as though this was news to him. "Maybe we should make it real. What do you think?" he answered playfully.

"Real or mock, I guess it is too late to stop it, right?" Chrissy asked seriously. "Is Mr. Hammond coming?" She dreaded that he might show. She hoped that the wedding would proceed without him. That would please her nicely.

"I haven't heard either way." He wouldn't dare show.

John left early so she couldn't ask any more questions. Jared was excited about his new suit and the fact that John would soon be his Daddy, which Chrissy never corrected. Explanations would come soon enough.

Chapter Twenty-Eight

Laura and Max came to help her get ready. Selma, who was supposed to help, arrived late due to the baby fussing over her feeding. A baby girl, Lucy Christine, was born the month before. Chrissy thought she was adorable.

After wishing her sister all the best, Selma left to be with her husband and daughter amongst the wedding guest.

Laura put the finishing touches on Chrissy's makeup and hair. Chrissy had been too nervous, so she appreciated Laura's help. She didn't know if Max and Laura were in on the reason for the wedding, so she didn't broach the subject.

Jared looked adorable in his new suit and shoes. He kept whizzing around, trying to hurry Chrissy. Max finally planted him in a chair and started questioning him on raising puppies to occupy him.

At last, they were ready. It was a beautiful warm evening, making coats unnecessary.

Max drove, letting Laura, Chrissy and Jared off at the front of John's home. Chrissy looked around. There seemed to be an awful lot of cars.

Laura was guiding Chrissy through the house, positioning Jared beside his mother and giving him instructions as to his role. Chrissy was in a daze.

They heard the wedding march, leading the way Laura proceeded to the terrace. When Chrissy cleared the doorway, she immediately noticed the guests on the lawn area surrounded by gardens with the

Alter, a canopy of flowers. Just like she and John had planned the wedding in make-believe that night after dinner.

Then her eyes swung to the Orchids Laura was handing her as they entered the terrace. Her eyes flew to John. This was no coincidence. Laura proceeded down the steps to walk down the aisle to the Alter, where John and Max waited.

Jared whispered. "Mommy, they are waiting."

Chrissy stepped forward, holding Jared's elbow he offered her. She walked through the guests without seeing them. Her total focus was on John.

Chrissy, a vision of loveliness, was walking towards him. The glistening sun accentuated the shimmers of color in her dress as she floated down the aisle with Jared. John was bursting with happiness that this lovely bride was coming to marry him. Knowing in his heart, he was a fortunate man. When Chrissy and Jared reached the Alter, the Minister asked, "Who gives this bride in Holy Matrimony?"

Jared said clearly in his own words. "I give my Mommy to my new Daddy,"

The statement invoked a chorus of laughter.

Jared gave Chrissy's hand to John. John accepted, saying, "Jared, your new Daddy truly accepts your Mommy as his bride, to love her and cherish her." John was looking deeply into her eyes as he said this. It was then Chrissy knew that this was for real. She squeezed John's hand in acknowledgment as they turned to the Minister.

Chrissy and John said their vows with deep sincerity while gazing lovingly into each other's eyes. John slipped the wedding ring on her finger, melding so naturally against the engagement ring, sealing their hearts together in love.

The Minister pronounced them man and wife. "You may kiss the bride."

John kissed Chrissy, letting everyone know how much he loved this woman. Releasing her, he picked up Jared, then swept Chrissy against his side and faced the guests.

The Minister introduced them. "With great pleasure, I introduce you to Mr. and Mrs. John Taylor and their son, Jared."

The guests broke into spontaneous applause.

Jared hugged John yelling. "Mommy, John is my Daddy now, and you are married, so it is okay to sleep together."

Chrissy and John's laughter rang out with loud clapping and exuberant laughter from the guests.

* *

Thanks for reading *Life's Unexpected Moments*. You can find my other works at website www.dorothycollins.ca.

CPSIA information can be obtained
at www.ICGtesting.com
Printed in the USA
BVHW091917231220
596244BV00005B/11